ARMS AND INSECURITY IN THE PERSIAN GULF

ARMS AND INSECURITY
IN THE PERSIAN GULF

JOHN MUTTAM

RADIANT PUBLISHERS

First Published 1984 in India by
Radiant Publishers
E-155 Kalkaji, New Delhi-110019

Printed in India by
Asia Composer
at Sunil Printers
WZ 555 Naraina, New Delhi-110028

To
Baby, Clara, Regi and Chellamma

Contents

List of Tables

Preface

Arms races present a variety of patterns which may be categorised and subjected to further analysis. Besides the quantitative and qualitative nuclear arms race between the United States and the Soviet Union at the global level, the superpowers carry on a conventional arms race either directly or by proxy at a regional level. As a matter of fact, the superpowers along with the Big Powers or developed nations, have been responsible for regional arms races.

The phenomenon of arms race, proposed to be analysed in this study, is basically related to developing nations in Asia, Africa and Latin America though the Gulf region has been chosen for a case study. In general, most of these countries do not possess any modern defence infrastructure or even defence potential; nonetheless, they are engaged in acquiring sophisticated weapons on a competitive basis from militarily industrialised nations—an exercise that has often accelerated the momentum of regional arms races. This study, while dealing with the dynamics of regional arms race, is restricted to the competitive conventional arms build-up by the developing nations.

A great deal has been written about the nuclear arms race and justifiably so in recent times. The scholarly contribution of Lewis F. Richardson, Philip Noel-Baker, Samuel P. Huntington, Colin S. Gray, Albert J. Wohlstetter, Geoffrey Kemp and others to the understanding of the complex arms race phenomenon, has been invaluable. There has been a spate of serious discussions and debates related to nuclear arms control. Bernard J. Beckhoefer, Thomas Schelling, William Epstein, David J. Singer, Donald G. Brennan and others have made in-depth analysis of the problems and prospects of arms control within the context of strategic power rivalries between the superpowers. But a more thorough-going analysis and study of the conventional arms race, especially the regional arms race, has been relegated to the background as a result of the present obsession with nuclear arms race and nuclear arms control debate. This does not mean that the problems of conventional arms race and conventional arms control among the superpowers are not receiving attention of the scholars.

Now that several arms control measures have been negotiated, keeping nuclear disarmament as the ultimate goal, it is worthwhile to pick up the problems of conventional arms race which is most manifest as a regional phenomenon and explore the possibilities and prospects of regional arms control. However, this does not mean that the control of nuclear arms race is successful.

The brisk arms trade by the developed nations with the developing nations and their arms policies have to be carefully examined in order to understand the seriousness of the conventional arms race and the ever increasing danger it poses to the developing nations. Regional arms races are undoubtedly a contributory factor to the present state of instability and insecurity in the developing nations. Therefore, it is necessary and desirable to inquire about the possibility of curbing regional arms races and also devise some regional arms control measures. The pertinent question is whether the time is opportune—in view of the superpower detente—to have a fresh look at the problem of arms control at the regional level and decide how to make a beginning in this direction.

It is equally important to know whether the big powers are prepared to accept some restraint in curbing regional arms races. For, the key to the control of regional arms race is the restraint to be exercised on the arms policies—regarding sale, transfer, assistance—of these Big Powers. It may be further examined whether the regional powers, particularly, the more dominant among them would be prepared to accept any restraint on their arms policies to produce successful arms control agreements as the regional arms races are often the cumulative outcome of the arms policies of the more ambitious and adventurous nations.

The current arms race in the Gulf area is the focus of this study. In this area, all the essential ingredients of a regional arms race are present: Great Power interest, regional backwardness, endemic interstate power rivalry, strategic importance, stockpiling of armaments, petro-dollar boom, all of which have already generated an explosive situation, leading for example, to the ongoing war between Iraq and Iran.

The main objectives of this study are: *a*) to conceptualise the regional arms race phenomenon; *b*) to briefly review Big Power rivalry in the Gulf region; *c*) to analyse the dynamics of armamentism in the Gulf region; *d*) to quantify the arms build-up in the Gulf region and to analyse the dangerous implications of such an arms build-up; *e*) to highlight the Iran-Iraq war as a consequence of the arms race; and *f*) to examine the prospects of arms control in the Gulf region.

The methodology followed in this study would be one of descriptive-literary approach and interpretation of the major inputs of an arms race potential in the Gulf region. Without using any mathematical model in this study, simple data analysis and quantification of the major inputs in the arms build-up through the arms supply by the USA, USSR, UK, France and other countries, would be attempted. Arms trade registers, prepared by authoritative sources like the Stockholm International Peace Research Institute, defence spending and percentage of Gross National Product for defence expenditures, etc., prepared by US Arms Control and Disarmament Agency, International Institute for Strategic Studies (London) and Centre for Defence Information (Washington, D.C.), will be extensively used. My visit to Iran in 1978-79 proved useful in getting a 'feel' of the region. Besides, discussions with some scholars of the area helped me to appreciate the arguments for the regional arms build-up from their perspective. Efforts have been made to make this study as comprehensive and objective as possible with the primary and secondary source materials available in India.

I would like to sincerely thank Dr. K. Raman Pillai, Professor and Head of the Department of Political Science, Kerala University and Dr. T.T. Poulose, Professor, Jawaharlal Nehru University, New Delhi, whose critical comments and suggestions at various stages of this study have been of immense value. Thanks are also due to Baby, my wife, whose moral support and encouragement kept me going while for a time disruptions in my studies tended to cast a shadow of discouragement over me. The kind cooperation and help, rendered to me by the library staff of the Department of Politics, Kerala University, Sapru House Library and Defence Institute Library, New Delhi, are gratefully remembered. Sincere thanks also go to Mr. Ramachandran Nair who prepared the typed-script, and to all my well-wishers and friends who have in one way or other helped me and encouraged me to complete this study expeditiously. Last, but not the least, I thank Radiant Publishers for their kind interest in publishing this book.

21 March 1984   JOHN MUTTAM

1

The Concept of Regional
Arms Race

There is an increasing tendency in almost all the developing
nations of the world to have an arms build-up similar to the
build-up of a buffer-stock of food grains. Such arms build-up
is apparently based on the national right of self-defence and
security of every sovereign State within the present international system.[1]

The arms build-up in the developing countries assumes a
competitive dimension when two States or a group of nations
enter into a virtual race for superiority at the regional level.[2]

In an inquiry into the arms race phenomenon, the
preliminary attempt will be: *a*) to examine whether or not the
concept of regional arms race is distinct from that of the
superpower nuclear arms race; and *b*) to analyse the nature
and dynamics of regional arms race.

PROBLEM OF DEFINITION

The works of eminent arms race experts have already facilitated the understanding of the arms race phenomenon in some
depth. The empirical framework of their study was mainly

focussed on the competitive arms build-up between great
European powers which ultimately ended up in two devastating
world wars[3] or on the contemporary nuclear arms race between
the United States and the Soviet Union.[4] Some of these
analysts attempted to define arms race within the broad
spectrum of strategic rivalries.

Thus according to Huntington, "an arms race has been
defined as a progressive, competitive, peacetime increase in
armaments by two States or coalition of States resulting from
conflicting purposes or mutual fears."[5] Colin S. Gray con-
ceives an arms race as a condition in which there should be
two or more parties perceiving themselves to be in an adversary
relationship, who are increasing or improving their armaments
at a rapid rate and structuring their respective military
postures with a general attention to the past, current, and
anticipated military and political behaviour of the other
parties.[6]

The basic components of an arms race, as brought out by
most of these definitions are that there should be an adversary
relationship between two or more rival nations with "conflicting purposes", and that the parties concerned should have the
capacity to increase the quantity and improve the quality of
their armaments. A definition thus conceived is very
appropriate in the case of the nuclear arms race in progress
between the United States and the Soviet Union. Their
opposition or adversary relationship stems from antagonism
based on opposing political systems, conflicting ideological
positions and several other factors.

The nuclear arms race has its origins in the Cold War.
The qualitative as well as quantitative arms race continues
unabated through every break-through in weapon technology
despite *detente*[7] and various arms control agreements including
Strategic Arms Limitations Talks (SALT)[8]. Even if the Cold
War is almost dead the arms race is not.[9] The very policy of
nuclear deterrence, mutual assured destruction, second strike
capability and "third strike" force has given a new lease to
the nuclear arms race.[10]

Strategic nuclear stockpiles of the two superpowers now
total over 50,000 nuclear weapons of varying size, shape and
deadliness. Their cambined explosive power is estimated to be

1,000,000 times the power of the bomb that destroyed Hiroshima in Japan in 1945 in a matter of seconds.[11] A single missile in the new MX weapon of the US carries 200 times the destructive force of the Hiroshima bomb. Missiles can carry the strategic nuclear weapons 6,000 miles in less than thirty minutes.[12] Still the two superpowers are investing well over $100,000,000 per day to upgrade their nuclear arsenals, though the existing stockpiles of nuclear weapons are enough to destroy the world several times over.

The two superpowers which are responsible for the nuclear arms race have geared the race to their global strategies and global commitments. They have immense economic resources and advanced weapons technologies to sustain unfalteringly a high degree of arms manufacturing capability.[13] The nuclear arms race would go on accelerating by every technological breakthrough and this fact makes each superpower somewhat suspicious of the other, i.e., "that one's adversary will gain a decisive military superiority through a technological innovation developed in secret research. This would have the other side vulnerable to attack and intimidation."[14] Expounding the US arms control policy, the former Secretary of State, Alexander Haig said: "just as arms control should not aim simply at reducing numbers, so it should not try simply to restrict the advance of technology. Some technological advances make everyone safer."[15] So the intense search continues adding new momentum to the global arms race.

Apart from the superpower arms race with a global dimension, it may be asked whether the competitive armament build-up of developing or non-industrialised nations could also legitimately be termed an arms race. If the analogy of 'race' could be used in the case of the arms build-up of the superpowers that would endanger the whole world, there is no reason why it could also not be applicable to the arms build-up of the developing nations at the regional level that tends to generate regional tension and often inter-state conflicts. Of course, it may be argued that the regional arms race is not autonomous. It is still regarded as a part of the global conventional arms race. However, the aim of this study is to examine whether or not a regional arms race could be considered a class by itself; whether or not it is distinct and unique from the global arms race.

Admitting that there are arms races[16] between non-industrialised nations in diverse regions of the world, can they be distinguished from the superpower arms race? Will the distinction between the two be essentially one of kind or one of degree in a single arms race scale? It is assumed here that it is possible to distinguish the two types of arms races as one of kind and not one of degree. It would appear that any attempt to apply the nature and characteristics of the superpower arms race to the regional arms race would in all likelihood run the risk of overlooking that distinction.

It has already been pointed out what essential components go to make up the superpower arms race. Attempts should now be made to find out what are those elements essentially required to constitute a regional arms race. If specific elements other than those recognized in the definition of an arms race between the superpowers could be discerned, then the distinction between the two as one of kind remains valid. If the distinction becomes evident as one of kind on the basis of recognising the differentiating elements, then the two earlier definitions of arms race need not necessarily be applicable to the regional arms race. Perhaps, another definition of the regional arms race is required to explain its peculiar characteristics.

If one tries to analyse the way the arms build-up takes place in developing nations, some of which are yet in their pre-industrial stages, one can easily recognise that their expensive arms build-up is fundamentally based on an element of competition. The competition of such a kind is a dynamic process tending to accelerate one's own military potentials which could either deter a potential aggressor or would presumably stand to maximise one's offensive capabilities in case of an open war. Against this background a competitive arms build-up by two developing States or a coalition of developing nations in a particular region is also in the nature of an arms race.

In so far as there is an element of competition in the regional arms build-up, it partakes the character of the global arms race, but with some essential differences in the level, intensity and duration. The competition between the super-powers is autonomous, self-sustaining, intense, vertical and horizontal whereas the one between developing nations is so dependent on external sources, uncertain, vicarious, sporadic and fluctuating.

A lack of self-sustaining economy severely inhibits developing nations to venture on an unlimited arms build-up. Inadequate organisational and managerial skill and capabilities heavily constrain the development and maintenance of large scale military and industrial complexes. To overcome these deficiencies the contending nations will have to depend on external sources.

The developing or non-industrialised States are often induced by interested industrialised nations to intensify or terminate the competition as they, by and large, depend on them for arms for their immediate needs of defence or to run an arms race with neighbouring States. In so far as the supplies of arms depend on the specific arms supply policies of the manufacturing nations, the developing nations cannot be sure of a steady arms build-up.

A decision to procure quality weapons in large quantities will also generally depend on the policy of the supplying nations and not necessarily according to the whims of the recipient powers. Hence, lesser powers lagging behind in the competition for arms cannot fully satiate their urge to have a rapid increase in quantity or improvements in quality of their armaments. An arms race at the regional level, whether horizontal or vertical, is seldom a consistent structural process of weapon development or arms deployment, intended to serve a definite military or tactical strategy, planned out exclusively by regional powers to meet local contingencies. In so far as the structural process of weapon development or arms deployment is dependent on the arms policies and arms transfers of weapon supplying powers, it is possible that the regional arms race participants might be compelled to abandon the process at certain levels. It might also become unavoidable for them to devise a totally fresh process of arms build-up, with no certainty whether or not it would be insulated against further structural gaps. Hence the local arms race tends to be sporadic and fluctuating.

In every developing State there is a basic structure of military defence with or without a military doctrine depending on its capabilities or self-reliance, however primitive it might seem to be. But in order to accommodate or assimilate more sophisticated or modern imported weapons systems this basic structure need to be altered. What most of the developing nations are doing is just that exercise of structural changes while engaging themselves in a competition of arms acquisition or an arms race. Hence, the capability to increase the force structure qualitatively and quantitatively does not appear to be one of the essential requirements of an arms race in the regional context.

An adversary relationship between two superpowers found in the nuclear arms race does not also appear to be empirically true to arms races in the regional milieu. An arms race may be initiated by a State due to certain domestic compulsions or simply because enough technology or money is readily available.[17] "It is possible that an arms race might develop without there being any driving political antagonism."[18] Further, "a quite autonomous arms increase may be matched by a fairly disinterested party solely as a precautionary move, and hence a cycle of close or intermittent armament interactions and previously unappreciated political antagonism may ensue."[19] Even the possession of sophisticated weapons is significant only to some nations in as much as it symbolises the determination to be power-oriented. By the very fact that a regional power decides to embellish its own stockpiles, the neighbouring States would be alerted either by suspicion or by prestige[20] but without leading apparently towards an adversary relationship.

It is not always likely that the mutual antagonism among some regional powers should lead to an arms race. The reasons for it are not hard to find. In most cases, developing nations in various regions of the world are not in a position to manufacture the arms they need. They have first of all no adequate industrial base and whatever base they may have, is so primitive as to produce only small arms which will be insufficient to sustain a war. Only in extreme cases these States are driven to a senseless arms build-up either through outright purchases from industrialised nations or through arms assistance given by a military alliance programme.

Evidently, therefore, the major elements in the global arms race of the two superpowers need not be present in an arms race at the regional level.

CHARACTERISTICS OF REGIONAL ARMS RACE

Firstly, it is not always necessary for the regional powers to be weapon producing States. Developing nations, depending on their economic resources and friendly relations with arms producing nations, can acquire large quantities of weapons and then initiate an arms race. Secondly, some developing nations, intending to run an arms race, have already the minimum technology and industrial base to keep the war machine in a state of readiness. This has been greatly facilitated by the transfer of advanced technology. Thirdly, there is an element of competitive arms acquisition by developing nations without there being *per se* adversary relationship between the arms race participants. Fourthly, regional arms races, in some cases at least, are strongly supported and sustained by militarily industrial powers.

DEFINING REGIONAL ARMS RACE

A regional arms race may, therefore, be defined as competitive arms acquisition by all or some of the countries belonging to a region—essentially controlled throughout by the arms exporters, in the absence of an autonomous, indigenous arms production process, at least for the present—through sale, aid or transfer from the weapon-supplier nations in pursuit of specific national objectives like regional balance, security, prestige or to wage proxy wars at the behest of outside powers. Four essential conditions follow from this definition of a regional arms race: first, a regional arms race is between two or more States or coalitions of States in a region; second, the element of competition spurs the arms acquisition; third, dependence on foreign source of arms supply is unavoidable; and fourth, a possible design to offset an existing regional military balance can be present.

Three basic factors may be examined to understand the nature and dynamics of regional arms race; one, arms acquisitions are often the result of domestic compulsions influencing regional powers and they are far more complicated than is generally assumed; two, the process of arms procurement initiated by various States of the region could also be due to regional factors; and three, regional arms races also occur on account of extra-regional factors, such as the arms supply policies of major powers.

NATURE AND DYNAMICS OF REGIONAL ARMS RACE

A. Domestic Factors

The competitive urge to acquire more and more weapons is generally associated with a number of domestic variables which are closely related to the survival of the developing nations themselves and the preoccupation of the ruling elite towards stabilising the specific type of political systems that have to acquire legitimacy among the people. To put it hypothetically, the more a State feels insecure either from potential disintegrating forces from within the system itself or from without, the more would its inclination to augment the military forces, irrespective of the cost this activity may entail. It is necessary to identify these domestic variables.

i) Security and Self-defence

Considered in terms of "practical needs and international status, the decisions to retain and develop military forces are acceptable."[21] The practical need of military forces for a developing nation arises more on account of its being confronted seriously with the problem of self-defence than on the mere consideration of international status which only a somewhat economically advanced country can think of. For the developing nations, self-preservation is more important than any other consideration.[22] If self-defence is accepted as one of the first principles of international politics, then there is no denying that each State is entitled to adopt such means as are available to it to ward off any possible threat to its existence either from corrosive forces within the system itself or from without. The right to self-defence presupposes that the developing nations should engage themselves in the development of an effective security force against potential and actual challenges to their existence as autonomous States. Therefore, conflict or inter-state war is an inescapable part of the burden of government. "To this end, they devote a portion of their available resources, or sacrifice some of their political independence, or both, to acquire military hardware and know-how from the world's suppliers."[23]

To keep the internal system stable, cohesive and immune from disintegrating influences, a variety of measures are prescribed according to the specific form of government that has been established in each State. One can pick up any one remedial solution from among the many options, as far as it is question of protecting internal security of a nation is concerned. But when the question devolves on defending a nation against possible external aggression or the threat of it, there are only two alternatives before such a nation. Either the nation that is being threatened with aggression decides possibly on an unconditional surrender to the aggressor or it accepts the challenge to take up arms to defend itself. The decision taken either way will have serious repercussions and risk involved in relation to the continued existence of a nation. While the first alternative may seem rather repugnant to be adopted by most of the nations, almost all nations will prefer to think in terms of the other alternative, regardless of possible costs and consequences. If the first alternative is repugnant to the honour of a nation, then there is no other way of safeguarding its autonomy, independence, social, economic and cultural values except by maintaining its defence forces adequately strengthened to repel potential aggressors. As there are always ambitious men seeking to extend their influence and push well beyond their own legitimate bounds, it has become of necessity for every State to take minimum precautionary measure in view of any emergency situation. For, "to build a national defence is to recognise serious differences, potentially incompatible goals of possible adversaries.[24] A nation will go to war whatever may be the cost, when it is actually attacked. Thus weapons for the twin purpose of defence and offence are accumulated in every State on a priority basis. But as far as the developing nations are concerned, weapons have to be imported from weapons producing countries to meet such basic requirements.

ii) *Radicalism* vs. *Traditionalism*

Besides the fundamental necessity of defending their freedom and autonomy, some of the developing countries are frequently threatened from within by forces, radical or revolutionary, challenging the structures of the socio-political system itself. The struggle for change within the system is essentially a struggle between the forces of modernism and traditionalism. The confrontation between the ruling elite and the radicals or revolutionaries is based on their respective views of socio-economic programmes to modernise the traditional society. Tension, thus created within nations will contribute to internal pressures, paving the way for acquiring weapons in order to suppress and crush dissident movements suspected of being a threat to the traditional ruling classes.

This is all the more true of despotic, military and monarchical regimes which are caught between the forces of traditionalism and modernism. On the one hand, it is necessary to have centralisation of power to promote social, cultural and economic reforms; on the other hand, centralisation in a monarchical or military regime with inflexible conservative values and ethnic overtones[25] "make it difficult or impossible the expansion of the power of the traditional polity and the assimilation into it of the new groups produced by modernisation."[26]

The utter inability of some political systems to stimulate conditions for the improvement of the standard of living through a rapid process of modernisation has belied the hopes and aspirations of young radicals who are gradually driven to insurgency and organised guerrilla activities resulting in civil strife and structural violence, threatening the traditional ruling clique. "The gospel of modernisation has released forces that produce ethnic cleavages, internal violence (civil wars, political excesses, and brutalities of military juntas) and armed conflicts between neighbours encouraged by the big powers."[27]

The perpetuation of the state of conflict between tradition and modernism is made easy within a developing nation when its ruling elite, unresponsive to the surging national aspirations, tends to oppress the radicals by force of arms. The psychological alienation they feel of being subjected to force of arms helps only to strengthen their determination to fight the oppressors on their own terms by acquiring arms from revolutionary and modern regimes in the neighbourhood which are only too willing to support them with military assistance and economic aid. Internal conflict behaviour within developing nations consists of such developments as demonstrations, riots, *coups d'etat*, guerrilla warfare, and national liberation movements, denoting the relative instability of the political systems.[28] For example, a survey study reveals that there were 274 military coups between 1946 and 1970 in the developing regions.[29] It indicates, not only the extreme incompetence of political leaders in those regions but also the precarious cleavages in the socio-political systems themselves.[30] The traditional ruling elite, in order to strengthen their position against exigencies of armed conflicts or insurrection, would do all that they can to acquire more weapons.

iii) Psychological Insecurity
Another crucial factor responsible for the arms build-up in developing nations is the psychological insecurity they experience as a result of the instability that ensued in the process of decolonisation and the national liberation struggle for independence.[31] It would seem that their security is assured by creating an adequate defence structure that would ensure their territorial integrity and political independence. Hence these States would seek to acquire arms either through economic and military aid or through outright purchases. Aggressive motivations may be absent in initiating such measures. However, nations do have a psychological need to prove that they are bigger, better or stronger than other nations.[32] Procurement of weapons acts as a confidence-building technique as far as these nations are concerned.

However simple these interpretations may be, an overt behaviour tends to symbolise potentially dangerous motives and intentions; the confidence-building measures of a particular nation may be misconstrued as an indication of hostile intentions for future plans of conflict. As in these matters, nations do not want to believe the explanations or clarifications of motives and intentions of arming nations, even a semblance of competition would signal the neighbouring States which are subjected to similar apprehensions to try to balance or outdo potential rivals in the procurement of armaments. All these activities become known to other nations or may be perceived and interpreted by them as threats.[33] Thus, an arms race conceived in terms of future plans of war or based on unfounded fears, germane to regional politics and military situations, tends to destabilise the entire region. The crucial point is that "no nation can afford to be less strong than a possible opponent. No State can afford not to participate in the resultant arms race if it wishes to protect its vital interests."[34]

The increase in arms build-up becomes sharper when fear of the unknown becomes a constant source of psychological insecurity. "When their interests conflict, part of each nation's strategy is to keep the other guessing as to its next moves and simultaneously try to convey the impression that it is powerful and indomitable. Since the unknown is an especially potent source of fear because one does not know how to combat it, to the extent that the exact scope and form of a threat is unclear, its capacity to arouse anxiety is increasing."[35] Hence it is natural for nations to exaggerate the perceived threats and over-react to them accentuating the arms race.

iv) Militarism
Countries which are subjected to military dictatorship are invariably more prone to attach higher priority in the procurement of arms. The perpetrators of most of the *coups d'etat* in various parts of the world are associated with the military junta. The junta has its own views about national interest and goals.[36] The military view on these matters may vary from the civilian view and this, according to Huntington, is due to the responsibility that leads the military to view the State as the basic unit of political organisation; to stress the continuing nature of the threats to the military security of the State and the continuing likelihood of war; to emphasise the magnitude and immediacy of the security threats, to favour maintenance

of strong, diverse and ready military forces; and to oppose the extension of State commitments and the involvement of the State in war except when victory is certain.[37]

Whether a military regime will always remain uninvolved in war except when victory is certain, is debatable, for military men who come to the helm of affairs are prone to adopt a military policy that is likely to be more aggressive than accommodative. They possess a feeling of insecurity and therefore are likely to exhibit aggressive traits and this is bound to create frictions and conflicts.

It has been argued that militarism in the new nations especially in Africa and Asia is impulsive or unanticipated.[38] Because of the weakness of civilian institutions and the break down of parliamentary forms of government the military officers develop a sense of public service and national guardianship as a result of their military training and experience.[39] While the *bona fides* regarding their altruistic spirit may not be called into question, it appears to be still a matter of controversy whether or not they can render effective political leadership. It is easier for them to seize power than to exercise power.[40]

It is very often true that countries ruled by the military junta are constantly plagued with internal political disturbances and instability. The feeling of insecurity, the perception of a hostile environment prevailing as a result of authoritarianism and dictatorship, the general atmosphere of instability, mistrust, and fear would naturally make these ruling classes think of acquiring more arms, a brutal exhibition of which, they think, would have a chastening influence over the minds and actions of dissidents and the so-called 'trouble shooters'. In order to escape from the problems of their own making, the military junta may follow an adventurist policy of attacking a neighbour in order to consolidate the internal forces and to forge a kind of national unity. But this would involve acquisition of weapons, the level of which may not match even the level of weapons of the country the junta may have planned to attack. What they hope perhaps by confronting a militarily stronger nation is neither a glorious victory nor an ignominious defeat, but possibly an intervention, diplomatic or military, of third parties to pull them out of the quagmire of their own making and to divert the attention of the people away from the numerous domestic problems at least for some time.

The governments that are faced with movements for social and political change tend to seek foreign assistance. The governments that are promised foreign assistance are less inclined to meet demands upon them. Very often conflict is promoted and not avoided by expectations of foreign intervention.[41] In politics, externalising internal problems is one of the ingenious tactics everyone would like to employ and the military junta seldom fails to adopt it indiscriminately.

v) Economic Factor
Economic backwardness and military weakness of developing nations cannot be seen as constraints on them to forego an extra zest for the accumulation of wepons. On the contrary, these seem to be latent conditions congenial for the free flow of economic aid and military hardware into the developing States. Because a nation is militarily weak it can obtain armaments either free of cost or at least to have them purchased at a commercially reduced rate. In this process of dependence on other States for arms requirements, very often, the recipient nations become obliged to the supplier nations in ways which could easily hamper the recipients' freedom to act autonomously in matters concerning their domestic economy.

With the transformation of empires and colonies into nations, neo-colonialism in the "form of economic dependencies and satellite States" is taking their places.[42] Economic dependencies are nominally independent States whose major economic activities are largely under the influence of a great power. Satellite States, on the other hand, are nominally independent States when their political life and foreign polices are in varying degrees under the control and influence of a more powerful State.[43]

Does it not appear a dichotomic situation where regional powers vie with one another to fulfill the wishes of foreign powers in order to secure more economic aid and armaments which will inevitably lead to a steady arms race in the region? Obviously, such an arms race is likely to be a strong stimulant for the regional powers to transform their own antagonisms and local disputes, if any, into regional conflicts.

B. Regional Factors

The nation States, with diverse political systems, cultural differences, conflicting ideologies and foreign policy objectives interact in a multiplicity of ways, giving rise to myriad patterns of interstate relationships which may be anything between the two extremes of co-operation and irreconcilable antagonism. While, on the one hand, reciprocative behaviour serves to provide nations a basis for peaceful co-existence and mutual respect in international affairs, hostile antagonism paves the way gradually towards open conflicts between nations on the other. As peaceful and harmonious coexistence of States is seldom a reality, there will arise the possibility of threats to the security of nations from potential aggressors within the regional system itself. A small nation, for example, may have reasons to fear if a big power or a developed nation in the neighbourhood, possessing disproportionate military strength becomes a source of either actual or potential threat to it.

The threat may be directed to achieve various kinds of goals[44] such as outright annexation of a piece of territory, conversion of a State into a satellite, imposition of an unpopular or puppet regime, encouragement to carry on subversive activities, open interference in the domestic affairs, and diplomatic or other pressures to follow a dependent foreign policy. Given the unequal distribution of power and the uneven spread of economic resources, the present international system provides conditions for every State, whether big or small, developed or developing, to build-up armaments as each sees and reacts to individual threat perceptions.

i) Conflict Potentials

A constant and fairly consistent process of arms acquisition initiated by various States of a region is necessitated by compulsions of diverse regional factors which are essentially centred on the crucial concept of conflict.

Conflict may be defined "as a situation of competition in which the parties are aware of the incompatibility of potential future positions and in which each party wishes to occupy a position that is incompatible with the wishes of the other."[45] According to Mack and Snyder a conflict relationship always involves the attempt to acquire or exercise power or the actual acquisition of or exercise of power.[46]

The latent conflict proclivities originate from generally identifiable psychological, economic, cultural, social, political, and religious sources.[47] However, the identification of a single cause, to which a conflict behaviour may be imputed, is empirically very difficult. A complex mix of all the causes may have a dominating influence in the precipitation of an open conflict. "The word conflict is used with the implication that war is a definite and mutually understood pattern of behaviour distinguishable not only from other patterns of behaviour in general but from other forms of conflict,"[48] such as say, rioting, mutiny, guerrilla activities and insurgencies.

An interstate conflict may be in the nature of a potential conflict or conflict formation. In the former case, it lies dormant and the situation may be described as an adversary, hostile or antagonistic relationship.[49] When relations deteriorate into tension between the political entities, it may result in an armed conflict in which case it may be described as an actual conflict. Political conflicts between States may meet with military response. The signals of such a response become evident when either one or both the States project overt signs of their antagonism.[50]

From the nature of conflict, two legitimate inferences can be made: one, every nation, as *de jure* or *de facto*, recognised or unrecognised component of the international system, is called upon to face a bewildering variety of situations affecting national security; and two, every nation believes that an adequate defence build-up is justified against national security threats.

Though national interests need not necessarily be conflicting, it is just possible sometimes that it can clash with the interests of some nations especially where vital national interests are involved. If the pursuit of such objectives by one State is diametrically opposed to the interests or security of its neighbour, then the latter would not hesitate to challenge the moves of the former.

Since unfriendly interactions among States are inherent in

the present international system, adoption of adequate measures of defence by every State against forces which might endanger national security is understandable. More belligerent States might seek "to extend the territorial limits of their sovereignty and to establish and impose upon the nations and peoples, with whom they are in conflict a political and economic order which is in the interest of the dominant party, race or nation."[51] Here again, on the one hand, an adequate defence against aggressors is fairly well recognised and accepted as legitimate; but on the other hand, what would constitute adequate defence often tends to be guided by considerations based on extremely subjective perceptions and calculations.

The perceived conflict relationship of nations induces them to acquire arms to be used in a future conflict. Secrecy in military affairs makes it inevitable that a potential enemy will usually be suspected of being stronger than it actually is. Consequently, rival States strive continuously to improve the quantity and quality of their arms. So it is that the arms race becomes based on the "hypothesis of the worst case", that is to say, one of two sides designs its programme of development on the assumption that its rival would be stronger.[52] Therefore, the period between the beginning of a strained relationship and the ensuing open conflict is characterised by activities of military preparations and acquisition of weapons by potential rivals; and the competition in arms acquisition and the ensuing tension can be dangerous.

ii) Hegemony

The ambition to establish political and military hegemony in a region by infusing ethnic and recist controversies in interstate relations, and playing up chauvinistic transnationalism with its appeal to regional solidarity, is one of the basic causes of conflict formation leading to a regional arms race.

The conduct of some of the newly independent nations clearly reflect the colonial traditions. In the kaleidoscopic international landscape, some of the emerging nations or developing nations attempt to project inflated images of themselves to the other nations belonging to the same region, betraying signs of regional hegemony.

One way of establishing hegemony is by obtaining a large

inventory of military hardware. Therefore, it is only natural that some of the developing nations are grossly preoccupied with the problem of augmenting their arms build-up qualitatively and quantitatively. A single State having hegemonic tendencies can destabilise and create tension in a region. Hegemonial intentions appear to be psychological imperatives behind adventurist policies based on mere self-interest. But such tendencies may not go unchallenged. There can be strong resistance from those nations which can hope to gain the support of any big power to initiate counter-measures and precipitate a regional crisis. For "self-interest as a national or international policy being sheer anarchy leads to blind and automatic war reactions".[53] It would seem politically and militarily imprudent on the part of the rest of the States in the region not to step up their defensive and offensive capabilities at least as a precautionary measure to guard against the establishment of absolute hegemony. Thus, once the process of acquiring arms has started by States of a region, it would assume the nature of a competition or an armament race and then reverting to the *status quo* will remain distressingly elusive.

Equally exacerbating is the ethnic-racist dimension which is pregnant with distortions in interstate relations to the extent that ethnically related nations work out schemes to harass and if possible attempt to destroy other nations, populated predominantly by a different ethnic or racial group. A conflict situation created by the logic of ethnicism between States is charged with a high degree of explosive emotionalism which has an inherent tendency to erupt with savage fury. Examples of nations waging war based on ethnic considerations are found throughout history. The extremely complex situations, where "tensions arise, is a consequence of the juxtaposition of historical, economic, religious or ethnic elements".[54] Even in our own times, ethnic considerations determine the arms policies of some regional powers.

Another interesting dimension of the problem is the somewhat esoteric concept of transnationalism, based on certain shared values. Of course, a relation based on transnationalism appears to be slender and weak especially in the case of the developing nations. Their national identity itself is in jeopardy because of their economic dependence and political instability.[55] Transnationalism can also be tinged with the stigma of ethnic fanaticism and religious affinities. But when there is an armed conflict or war, there seems to be a tacit understanding among the member States that if one among them is attacked by an aggressor or if a common danger looms over all of them, the entire group will undertake collective measures to face the aggressor or deal with the common enemy. Each nation in the group is prepared to contribute what it possibly can to the common defence, for, in a conflict, victory over the enemy is victory for all and defeat is considered a misfortune for each one of them. A complex multi-lateral arms race begins when nations belonging to a transnational group perceive that a common enemy is to be fought. Transnationalism is, however, an unpredictable political variable especially when it is known that its contents are more supported by feelings than by principles in interstate relations.

iii) Territorial and Boundary Disputes
Mere disputes among States would simply denote diverse competitive interests. The actual use of force is absent in such disputes. They are generally concerned with incompatible political issues. Disputes can also arise out of border incidents, relating to territorial or boundary questions. Presumably, they are comparatively easy to settle because the causes are easily identifiable and because they involve specific grievances.[56]

Most of the territorial and boundary disputes concerning the developing nations are colonial legacies and they are of a different genre from those described above. To suit their administrative purposes, the empire builders in the past cut and divided kingdoms and principalities which, most often, changed the original boundary line beyond identification. However, after "empires have fallen on evil days and nations have arisen to take their place,"[57] efforts are being made to find out the exact extent of their jurisdiction over territories. Nations which are contiguous and whose boundary lines are imaginary and artificial find it more difficult to prove their claims and counter-claims.[58]

With decolonisation after the Second World War, many developing nations were locked up in interstate boundary and territorial disputes. Some of them even went to war on the question of border disputes.[59] Now and then, they aroused national emotions to challenge the opponent either openly or by subversion. For, issues settled by the verdict of arms is no settlement as far as the aggrieved nation is concerned. Nor can the victor hold in peaceful possession what he had achieved by the use of arms. Hence the natural course open to both sides would be to further strengthen their forces by a spiral of arms race for another round of conflict over the same issue.

C. *Extra-regional Factors*

Extra-regional factors would mean those specific determinants which have a direct or indirect bearing on the course of arms build-up in various regions and on which would greatly depend the intensity and duration of regional arms races. However compelling may be the domestic and regional factors in creating a climate for an arms race between two States, without the synchronisation of extra-regional factors, an actual arms race is very difficult, if not impossible, to take place. The influence of extra-regional factors in the initiation of regional arms race is indeed significant. An intensive and prolonged regional arms race may sometimes be directly due to extra-regional factors which are generally beyond the control of regional powers. It is, therefore, essential to discern these extra-regional factors which lie behind the regional arms race and which are responsible to a very large extent in aggravating a regional arms race.

i) *Superpower Rivalry*

The likelihood of a regional arms race is greater where the superpowers take a keen interest in supplying arms to the regional powers under one pretext or other.

Armaments constitute an integral part of the arms race. It has already been established that developing nations, even if they have the will to run an arms race, do not have the necessary pre-requisites such as resources, industrial infrastructure, technology, and expertise to run an arms industry. The only possibility, therefore, by which they can think of enhancing their power position and subsequently embark on a serious competition with another in the region, is to acquire weapons from developed nations, particularly the superpowers. Hence the major arms producing nations have a definite role in the arms build-up of developing nations.

According to Kemp, the reasons for transfer of weapons to developing nations are mainly three: "A supplier country may consider the transfer of arms in the economic interest; or it may conclude that political and strategic considerations justify such a transfer; or its economic, political and strategic interests may converge to make the transfer of arms acceptable from a policy standpoint."[60] Hence it is evident that the weapon suppliers have been deliberately feeding the arms race of developing nations.

With their unlimited arms production, the superpowers have injected a dynamic element into international politics. It has its crisis points as some have observed along what has been called "the international shatter zone" where the main opposing forces are in direct contact.[61] Further, it takes the form of a tireless race for allies, raw materials, bases and armaments; in political terms, it requires a constant search for victory; in psychic terms, it calls for the pursuit of absolute hegemony over the adversary. This was the case of French and British nationalism in the Napoleonic era. Today rival nationalisms of a global dimension are of the American and Russian type.[62]

The objective of superpower nationalism is not to paint new colours across the atlas, but to win friends and influence people.[63] What they seek above all is allegiance.[64] Allegiance is unlikely to be won by sprinkling hydrogen bombs on foreign populations or even by hurling massed divisions of tanks and guns against them; the use of such crude weapons is not normally an attractive instrument of policy.[65] However, it does not necessarily follow that they will remain unconcerned in such situations where their vital interests are affected or at stake. The United States and the Soviet Union will not possibly confront each other in an open war (which would be a game of mutual suicide) to achieve their objectives though they have been fighting proxy wars in various part of the world.[66]

The more the superpowers get themselves involved in the regional politics of developing nations, the greater is the possibility of a regional arms race occurring there. Direct as well as indirect involvement in regional politics appears to be a 'must' for the realisation of their global objectives. Regional political conflicts are the levers through which superpower rivalry is introduced into a region.[67] When once the superpowers get a foothold in a particular region, they endeavour strenuously to strengthen that hold politically as well as militarily. The surest way of making themselves acceptable to local powers, they well know, is by supplying weapons in bulk to fight out old antagonisms among themselves.[68]

Lewis Richardson aptly observed long ago that arms races arise as a result of political conflicts, are kept alive by them and subside with them.[69] A developing country A having political conflicts with another developing country B in a region R, no doubt is capable of starting an arms race, at least at a primitive level as every country has some form of military power at its disposal. But it cannot escalate the arms race to the level of competition in more sophisticated armaments whatever may be the nature and intensity of their hostile relationship. But political conflicts among developing nations are a set of variables, easily manipulable in the overall framework of the global strategies of superpowers in which they stand to derive great advantages from these conflicts. Superpower X on agreed terms and conditions offers large quantities of weapons to the country A and superpower Y offers weapons to the country B to offset the weapons given to A by the rival and this starts off the arms race in a region. As the superpowers X and Y endeavour to sharpen the political conflicts, A and B would demand for more weapons and they would be given further, provided they are prepared to pay the political or strategic price. Therefore, it may be said the regional arms races arise as a result of big power machinations and are kept alive by them and are likely to subside only by their exercise of control over the arms transfers to developing nations. An exercise of total control over the arms transfer policies by the superpowers or other arms exporting countries is very unlikely to materialise for a long time to come without endangering their own economic positions in the process, let alone their global objectives, prestige, and influence in the developing regions of the world.

ii) *The Alliance System*

The alliance systems worked out by the two superpowers at the start of the Cold War are themselves instrumental for the transfer of weapons in large scale to vulnerable regions. Under CENTO and SEATO, for example, some of the developing nations which were closely associated with them were provided with military assistance and economic aid. Moreover, it was a strong incentive for them to become partners in an alliance system and also to stimulate a regional arms race. The *raison d'etre* of a developing nation's concern for entering into an alliance with a great power is not so much to subscribe to its global policies as to maintain its own internal security or legitimate self-defence; it also helped to build up a deterrent force against a neighbouring State.[70] The arms thus obtained, if necessary, could be used in a future conflict against an adversary. In the 50s and 60s weapons were supplied to under-developed countries to win their allegiance. However, that situation has now considerably changed. Some of the beneficiaries have changed camps for their own reasons, and many of them have adopted a non-aligned stance; they also have begun to diversify their weapon procurements.[71]

The involvement of the superpowers directly or indirectly in Korea, Vietnam, Cambodia, the Indian subcontinent and the Middle East enabled the local powers to acquire lethal weapons of mass destruction and the wars fought in those places were bloodier than anyone could have ever expected. It has been observed that wherever any developing country has joined an alliance system after World War II, it has led to a regional arms race precipitating unstable socio-political conditions and local wars.

iii) *Limited Wars*

The superpowers have a common interest in maintaining the stability of the centre as against the periphery. When their vital interests are deeply involved or their hegemony is challenged in the respective spheres of influence, they communicate to each other of their intentions in an effective manner by fighting proxy wars. In other words, because of the fearsome realisation that a thermo-nuclear war between the superpowers would bring down total destruction, local quarrels and disorders far from the capitals of the great powers would be exploited wherein the proxies function as a tool to test the will of the one superpower.[72] They are prepared to permit a certain amount of violence and strife at the periphery that happens to be the developing regions.[73] In fact, the concern of the superpowers to maintain the central balance and even to hold a balance of power in particular regions, assumes that regional wars may be permitted within the limiting parameter of the escalation threshold.

According to Ruth Sivard, of the more than 120 armed conflicts between 1955 and the early part of 1979 all but six occurred in developing nations. It is further observed that when foreign arms moved into at least 100 developing countries, violence also was on the rise. More nations had arms and more used them either internally or against foreign enemies. A study by Kende also has drawn the conclusion that there has been a close relation between those wars and arms trade or arms supply by big powers.[74]

iv) Arms Sales Competition

Militarily developed nations are also engaged in a keen competition to sell their armaments in different parts of the world. Caught up in a fierce competition are the United States, the Soviet Union, France and Britain.[75] The imperatives of the arms trade have almost relegated to the background the earlier considerations of supplies of weapons based on East-West strategic rivalries. Until lately, close allies and friends only were eligible for military assistance and economic aid. However, at present anyone could fetch weapons in the arms sellers' market. The developing countries are not less tempted to buy weapons even if they have to forego scarce resources for other developmental purposes. They can even gainfully bargain in the arms sellers' market. Each year, the weapons transferred are not only more numerous but also are more sophisticated and deadly.[76] If one is unwilling to sell particular types of weapons, the developing nations would threaten to seek alternate sources of supply which would ultimately strengthen their bargaining position.[77] Commercial considerations do not generally discriminate between customers, for war business is real 'big business'. Hence it is interesting to note that even mutually antagonistic and warring nations are supplied with weapons originating from a single source.

Armaments are a key currency in international politics as well as international trade.[78] What, in turn, the arms merchants are expected to reap after the sale of weapons to different developing nations are a mix of many blessings: political benefits, opportunities of employment and the balance of payment. "Arms sales abroad are encouraged, since greater sales reduce the per unit cost of weapons for the country which manufactures them; often R and D costs are recovered from the sale of new weaponry abroad."[79] The export of sophisticated weapons is accompanied by an export of military technical instructors which would aggravate existing tensions. It is an open secret that major powers sell weapons to suit their own foreign policy or self-interests, rather than to benefit the economies of the recipient countries. Arms sales particularly to oil producers have acquired recently an aura of respectability.[80]

According to Freedman an aggressive American sales policy helped to create a climate of fierce competition for large orders which the British and the French felt they had to meet. The setting up of the Defence Sales Organisation within the Ministry of Defence in 1965, to promote British military wares, was one response to this challenge.[81] The competition for this growing market was intensified by the flow of petro-dollars into the Middle East and the desire of the Western powers to regain some of them through a trade in arms.[82] Economic considerations more than strategic or foreign policy demands have become the major support for French arms transfers.[83] In short, the commercial competition abetted and stimulated by the military industrial complexes of the developed nations has substantially contributed to an acceleration of regional arms races.[84]

In sum, regional arms races are autonomous phenomena. The countries concerned are in most cases incapable of producing even a fraction of the arms they wish to possess. They have either to buy arms from other powers or belong to a military alliance system; in either case, they probably are expected to pay an invisible political and/or strategic price.

Normally an arms race is generated in regions in whose conflicts the major powers have more than a normal involvement. This involvement can be traditional (historical) or of contemporary vantage. As for instance, the Middle East, particularly the Persian Gulf region has been a cockpit of big power rivalry for several centuries. More recently, the arms transfer policies of the big powers, explicitly encouraging militarisation of the Gulf area represent a more virulent syndrome of their involvement in the region. Hence an attempt is made to briefly review the big power rivalry in the Persian Gulf region in the following pages.

REFERENCES

1 F.S. Northedge, ed., *The Use of Force in International Relations* (London: Faber and Faber Limited, 1974), p. 17.

2 Country groupings and regions are essentially geographical. "It should be noted, however, that only the United States and Canada are represented in 'North America' and that Mexico is included with Central and South America as 'Latin America'. Similarly, Egypt is assigned to the 'Near East' with other Asian countries, rather than to 'Africa'. In addition, the 13n ations which comprise the Organisation of Petroleum Exporting Countries (OPEC) are displayed as a group. These are geographically disparate: Iran, Iraq, Kuwait, Qatar, Saudi Arabia, and the United Arab Emirates in the Near East; Indonesia in East Asia; Algeria, Gabon, Libya and Nigeria in Africa, Ecuador and Venezuela in Latin America". See U.S. Arms Control and Disarmament Agency, *World Military Expenditures and Arms Trade*, 1963-1973 (Washington, D.C.: U.S. Government Printing Office, 1975), p. 4.

3 Richardson illustrated his model by examples of conventional arms races, especially the arms race preceding World War I; and the abstract models deal with two or more participants, without specification of their status (superpowers or regional powers). See Lewis F. Richardson, *Arms and Insecurity* (Pittsburg: The Boxwood Press, 1960).

4 For a very lucid exposition of the nuclear arms race and its possible consequences, see Philip Noel Baker, *The Arms Race: A Programme for World Disarmament* (London: Oceana Publications' 1958).

5 Samuel P. Huntington, "Arms Race: Pre-Requisites and Results",

reprinted from *Public Policy* (1958) in Robert J. Art and Kenneth N. Waltz, eds., *The Use of Force* (Boston: Little, Brown and Company Limited, 1971), p. 366.

6 Colin S. Gray, "The Arms Race Phenomenon", *World Politics* (Princeton), Vol. XXIV, no. 1, October 1971, p. 40; See also Teresa Clair Smith, "Arms Race Instability and War", *The Journal of Conflict Resolution* (Beverly Hills), Vol. 24, no. 2, June 1980, pp. 253-84.

7 Robert G. Kaiser, "US-Soviet Relations: Goodbye to Detente", *Foreign Affairs*, Vol. 59, no. 3, 1981. Reprinted in *Strategic Digest* (New Delhi), Vol. XI, no. 5, May 1981, pp. 434-50.

8 For an analysis of the multilateral arms control agreements, see SIPRI, *Arms Control: A Survey and Appraisal of Multilateral Agreements* (London: Taylor and Francis Ltd., 1978).

9 Jerome B. Wiesner, "The Cold War is Dead, But the Arms Race Rumbles On", *Bulletin of the Atomic Scientists*, (Chicago), June 1967, p. 6.

10 Max Lerner, *The Age of the Overkill* (New York: Simon and Schuster, 1962), p. 47; See also Francis, P. Hoeber and William Schneider, Jr. eds., *Arms, Men and Military Budgets: Issues for Fiscal Year 1978* (New York: Crane, Russak & Company, Inc., 1977), p. 27.

11 Ruth Leger Sivard, *World Military and Social Expenditures, 1980* (Virginia: World Priorities, 1980), p. 5.

12 *Ibid.*, p. 8; see also "Secretary of Defense Brown on American Military Strength", USICA, *Backgrounder* (American Center, New Delhi), October 10, 1980, pp. 8-10.

13 Laurence J. Korb, "The FY 1980-1984 Defense Program: Issues and Trends", *AEI Foreign Policy and Defense Review* (Washington, D.C.), Vol. 1, no. 4, 1979, p. 53.

14 Richard A. Falk and Saul H. Medlowitz, eds., *The Strategy of World Order, Vol. IV* (New York: World Law Fund, 1967), p. 8; also see "Military Research and Development: The Driving Force behind Armaments", *Bulletin of Peace Proposals* (Oslo), Vol. 1, 1978, p. 38.

15 "Secretary Haig Outlines US Arms Control Policy", *Official Text*, USICA (American Center, New Delhi), July 15, 1981, p. 6.

16 F.O. Miksche, "Arms Race in the Third World", *Orbis* (Philadelphia), Vol. 12, no.1, Spring 1968, pp. 161ff; Also see John H. Hoagland, "Arms in the Developing World", *Orbis*, Vol. 12, no. 1, Spring 1968, pp. 167ff. For a development of the structural aspect of a regional arms race with particular reference to the Arab-Israeli rivalry, see J.C. Hurewitz, *Middle East Politics: The Military Dimension* (New York: Frederick A. Praeger, 1969), Chapters 24 and 25.

17 Colin S. Gray, "The Urge to Compete: Rationales for Arms Racing", *World Politics*, Vol. 26, no. 2, January 1974, pp. 219-24.

18 Gray, n. 6, p. 41.

19 *Ibid.*

20 William Gutteridge, *Military Institutions and Power in the New
    States* (London: Pall Mall Press Ltd., 1964), p. 70.

21 Gutteridge, n. 20, p. 67.

22 "The right of self-preservation . . . is a right which belongs to
    States . . . it includes the protection of State, its honor, and its
    possessions, and the lives and property of its citizens". Lt. Com.
    Bruce Harlow, U.S.N., 'The Legal Use of Force—Short of War'
    UNIP, November 1966, quoted in James Cable, *Gunboat Diplomacy*
    (London: Chatto and Windus, 1971), p. 126; See also Northedge,
    n. 1.

23 Gavin Kennedy, *The Military in the Third World* (London: Gerald
    Duckworth and Company Ltd., 1974), p. 253.

24 Albert Wohlstetter, "Is there a Strategic Arms Race", *Foreign
    Policy* (Washington, D.C.), no. 15, Summer 1974, p. 3.

25 For an interesting view of how ethnically-designed militaries are
    frequently used by governments as vehicles through which to exert
    and maintain their authority, see Cynthia H. Enlone, "The Military
    Uses of Ethnicity", *Journal of International Studies* (London), Vol. 4,
    no. 3, Winter 1975-76, pp. 220-35.

26 Samuel P. Huntington, *Political Order in Changing Societies* (New
    Haven: Yale University Press, 1968), p. 177.

27 Rajni Kothari, *Footsteps into the Future* (New Delhi: Orient Long-
    mans Limited, 1974), p. 3.

28 Ivo K. Fierabend and Rosalind L. Fierabend, "Aggressive Beha-
    viours within Politics 1948-1962: A Cross-national Study", *Journal
    of Conflict Resolution* (London), Vol. 10, no. 2, 1966, p. 249.

29 Richard, P.Y. Li and William R. Thompson, "The Coup Contagion
    Hypothesis", *Journal of Conflict Resolution* (London), Vol. XIX,
    no. 1, March 1975, p. 87.

30 R.J. Rummel, "Dimensions of Conflict Behaviour within Nations,
    1946-1959", *Journal of Conflict Resolution*, Vol. X, no. 1. 1966, p. 65.

31 George C. Abbott, "Size, Viability, Nationalism and Politico-Econo-
    mic Development", *International Journal* (Toronto), Vol. 25,
    1969-70, p. 54.

32 J.W. Fulbright, *The Arrogance of Power* (New York: Random
    House, 1966), p. 5.

33 Richardson, n. 3, p. 75.

34 John W. Spanier and Joseph L. Nogee, *The Politics of Disarmament,*
    (New York: Frederick A. Praeger Inc., Publisher, 1962), p. 13.

35 Jerome D. Frank, *Sanity and Survival* (New York: Alfred A. Knopf,
    Inc., and Random House, Inc., 1967), p. 116.

36 For political role of the military, see William Gutteridge, "Arms
    Control and Developing Countries", in Frank Barnaby and Carlo
    Schaerf, eds., *Disarmament and Arms Control* (New York: Gordon
    and Breach Science Publishers, 1972) pp. 136-37.

37 Samuel P. Huntington, *The Soldier and the State* (Cambridge: The Belknap Press of Harvard University, 1967), pp. 64-65. For an analytical view of the military mind, see *ibid.*, pp. 59-79.

38 Jacques Van Doorn, *Armed Forces and Society* (The Hague: Mouton and Co., N.V. Publishers, 1968), p. 28.

39 *Ibid.*

40 For a series of case studies on the role of the army in politics, see Henry Bienen, ed., *The Military Intervenes: Case Studies in Political Development* (New York: Russell Sage Foundation, 1968); See also H. Jesse Kochar, "Coup d'etat", *Sunday Standard* (Cochin), August 31, 1980.

41 John W. Burton, *Conflict and Communication* (London: Macmillan and Co. Ltd., 1969), p. 93.

42 Charles O. Larche, Jr., and Abdul A. Said, *Concepts of International Politics* (Englewood Cliffs: Prentice Hall Inc., 1964), p. 147.

43 *Ibid.*

44 V.V. Sveics, *Small Nation Survival* (New York: Exposition Press, 1970), pp. 25-26.

45 Kenneth E. Boulding, *Conflict and Defence: A General Theory* (New York: Harper and Brothers, 1962), p. 5.

46 Mack and Snyder, in Ralf M. Goldman, "A Theory of Conflict Process and Organisational Offices", *Journal of Conflict Resolution*, Vol. X, no. 3, 1966, p. 335.

47 For a detailed analysis of the causes of conflict, see Warner Levi, "On the Causes of War and the Conditions of Peace", *Journal of Conflict Resolution*, Vol. 4, no. 4, 1960, pp. 411-20.

48 Quincy Wright, *A Study of War* (Chicago: The University of Chicago Press, 1965), p. 9.

49 "Antagonism is related to latent conflict", See Feliks Gross, *World Politics and Tension Areas* (New York: New York University Press, 1966), p. 25.

50 Vilhelm Aubert, "Competition and Dissensions: Two Types of Conflict and Conflict Resolution", *Journal of Conflict Resolution*, Vol. 7, no. 1, 1963, p. 26.

51 Leon Bramson and George W. Goethals, eds., *War* (New York: Basic Books, Inc., 1967), p. 244.

52 Report of the Secretary General, *Economic and Social Consequences of the Arms Race and of Military Expenditures* (New York: United Nations, 1972), p. 15.

53 Kirby Page, *Must We Go to War* (New York: Farrar and Reinehart, 1973), p. 206.

54 K.J. Holsti, *International Politics* (New Jersey: Prentice Hall, Inc., 1967), p. 443.

55 "The question of orientations to the national political system as a whole constitutes one of the most serious developmental problems in the political culture of the new nations.... At some point in the history of any new nation, as loyalty to the traditional subnational

units conflict with national loyalties and goals, the issues of national identity are likely to become paramount". See G.A. Almond and G.B. Powell, Jr., *Comparative Politics: A Developmental Approach* (New Delhi: Amerind Publishing Pvt. Ltd., 1975), p. 52.

56 K.J. Holsti, "Resolving International Conflicts: A 'Taxonomy of Behaviour and Some Figures in Procedures", *Journal of Conflict Resolution*, Vol. 10, no. 3, 1966, p. 272.

57 Rupert Emerson, *From Empire to Nation* (Cambridge, Mass: Harvard University Press, 1960), p. 3.

58 Some would categorise claims as legal, emotional and accidental. For a detailed analysis of this, see Shimon Tzabar, *The White Flag Principle* (London: The Penguin Press, 1972), pp. 32-37. Tzabar gives an example for legal claim, the India-China border dispute; for emotional claim, Israel's claim to Jerusalem; and, for accidental claim, the dispute on the Ussuri River on 31 March 1969, See *Ibid*.

59 For a very interesting account of the boundary problems, see Carl Costa Widstrand, ed., *African Boundary Problems* (Uppasala: The Scandinavian Institute of African Studies, 1969), pp. 22-32. Frontier conflicts of recent times have led to large-scale war, partly due to the intervention of outside parties, See Evan Luard, ed., *The International Regulation of Frontier Disputes* (London: Thames and Hudson, 1970), pp, 225-26.

60 Geoffrey Kemp, "Arms Traffic and Third World Conflict", *International Conciliation* (New York), no. 577, March 1970, p. 12.

61 Charles O. Lerche, Jr. and Abdul A. Said, n. 42, p. 149; See also Paul H. Nitze, "Strategy in the Decade of the 1980s", *Foreign Affairs*, (New York), Vol. 59, no. 1, February, 1980, pp. 82-101.

62 *Ibid.*

63 John W. Burton, *Peace Theory: Preconditions of Disarmament* (New York: Alfred A. Knopf, Inc., 1962), p. 16.

64 Kamaleshwar Sinha, *Zulfikar Ali Bhutto* (Delhi: ISSD Publications, 1972), p. 105.

65 Evan Luard, *Conflict and Peace in the Modern International System* (London: University of London Press Ltd., 1970), p. 187.

66 *Ibid.*, p. 186.

67 Arms races arise from regional tensions. The quarrels from which they stem normally predate the involvement of interested extra-regional powers. But in regions where in the past years Britain and France abandoned their dependencies one after another, the United States and the USSR could hardly have failed to become rivals. See J.C. Hurewitz, no. 16. p. 11.

68 John Muttam, *U.S. Pakistan and India: A Study of U.S. Role in India-Pakistan Arms Race* (New Delhi: Sindhu Publications Ltd., 1974), p. 63.

69 Lewis F. Richardson, n. 3, p. 13.

70 David D. Newsom, "America Engulfed", *Foreign Policy* (Washington, D.C.), no. 43, Summer 1981, p. 21.

71 Ruth Leger Sivard, n. 11; See also Shirin Tahir-Kheli, "Proxies and Allies: The Case of Iran and Pakistan", *Orbis* (Philadelphia), Vol. 24, no. 2, Summer, 1980, pp. 339-52.

72 Lincoln P. Bloomfield and Amelia C. Leiss, *Controlling Small Wars: A Strategy for the 1970s* (New York: Alfred A. Knopf, 1967), p. 3.

73 Harry G. Shaffer and Jan S. Prybyla, ed., *From Underdevelopment to Affluence: Western Soviet and Chinese Views* (New York: Appleton-Century Crofts, 1968), p. 49.

74 Ruth Leger Sivard, *World Military and Social Expenditures, 1979* (Virginia: World Priorities, 1979), p. 8; See also Istvan Kende, "Wars of Ten Years (1967-1976)", *Journal of Peace Research* (Oslo), Vol. XV, no. 3, 1978. Reprinted in *Strategic Digest* (New Delhi), Vol. XI, no. 3, March 1981, pp. 197-214.

75 Ron Huisken, "The Development of the Conventional Arms Trade", in Robert O' Neill, ed., *Insecurity* (Canberra: Australian National University Press, 1978), p. 40.

76 *Weekly Compilations of Presidential Documents*, Vol. 13, no. 21, May 23, 1977.

77 George Thayer, *The War Business* (London: Weidenfeld and Nicolson, 1969), pp. 231-33.

78 Lawrence Freedman, "Britain and the Arms Trade", *International Affairs* (London), Vol. 54, no. 1, July 1978, p. 378.

79 M.A. Husain, "Third World and Disarmament: Shadow and Substance", *Third World Quarterly* (London). Vol. II, no. 1, January 1980, p. 96.

80 *The Hindu* (Madurai), April 29, 1981.

81 Lawrence Freedman, n. 78, p. 383.

82 *Ibid.*, p. 383.

83 Edward A. Kolodziej, "France and the Arms Trade", *International Affairs* (London), Vol. 56, no. 1, January 1980, p. 61.

84 For a deeper understanding of the role of military industrial complexes in stimulating the arms trade, see Carrol W. Pursell, Jr., *The Military Industrial Complex* (New York: Harper and Row, Publishers, 1972); and Sam C. Sarkesian ed., *The Military Industrial Complex: A Reassessment, Vol. II* (Beverly Hills: California Sage Publications, Inc., 1972).

2

Big Power Rivalry in the Persian Gulf: A Historical Perspective

The area that is involved in this study is the Gulf region which includes the States of Muscat and Oman, the United Arab Emirates (UAE), Qatar, Bahrain, Saudi Arabia, Kuwait, Iraq and Iran[1] (For details of area and population, see Table 1).

TABLE 1

Area, Population and Armed Forces of the Gulf

Country	Area sq. miles	Population	Total armed forces
Iran	628,000	41,500,000	2,000,000
Saudi Arabia	972,000	8-12,000,000*	51,500
Iraq	172,000	14,300,000	517,250
Kuwait	5,000	1,450,000	12,400
Oman	82,000	970,000	23,550
Qatar	4,000	260,000	6,000
Bahrain	230	400,000	2,700
UAE	32,000	1,130,000	49,000

*estimated

Source : Adapted from *The Military Balance 1983-1984* (London, 1983).

From ancient times the Gulf region was considered important by different nations having diverse interests in the region. For the Greeks and the Romans, the land of the South Arabians which produced frankincense and spices was fascinating. The ancient trade route to the markets of India and Somaliland lay across the Gulf region. For the colonial powers the sealanes around the Arabian Peninsula provided an arena of rivalry. They too were, at first, interested in the promotion of trade and commerce. The Portuguese were the first to arrive on the scene towards the end of the fifteenth century. They occupied a very strategic spot in the region, namely Hormuz on the Persian side of the Gulf. Their influence however lasted only till 1622 when, with the help of the English who too initially came there as merchants, seeking trade and fortune, the Shah Abbas I of Iran recaptured Hormuz, the citadel of Portuguese power, and opened the markets of Persia and Arabia to English commerce.[2] Britain first became interested in the area as a consequence of its drive for paramountcy in the Indian Ocean. British factories competed with French and Dutch establishments and eventually[3] supplanted them too. Britain's complete sway over the Gulf region was relatively established by 1770 after the British annexation and conquest of India.

BRITAIN'S INTERESTS

The evolution of British influence in the Gulf region had passed through three general stages before it officially ended in 1971, according to Mohammed Khalifa. First, there was an infiltration stage on a purely trading basis along with other European powers through the 16th, 17th and 18th centuries. This was followed by a period of defensive penetration during which Britain sought to protect the sea lanes to its newly acquired empire in India through a system of maritime control. This era took up the last few decades of the 18th and most of the 19th centuries. It was also during the latter century that the third stage of British presence began with the continued consolidation of their position which finally led (in the 1890s) to a virtual British monopoly of foreign control in the area that continued until independence.[4]

After the annexation and conquest of India, Britain was convinced of the "necessity for protecting the Indian sea route and to a lesser extent, the overland route to India by way of the Euphrates and Persian Gulf, from the attacks of pirates."[5] The Middle East was considered the lifeline to the empire and hence all approaches to this area came strictly under British control.[6] With the successful elimination of all Western powers from the region, the British was in a position to undertake to safeguard the trade routes to India, mainly by way of entering into special truces with several Sheikhdoms in the Gulf. For 150 years Britain's only material interests in the coast, according to Hawley were: (a) to end piracy which looted their trade ships; (b) to exclude other foreign powers whose ambitions threatened the security of the Indian Empire; (c) security of the communications system that passed through the Gulf; (d) to abolish the slave trade which was rampant in the area; and (e) after 1947 with Indian independence, British interest in the area induced them to involve in the internal affairs of the States.[7]

The pirate-controlled Gulf posed many problems to the Sheikhdoms which lacked both adequate resources and naval capability to exterminate piracy from the Gulf waters. There were frequent depredations of piracy on British ships. To protect their own interests the British navy moved in, rounded up the pirate ships and burnt the entire pirate fleet in the harbour of Ras al-Khaima. The Gulf was thus freed of piracy. According to the truces which were signed with the various Sheikhdoms, Britain recognised their ruling rights and the Sheikhs accepted British protection. The entire history of the long relationship between Britain and the Trucial States, Bahrain and Qatar has been based on the general Treaty of the Cessation of Plunder and Piracy by land and sea of February 5, 1820 and the perpetual Maritime Truce of May 4, 1853. Britain's principal role throughout was to maintain the Trucial system and to police the Maritime Truce.[8]

It was Britain's responsibility to provide external defence of most of these Gulf States.[9] In practice, even the serious internal law and order problems were dealt with by Britain. The relatively small armies of these States insofar as "they had a function at all, acted either as an internal peace force, or as auxiliaries to and under the command of European forces.[10] But, despite Britain's protectorship over these Sheikhdoms, interstate disputes and conflicts continued to exist which, of course, were the key factors that helped British diplomacy to succeed in maintaining the special position of Britain in the area. "The states were allowed to fight each other at will, provided there was no breach of Maritime Truce".[11]

The State of Oman attached particular importance to its relations with Britain in the 19th century in view of its pre-eminent position in Arabia and its willingness to work with the British. Oman became instrumental in preventing piracy against British shipping, in securing facilities for British steamers stopping at Muscat, and in providing guarantee for the establishment of Indo-European Telegraph in 1864.[12] Between 1929-32 Britain developed imperial airways with bases at Shinas, Suhar and Muscat.[13] By 1920, Britain exercised complete military and political control over Oman by stationing a battalion of the Indian army and the appointment of an Englishman as *de facto* ruler of the State.[14]

With the British paramountcy in India, Britain could effectively dominate the Gulf region. The importance of the Gulf was four-fold:[15] commercial, political, strategic, and navigational. The Gulf was used for all legitimate trade and shipping by all nations. From the middle of the nineteenth century, Britain maintained a small but adequate naval presence to ensure the peaceful use of the Gulf waters. But the British strategy was to insulate the region against any hostile power and keep it always under unchallenged British supremacy. For, by now, not only Britain came to realise increasingly the importance of retaining the dominance of this strategic area by every device available to it, but also other nations like France, Russia and Germany felt the need to make their presence there. However Britain outmanoeuvred them and forced them to sign formal agreements recognising British supremacy in the area.[16]

During World War I, when Iran faced severe internal political, economic and constitutional problems there arose an intense rivalry among Russia, Britain and Germany. Throughout the nineteenth century Russia and Britain clashed repeatedly in Iran to obtain imperial privileges of one sort or another.[17] But, it is significant to note that from the beginning of the 19th century up to Churchill's intervention in Greece in 1944 Britain had constantly bargained and fought to prevent continental great powers, primarily Russia, from gaining a foothold in this region.[18]

FACTORS LEADING TO BRITAIN'S WITHDRAWAL

However, the peace-keeping role and the special position Britain enjoyed in the Gulf could not survive the vicissitudes of history. There were several factors responsible for it.

First, after World War II, the British empire itself was in the process of disintegration. Under the pressure of decolonisation and declining economic and military power, Britain was reduced to a secondary power and decided to reduce and wherever necessary withdraw its military presence. As a result of this policy of withdrawal especially from India, the mainstay of British military power east of Suez, Britain appeared to have lost its credibility as a great power. Without the Indian empire, Britain could not sustain its power in the Gulf and hence Indian independence in 1947 considerably weakened British position in the area.

Secondly, the triumph of the Indian national movement against British colonialism accelerated similar movements elsewhere. "It was during the intervening period between the First and Second World Wars that Arab political consciousness truly developed, nationalist parties came into being and massive struggles for independence were launched. Roughly during the same period, Indian political movements also forged ahead and political parties became truly representative of the people".[19] Arab nationalism was the rising tide which swept across the Middle East and the Gulf region. Earlier it had begun to be an effective counterforce to the policy of imperial domination even under the Ottoman empire. "The espousal of nationalism encouraged the principle of self-determination and both led to the struggle for independence from foreign rule."[20] Arab nationalist movements gathered momentum in the 1940s and as a result Syria and Lebanon which were Mandated territories achieved the status of independent republics in 1946; in

1948 the British troops were withdrawn from the Mandated territory of Palestine; in 1951, the Anglo-Egyptian treaty was denounced; in 1953, Libya was proclaimed an independent kingdom.[21]

Arab nationalism played a major role in Egypt in checking British imperialism which basing itself there expected to control the entire Arab lands. However, it received a great rebuff in the liquidation of the monarchy through a revolution in 1952. The Iraqi revolution in 1958, which again was one of the finest results of practical Arab nationalism, ended Britain's political role there; and in 1961, Kuwait regained her complete independence from British protection. Besides, a consciousness of the past glory of the Muslim empire and of the brilliant cultural achievements of the Arabs suggested a future possibility. Political awakening came in the wake of intellectual awakening. Political passivity gave way to political activity; for once in centuries change became a desideratum.[22] In fact, through the influence of European liberalism, there had emerged what was termed Islamic modernism which was a conscious attempt to combat European influences on the Muslim World by means of a restatement and re-implementation of the principles of Islam.[23] The traditionalists as well as the modernists were resentful of foreign domination and distrustful of imperialist intentions in the Arab lands. Concerted pressure was being steadily built up against Britain to vacate the area particularly after the Suez fiasco in 1956. Thus Arab nationalist pressure was one of the contributory factors for British 'withdrawal, from the Gulf region.[24]

Thirdly, pan-Arabism by now had come to inspire Arab leaders like Nasser to effectively organize opposition against foreign domination. Pan-Arabism, according to Cecil Crabb, was a natural reaction against former colonial subjection and it was sustained by many forces of which three have been of lasting historical significance: a common language—Arabic, a common religion—Islam, and common racial ties—Semitic.[25] Nasser was not merely an Arab nationalist interested only in the liberation of Egypt from foreign domination.

"Arabs are a single nation," he asserted, and that "every Arab speaking country is our country, and our country absolutely must be liberated. Widely separated in space, we are united by community of sentiments, as also by our common origins, by the bond of religion and language."[26] Nasser's vision of pan-Arabism found wide support all over the Middle East. His historically bold step in nationalising the Suez Canal followed by an effective resistance to the combined attack by the forces of Britain, France and Israel in 1956[27] galvanized pan-Arabism and national liberation movements. The Suez crisis produced strong reactions in the Gulf. The British Adviser in Bahrain was asked to leave in 1957. Even young students in the schools of the Trucial States demonstrated, expressing their sympathy with Nasser's resoluteness against foreign aggression.[28] Pan-Arabism as an effective movement has been constantly trying to dislodge all incursions of foreign influence from the Gulf region as well.

Fourthly, political polarisation and left radicalism also quickened the process of British withdrawal from the Gulf region. The strategic importance of the region because of the world's largest oil reserves added to the self-confidence of the nations[29] and strengthened their resolve to exploit this abundant natural resources and not to allow it to be exploited any more by colonial and neo-colonialist powers.

Even Iran could not remain isolated from the main stream of national upheavals. Iran began to assert its independence from foreign influence in early 1950s. The expropriation of the Anglo-Iranian oil company by the Mossadeq government in 1951 was a clear manifestation of this spirit.[30]

Fifthly, an important factor which compelled an early British withdrawal from the Gulf was the American intrusion in the Middle East after World War II, attracted greatly by the oil interest. To further its economic, political and strategic interests, the US exploited to the maximum the existing raging local nationalism against British colonialism. According to Marlowe, every successive British withdrawal from the Middle East had been hastened by the United States.[31] Marlowe quotes instances to prove his point: *1*) British withdrawal from Palestine was hastened by US support for it, accompanied by a refusal to assist in implementing a pro-zionist policy in Palestine. *2*) The expulsion of the Anglo-Iranian Oil Company from Iran in May 1951 and its eventual replacement by an international consortium with a 40 per cent American interest was effected by American diplomatic support for the Mossadeq Government. It has been lately disclosed by the British government that Britain had planned an invasion of Persia following the depossession of Anglo-Iranian Oil Corporation in which Britain held a major stock interest. But the US refused to back the venture.[32] *3)* The US did not support the military policy of Britain on the Suez Canal zone; British withdrawal was hastened by US lack of cooperation. *4)* The US refused to join the Baghdad pact although this pact had been regarded by the Americans themselves as an integral part of American inspired defence system in the Middle East.

The US, motivated by its own political, economic and strategic interests, constantly militated against British continuance in the area. Pushing their English and French competitors out of the Arab markets, the US monopolies came to establish their control over the economy of the Arab countries. Up to the Second World War the English monopolies controlled 80.9 per cent of Middle Eastern oil and the US 12.8 per cent. In 1952 the US share in Middle Eastern oil output was to the tune of 66 per cent of the total, an increase at the expense of Britain.[33] All these instances indicate that after the Second World War, the US had stepped up its assault on the positions of Britain and France in the Middle East and North Africa in an attempt to oust them and thereby become the dominant power in these important areas.[34]

Sixthly, Britain's resolve to relinquish its military presence in the Gulf region was also induced by its declining economic position besides its weakened military power. In a debate on the issue of withdrawal from the Gulf region, Harold Wilson emphatically stated in the House of Commons: "It is not only in our interests but in those of our friends and allies for this country to strengthen its economic base quickly and decisively. There is no military strength whether for Britain or for our alliances except on this basis of economic strength, and it is on this basis that we best ensure the security of this country."[35]

EARLY US INTEREST IN THE GULF REGION

Historically, the United States is a latecomer to the Middle East in general and the Gulf region in particular. Until the

First World War the American interest in the Middle East was said to be cultural; and during the inter-war period it was commercial, mostly because of the Arab oil wealth; the realisation of the crucial importance of oil in the war greatly attracted American interests there in a big way.[36] Oil was first discovered in Iran in 1908. By 1913 the British government acquired the controlling interest in the Anglo-Iranian Oil Company. In 1927 the biggest oil producing field in Iraq was discovered—the Kirkuk oil field. The discovery of oil in Bahrain in 1932 stimulated further search for oil in the Arabian peninsula. A large concession by Saudi Arabia granted in favour of Standard Oil Company of California and Texas Oil Company in 1933 produced good results. By 1939 American oil interests in the Middle East had become one of the most important of American foreign investment.[37]

According to Crabb, the US had no foreign policy at all for the Middle East before the Second World War because it thought it had no vital interests in the far away and backward region.[38] However towards the end of World War II, it was more than clear to the US administration that oil was an important ingredient in any war efforts and that this commodity could be easily exploited in huge quantities from the Gulf region, particularly Saudi Arabia.

The lend-lease arrangement which US pursued successfully with Saudi Arabia in 1943 was mainly due to the clear machinations of the Texas Oil Company and Standard Oil Company of California to further their oil control and pre-empt possible British influence in Saudi Arabia. The arguments in favour of the lend-lease deal were chiefly two: firstly, American home reserves were being rapidly exhausted and that there would be a shortage of crude oil for meeting the requirements of the US armed services and the essential industrial and civilian economy by the end of 1944. Secondly, Saudi Arabian oil was important to the national welfare of the US. But the Britsh influence there, which the US oil companies surmised was jeopardizing American interests in Arabian oil reserves, had to be counteracted.[39] Through an elaborate process of political bickerings and diplomatic bargainings there emerged the Anglo-American Oil Agreement of September 24, 1945, stipulating equal access to the

Americans in what was till then a British monopoly for oil exploration.[40]

America was the only big power that emerged unscathed by the Second World War. With abundant resources at its disposal, the United States became the most prosperous nation and militarily the strongest of all. Since then, it presumed it could safely exercise the role of a world police-man. But, the rapid rise of the Soviet power was a challenge to American supremacy and tended to militate against the global objectives of the United States. The irreconcilable antagonism of the Cold War politics and ideological confron-tation between the United States and Soviet Union began to express themselves in bloc rivalries everywhere. The United States soon recognised that the Gulf countries, particularly Iran and Iraq could become vulnerable to Soviet military penetration and its own oil interests would be seriously undermined. The predominantly US economic interests in the area were assumed to be closely related to the strategic concern which evolved subsequently as a new phase in US Soviet relations. Henceforward, US presence in the area came to be interpreted in terms of the security of the countries in the region against any potential threats from the Soviet Union. According to Marlowe, the communist threat as applied to the Middle East was a mere excuse for Western intervention and that the United States, with its superior resources, had simply taken over from the British and French and that "the common aim of all three was to make the Arab countries the instruments of their policies and the servants of their economies."[41]

With the decline and fall of the British empire, when it retreated to the British Isles, the United States, through its alliance system and economic and military assistance pro-grammes succeeded in acquiring a number of strategic bases all over the world. The Eisenhower Doctrine was formulated underscoring the need to use US forces in the Gulf region or anywhere "to secure and protect the territorial integrity and political independence of such nations requesting such aid against overt aggression from any nation controlled by inter-national communism". In the Middle East and the Gulf region, however, Britain despite all its economic problems continued to have a minimal presence in collaboration with the United States which again was construed to exclude any Russian presence within the Gulf itself.[42] Iran and Iraq were persuaded to join the military alliance system, purported to contain the so-called Soviet expansionism and in return they received economic aid and military assistance. First, the Baghdad Pact came into being; but later as a result of the Iraqi revolution in 1958 Iraq withdrew from the pact. Hence forward it became known as the Central Treaty Organisation with its headquarters at Ankara. These military pacts provided the opportunity for the United States to play Cold War politics in the Gulf region.

The unobstrusive penetration of the United States into this area reduced considerably Britain's economic burden. However, this was done within the overall framework of the US global strategy to promote its own interest in the region. The compulsions of global strategy seem to have induced the United States to have a joint strategy of the Anglo-American presence against the Soviet Union. A combined Anglo-American naval presence in the Gulf region, in which the British role was stipulated to be nominal, was the strategy that was favoured by America.

It should be remembered that from the early 1960s the US manifested its presence in the Gulf region by taking over the former British naval base at Bahrain. In fact, the American forces had been using facilities supplied by the British in Bahrain for over a quarter of a century and the new agreement according to Burrell was in fact equivalent only to change of landlords.[43]

THE THEORY OF POWER VACUUM

When the British withdrawal from the Gulf actually took place in 1971, the US was not able or unwilling to assume British responsibilities because, first of all the American public was caught up in the 'Vietnam Syndrome' as a result of the traumatic experience of US forces in the Vietnam war. Secondly, any attempt to substitute Britain in the area would have been strongly opposed by nationalistic resistance movements which took a variety of forms in these countries.

The same radical Arab forces which compelled Britain's withdrawal were also at work against the US for a long time. Hence the advance of American imperialism into this area and its constant search for spheres of influence motivated by its own conception of world leadership and its unabated quest for natural resources to lay hands on, became increasingly difficult.

Britain's decision in 1968 to withdraw militarily from the area by 1971 was an important development which set the entire region into a new political awakening. The littoral states in the Gulf hoped for a new era of independence and self-determination. They felt confident in managing their own affairs unfettered by vested foreign interest. Even the late Shah of Iran maintained that the security of the Persian Gulf was the responsibility of the littoral states and that great powers should keep out of the Gulf area.[44]

In the context of the changed situation, a number of Sheikhdoms which depended on Britain for their external defence became aware of their responsibility and created a flutter of political re-alignment of forces. They initiated a process of adjusting themselves to a new regional set up which would be politically viable to absorb the shocks of a regional rebirth. Seven Sheikhdoms—Abu Dhabi, Dubai, Sharjah, Ras al-Khaima, Fujairah, Ajmen and Umm al-Quwain—federated into what is now known as the United Arab Emirates (UAE). Saudi Arabia was politically very active in the formation of the federation. Its attempt to include the Sheikhdoms of Bahrain and Qatar, however, did not succeed. They opted to maintain their autonomy. These developments made it clear that the US would not get local support for an intimidating military presence in the area.

However, the theory of power vacuum was advanced by the West as a facade providing an opportunity for the US to embellish its naval presence in the Indian Ocean-Persian Gulf area following the British withdrawal in 1971.[45] The British decision to withdraw its troops from the Gulf was immediately taken to mean the end of the special position which Britain enjoyed there for more than 150 years.

It meant strategically that as an external power guarantee-ing the security and stability of the region in return for certain political and military rights, Britain has ceased to be the 'guardian' of the region. In other words, Britain's responsibility of maintaining the regional security and stability that arose from the colonial treaty relationship with the Gulf States no longer existed because of historical reasons. This led to the propaganda that a power vacuum[46] would be created and conditions of instability and scramble for power would follow.

What is meant by a power vacuum? According to the traditional sense, a power vacuum is described as a "geographical region that is militarily and politically weak and hence invites military or subversive incursion from abroad."[47] The colonial powers in the past followed the policy of annexation and conquest of strategically and economically important territories in Asia and Africa. Historically, therefore, military might of the colonial power substituted for the defencelessness of militarily weak States.

In the traditional sense, power vacuum was understood as the absence of a formidable power which could withstand the onslaught of colonial penetration into African or Asian nations. As long as there was the presence of a colonial power, nobody raised the question of a power vacuum. It was also taken for granted that the external power undertook the responsibility of maintaining the security and stability of those regions which came under their complete sway.

However, it should be said that the theory of power vaccum is of recent origin. It has been introduced as an *ex post facto* justification of a certain situation in which the colonisers as the dominant powers were forced to withdraw militarily for historical reasons. This theory can be said as the conceptualisation of a historical development, namely the withdrawal of imperial powers. It was conceived by the colonial powers recently and was offered as an intellectual explanation to the phenomenon of the disappearance of the great power presence from any region in Asia or Africa.

The power vacuum theory viewed in the traditional sense is to be discarded because it assumes that after the withdrawal of the colonial powers, there is the possibility of a region reverting to a situation of instability and insecurity; and it seeks to rationalise *ex post facto* a situation which does not take into account the structure of power obtained after decolonisation in various regions of Asia and Africa.

The power vacuum theory is to be rejected on other grounds too: *i*) this theory implies or assumes that an external power which is also a great power is required to maintain the stability and security of the region; *ii*) it also implies that there is no significant single or combination of powers locally available, capable enough to maintain the stability and security of the region concerned in the absence of such an external power; and *iii*) it further implies that when a colonial power which came into a region vacates it, any other external power may automatically step into the shoes of a receding power. However, when the colonial powers withdraw indepen dent local powers emerge and it will be their individual or collective responsibility to ensure the security of the region.

Even within the framework of the given definition of power vacuum, it is possible to argue that its application to the Gulf situation, following Britain's relinquishment of its traditional role as the protector of the small Sheikhdoms seems inappropriate and irrelevant. The two basic components of the definition are a region's military defencelessness and political weakness. Firstly, it may be argued that the kind of military defencelessness of the States bordering the Gulf, as of today existed even during the period of British protectorship of the region. For, despite Britain's peace-keeping role there, a number of conflicts plagued this region and Britain could do very little to settle them nor could it have any practical control over them.[48] The Saudi seizure of Buraimi in 1952, the Iraqi threat to annex Kuwait in 1962[49] and the externally supported challenge to the authority of the ruler of Bahrain in 1964 were all instances where Britain proved least useful in settling them. Britain's failure in solving local issues has been attributed to its disruptionist policies towards the Middle East. For, according to Marlowe: The "British decision which was in effect a conscious decision to swim against instead of with the tide, to resist instead of attempting to cooperate with the forces of nationalism in the Middle East, to perpetuate the divisions rather than to encourage the unity of the Arab States, to sustain reactionary rather than to come to terms with progressive forces in the Arab world was no doubt in part the instinctive reaction of a declining imperial power in retreat before the forces of nationalism".[50] It should be noted, further, that the decrease in the incidents of local conflicts after Britain had relinquished its responsibility of this region, has brought about a qualitative change in the situation.[51] The regional powers themselves have manifested their confidence and resolve to maintain regional security and stability.

Political weakness or social backwardness which constitutes another aspect of power vacuum in the conventional sense when applied to the Gulf region becomes irrelevant. For, the concept of political weakness itself tends to be rather relative. If it is taken to mean a lack of a high level of bureaucratic structure of management, then, it would be that this region suffered such weakness.[52] But if it is taken to mean that the States in this region lacked the political will to manage their own affairs, then, this concept certainly contradicts a number of developments following Britain's decision to withdraw from the region. The will of the seven tiny Sheikhdoms of the region which were under the British protectorate for years to federate and the political arrangements of Bahrain and Qatar to constitute separate independent sovereign states did clearly demonstrate the ability of these nations to identify their national and regional interests and to make efforts to achieve them through legitimate political means. These activities may be viewed only as signs of political maturity and not that of political weakness.

The purpose of the UAE federation is to cement ties between them in all fields, to coordinate plans for their development and prosperity, to reinforce the respect of each one of them for the independence and sovereignty of the others, to unify their foreign policies and representation, and to strengthen the collective defence of their countries with a view to safeguarding their security, safety and mutual interests in such a manner as to ensure the fulfillment of their aspirations and realise the hopes of the greater Arab land.[53]

The readiness and speed with which they sorted out their problems to live in harmony belie the prophets of doom who were predicting increased tension and instability in the area after the British withdrawal.[54] Hence the power vacuum theory appears to have been advocated to justify an increased US naval presence in the Indian Ocean-Persian Gulf area as Britain decided in 1968 to abdicate its beleaguered military presence in the region. Immediately following the British decision to withdraw, the US navy started regular deployment of carrier task forces to the Indian Ocean and the Gulf.[55] At the same time, the US speedily initiated the process of developing the base at Diego Garcia and obtained the 'use' of Masirah island, off the coast of Oman, a sultanate on the extreme south-east tip of the Arabian Peninsula.[56] The Royal Air Force (RAF) maintained a base here since 1958 under a secret agreement[57] with the ruler of Oman that provided for landing rights to other friendly powers.[58]

Burrell and Cottrell are of the view that the US decided to continue a naval presence in the Gulf since the British withdrawal, and there were potentially serious psychological and political disadvantages in any decision to withdraw from its long established position in the area.[59] This appeared to have been the third instance of a maritime power's success in corroborating the historical theory that command of the sea is the pre-requisite of power in the Gulf.[60] This did not mean that the US wished to hold any commitment that would give the appearance of reversion to anything remotely resembling the former great power stranglehold on the region.[61]

US OBJECTIVES IN THE GULF

The US has developed, over the years, definite interest in the Gulf region. It is centred on the one commodity, oil. As Britain withdrew in 1971, the US seemed to have defined its objectives in the Gulf which were mainly four[62] and even after a decade they remain the same:

   i) to support indigenous efforts to ensure regional security, to provide stability and to foster orderly development without outside interference;

   ii) to assist peaceful resolution of territorial and other disputes among the regional powers and the opening up of better channels of communication among them;

   iii) to ensure continued access to and protection of the Gulf oil supplies, to maintain reasonable rates and supply of sufficient quantities of oil to meet US needs and those of its European and Asian allies; and

iv) to protect US commercial and financial interests and investments in the Gulf region.

To achieve these objectives, the US applied the Nixon Doctrine of the late 60s which revolved round the principle of allowing surrogates to guard American and Western interests in peripheral regions instead of direct involvement as was the case in Vietnam.[63] This was a new approach and a fresh basis for a new relationship with the States of the Gulf thereby making it expedient in exploiting the sources of energy and raw materials "at unfair prices out of all proportion to the rising prices of finished products in developed countries.[64]

But what gave a big jolt to the US and its allies was the use of Arab oil as a political weapon to achieve definite political goals[65] and the decision of the members of OPEC (Iran, Iraq, Kuwait, Saudi Arabia, Qatar and Abu Dhabi) belonging to the Gulf region to hike the oil price at the wake of the Arab Israeli conflict in 1973.[66] Since then, oil politics injected a new dynamism and orientation in international relations.[67] Several highly industrialised western nations primarily depending on the oil supply from the Gulf region realised for the first time their vulnerability to instant shortages of energy supplies. This single factor drove a wedge in the NATO alliance and divided the western nations in their attitude towards the Arab-Israeli conflict.

With regard to the US objective of having access to the Gulf oil supplies at *"reasonable prices"* and in *"sufficient quantities"* to meet US needs and those of its European and Asian friends and allies,[68] the question arises as to who should decide what is "reasonable" price. And what happens if the Gulf States refuse to oblige the US or its allies? Ever since the Arab States of the Gulf region ventured to use the oil weapon in the Arab-Israeli conflict in 1973,[69] the United States seriously considered retaliation by using food as a counter-weapon through an embargo on the Arabs[70] and also considered the use of force in the event of "some actual strangulation of the industrialised world" by an oil cartel as was stated by the then Secretary of State, Henry Kissingar.[71] Since then, the United

States has been increasingly linking up its national security interests with the flow of oil from the Gulf region. According to Maxwell the oil issue affects American security in a vital sense and leads to retarded economic growth, higher costs of industrial production, new deficits in international payments, increased inflation, disaster to NATO allies and Japan and decline in the effectiveness of the NATO alliance.[72] According to David Holden : "The United States has discovered a new dependence upon Middle East oil and has moved discreetly towards the creation of a protective screen around the Gulf oil-fields that will replace the old British presence."[73]

Oil was the only reason that brought US into the Persian Gulf and its present and future interests lay solely in the exploitation of oil from this region. The Middle East in general contains 60 per cent of all the planets proven petroleum resources and 75 per cent of all the oil in the world internationally available.[74] Saudi Arabia alone possesses 26 per cent of the planets proven petroleum resources—a third of all the oil in the world internationally available.[75] About 80 per cent of the non-Communist world's oil is produced by the Organisation of Petroleum Exporting Countries and of this the Islamic member states control 72 per cent with Saudi Arabia having the largest share of 20 per cent. More than half of oil needs of the Western world and Japan are met by supplies from the Gulf countries.[76] (For details of oil reserves of Persian Gulf countries, see Table 2).

TABLE 2

Reserves of Persian Gulf Countries

	Proven reserves (thousand million barrels)	Oil life (years)
Saudi Arabia	148.6	48
Kuwait	68.0	73
Iran	64.5	29
Iraq	34.3	50
Abu Dhabi	29.5	57
Qatar	—	—
Oman	—	—

Source: Elie Kedorie and Sylvia G. Haim, eds., *Towards A Modern Iran* (London: Frank Cass, 1980), p. 245.

It should be remembered that the wonderful success of the Marshall plan in Europe at the wake of the Second World War was due in part to the oil supply from this region at so cheap a rate as one dollar per barrel of oil (this price remained the same until 1970). At present, the 'oiling' of NATO depends very heavily on the oil supply from this region. Not only the West European powers but also the US itself is increasingly becoming dependent on Persian Gulf oil. The US imports more than one million barrels of oil a day from Saudi Arabia, the largest single contributor to US oil imports.[77] France obtains 60 per cent, Portugal 80 per cent, Italy and Britain 50 per cent and West Germany 35 per cent.[78] Hence, the US views the Persian Gulf area as vitally important for itself; particularly, it is interested in the uninterrupted flow of oil from this region to the US as well as to its allies in the West. (For details of crude oil production in the Persian Gulf region, see Table 3).

TABLE 3

Crude Oil Production in Persian Gulf Countries

Persian Gulf Producers	Production per day	1972	1974	1975
Kuwait	'000 barrels	2,753	2,278	1,937
Saudi Arabia	,,	7,344	8,210	6,827
Iran	,,	5,896	6,058	5,677
Iraq	,,	2,018a	1,871a	2,044a
Abu Dhabi	,,	1,308	1,418	907
Qatar	,,	517	519	481
Oman	,,	293	291	302

a=partly estimated

Source: Adapted from Elie Kedorie and Sylvia G. Haim, eds., *Towards a Modern Iran* (London: Frank Cass, 1980), p. 245.

The policy of the United States, despite its recent foreign policy set-back in Iran, is backed up with an operational military presence in the neighbouring Indian Ocean area to manipulate and influence situations. Such a presence is a coercive presence that would have serious impact on the shaping and controlling of important geopolitical features of the area in which a crisis may come to a head.

One of the implications of the US oil policy seems to be a warning to the Arab States that national sovereignty over national resources and national competence to dispose them of are to be exercised with restraint. Intimidation of the Gulf states, despite the power of their petro-dollar, seems to be another implication. What exactly is meant by "sufficient quantities"? Even this seems to be determined by the US dictates and not by the oil-producing nations, as long as the United States will be involved in the oil politics of the Gulf region.

USSR AND THE GULF

The interest of the United States and Western powers in the Gulf region is matched by the Soviet interests—political, strategic and economic—in the Indian Ocean-Gulf region. To understand the increasing influence of the Soviet Union in the area, it would be necessary to go into the very genesis of Soviet policy towards the developing world.

Since the death of Stalin in 1953, post-war international relations entered a new phase.[79] Instead of the rigid and dogmatic approach of Stalin, the new leadership in the Kremlin took a more flexible line in foreign policy.[80] It realised that the old concept of world revolution through war in favour of an ideology proved unworkable in the new environment dominated by nuclear weapons. Nuclear diplomacy based on the peaceful coexistence of communism and capitalism was adopted as a foreign policy posture of the Communist Party of Soviet Union. Evidences strongly suggest that Soviet foreign policy objectives revolved primarily around preserving the USSR's position as a superpower and not around spreading marxist ideology in the non-communist world.[81] With the Mutual Assured Destruction (MAD) capabilities of both America and the Soviet Union, a general nuclear war would mean sure extinction of both the systems. A policy of national suicide would not be entertained by any sane government. However, the new outlook in Soviet foreign policy deliberately avoided both an all-out war and an all-out peace. Like Stalin, his successors had two reasons for avoiding an all-out war. The first is doctrinal: "Their central belief teaches them that they are the wave of the future, that the capitalist order is in decay and that time is on their side. The other is a readiness to risk war at the periphery, 'limited engagements' 'calculated risks', for, in their activist theory, history helps only those who help her, but not to jeopardize their power centre, the loss of which in all-out war might change the course of history.[82]

The Soviet Union fully exploited the nuclear stalemate to penetrate the developing world at the expense of the United States. Just as the United States utilised military and economic aid as intruments of its foreign policy, the Soviet Union also relied increasingly on aid and trade to acquire political influence but the style and form of this policy differed basically from that of the USA.[83]

The new trend in Soviet foreign policy initiated by Kruschchev was found favourable to the developing nations. The Soviet emphasis was on the development of "national industries especially, machine-building". The Soviet Union also wanted to establish extensive commercial intercourse with the industrially underdeveloped countries, irrespective of their social systems, on a basis of equality, mutual benefit and respect for one another's sovereignty. National sovereignty and independence are indispensable conditions for the solution of all the complex economic problems which control these countries.[84]

The trade and aid programme envisaged for the developing countries by the Soviet Union had three main objectives from the ideological point of view. Firstly, these were intended to help the poor nations to liberate themselves politically and economically from the West. Secondly, it was also meant to persuade the newly independent nations to accept the socialist path of economic development and abandon the capitalist path. Finally, it would promote the growth of revolutionary social and political conditions in the new States.[85] Accordingly, there are three types of Soviet activity in the developing world: *i*) denial of influence in neutral areas to adversaries, particularly to the United States; *ii*) intrusion into opponent's spheres of influence; and *iii*) promotion of socialist revolution.[86]

However, the "dialectics of the Soviet interest in the
Middle East"—and indeed in the Gulf region—"follows the
same route as that previously travelled by the British, French
and Americans. They must look for local security and stability
that will not threaten their interests; they must find friendly
regimes who will work with them and not with others; they
must help to build the armed forces and the economic bases
of these friendly regimes; they must support them diplomati-
cally in their disputes with others and possibly also militarily,
so long as this produce no complication".[87]

For the realisation of these three objectives in the Arab
countries and in the Gulf region, the Soviet Union picked up
the most sensitive political issue namely the Arab-Israeli conflict. It became easy for the Soviets to gate-crash into the
Arab world because of the US support for Israel which made
the Arabs more and more wary about US intentions in West
Asia. Besides, a new surge of Arab nationalism and pan-
Arabism demanded urgent solution of the Arab-Israeli
problem.

The Soviet Union befriended a number of Arab States,
like Egypt, Syria and Iraq. In trying to support the Arab
cause in the Middle East, the Soviet Union gained the confidence not only of the radical Arab States but also some of the
conservative regimes of the Gulf region. Though many of
these conservative Arab States are known for their pro-west
policies, their common problem has been the American
guarantee to the existence of Israel. Hence, the Arabs were
skeptical of any timely American support against Israel. That
made the Soviet entry into the Arab world quite easy. The
Soviet policy towards the region is governed by the following
factors:

1) The Gulf region does not appear to constitute an area
of great strategic importance to the Soviet Union. Its significance arises from the fact that it is contiguous to the
Mediterranean which is indeed strategically important to the
Soviet Union. Otherwise, basically the Soviet Union adhered
to strategic negativism as a keynote of its policy which sought
to deny the area to various western forces.[88]

2) The Gulf oil resources are of no direct concern to the
Soviet Union or to her East European allies as they are self-

sufficient in oil.[89] It should be remembered that the Soviet Union is the world's single largest oil producer.[90]

3) The Soviet Union can control the vital routes to the Gulf in a crisis situation and create trouble for the West. In any future conventional war, Moscow would be able to shut off the flow of Middle East petroleum whether or not it controlled the area prior to the outbreak of hostilities. The strong probability is that in peace the oil will flow to Western Europe and in war it will not, no matter whether the Soviets or the Arabs control it.[91] Besides if the Soviet Union were to prevent Western access to the Gulf oil, it can easily do so by a land based operation from the north. It has no need to undertake a naval blockade of the Gulf from the southern side.[92] It should be noted that the Soviet Union has now acquired greater strategic advantage by establishing its military presence in Afghanistan.

4) The Soviet Union has not been spreading thin all over the Gulf region, like the United States, by supplying armaments and sending military advisers with the intention of influencing the recipient country's domestic and foreign policies. The Russians learnt from their experience with Egypt that it was not advantageous and can even become a liability. The United States, it seems, has not learnt such lessons from its traumatic experience in Iran in 1979. On the other hand, the Arabs are waveringly inclined towards maintaining equidistance from both the superpowers with a view to limit the possibility for influence in the Gulf region.[93]

5) The Soviet Union's interest is perhaps to undermine the credibility of the US and the West in this region and it is trying to do this by supporting the Arabs in their conflict against Israel. The expulsion of US, first from Iraq in 1959 and then in 1979 from Iran, must in part be considered the results of the slow and invisible ideological process that was set in motion by USSR in the early 1950s against dictatorial regimes in the Gulf, supported by western weapons and personnel.

What is important for the Soviet Union is not to make these countries allies or satellites but not to lose them as sympathisers and friends. Hence it is extremely cautious in its approach towards the countries of the Gulf. Some would argue that the Soviet policy towards the Gulf is invariably tied up with their objectives in the Indian Ocean.[94]

Among the countries of the Gulf area, Iraq was considered more important by the Soviet Union because of its radical regime. The Soviet Union wields great influence in this crucial state of the region which is bordered on the east by Iran (an ally of the US until 1979), and the west by Turkey, a NATO partner. Hence, the Soviet Union did show great interest in strengthening Iraq militarily and gaining access to the Iraqi port at Umm Qasr. Massive Soviet economic and military aid was given to Iraq. Through Iraq, the Soviets have also been giving both military and economic assistance to guerrillas and insurrectionary forces in various parts of the region where the conservative monarchical regimes are totally opposed to Soviet penetration.

In the final analysis, it would seem that just as the US is interested in establishing military bases in the region, the USSR is interested in fostering and encouraging a pro-Soviet orientation among Arab nationalist movements that would set the stage for changes in the age-old political system of the region.[95]

Judging from the US global strategy and specific Gulf policies, despite the 1979 debacle in Iran, it is determined to make its presence felt in this sensitive area. To some regimes in the region, like Oman and Saudi Arabia, this presence is a boon; to some others, like the United Arab Emirates, Kuwait and Bahrain, it serves their interest; perhaps Iraq alone is sympathetic to the Soviet Union. The theory of power vacuum in the Gulf was fundamentally the basis by which the US was able to encourage the regional powers to tolerate its presence. Along with this presence came a large supply of sophisticated weapons which were presumed to be necessary for national defence and regional security.

Since the so-called British withdrawal in 1971, the Gulf States have been keen in acquiring large quantities of sophisticated weapons from wherever possible. The Gulf region became a weapon sellers' market particularly following the oil price-hike in 1973. USSR, UK, France and West Germany competed with the US in the sale of weapons.

A conglomeration of causes such as great power rivalry,

strategic significance of the area and other regional factors
capable of creating regional conflicts, have contributed to a
gigantic arms build-up in the area which has assumed the
character of a regional arms race.

REFERENCES

1 The Gulf region is not synonymous with the Middle East. The
  Middle East comprises the following States: Syria, Israel, Jordan,
  Iraq, Saudi Arabia, Kuwait, Bahrain, Qatar, United Arab
  Emirates (UAE), Oman, North Yemen, South Yemen, Egypt, Sudan,
  Turkey and Iran. Culturally, the Middle East embraces a society
  and civilisation found not only in that region but also in a number
  of adjacent localities such as Afghanistan, Pakistan, Libya, Tunisia,
  Algeria and Morocco, see Sydney Nettleton Fisher, *The Middle East*
  (New York: Alfred A. Knopf, Inc., 1968), p. 3.
2 J.B. Kelly. *Britain and the Persian Gulf, 1775-1880* (London: Oxford
  University Press, 1968), pp. 1-2.
3 J.E. Peterson, *Oman in the Twentieth Century* (London: Croom
  Helm, 1978), p. 137.
4 Ali Mohammed Khalifa, *The United Arab Emirates: Unity in Fragmentation* (Colorado: Westview Press, Inc., 1979), p. 117.
5 John Marlowe, *Arab Nationalism and British Imperialism* (London:
  The Cresset Press, 1961), p. 100.
6 Benjamin Shwadran, *The Middle East, Oil and the Great Powers*
  (London; Atlantic Press, 1955), p. 7.
7 Donald Hawley, *The Trucial States* (London: George Allen &
  Unwin, 1970), p. 7.
8 Hawley, n. 7, p. 18.
9 Roy E. Thoman, "The Persian Gulf Region", *Current History*
  (Philadelphia), January 1971, p. 38.
10 Marlowe, n. 5. p. 100.
11 Hawley, n. 7, p. 171.
12 Peterson, n. 3, p. 137.
13 *Ibid.*, p. 139.
14 *Ibid.*, p. 148.
15 J.A. Saldhana, *Precis of Correspondence of International and British
   Policy in the Persian Gulf, 1872-1905*, India Office Records
   (Calcutta, 1906), pp. 33-36.
16 Muhammad Morsy Abdullah, *The United Arab Emirates: A Modern
   History* (London: Croom Helm, 1978), p. 26. France, Russia,
   Germany and the Ottomans formally signed agreements with
   Britain in 1904, 1907, 1912 and 1913 respectively, see *Ibid.*
17 Fisher, n. 1, p. 464.
18 Henry L. Roberts and Paul A. Wilson, *Britain and the United States*
   (London: Broadwater Press, 1953), p. 182.

19 Maqbul Ahmad, *Indo-Arab Relations* (New Delhi: Indian Council of Cultural Relations, 1969), p. 166.

20 Philip K. Hitti, *History of the Arabs* (London: Macmillan, 1970), p. 753; See also Cecil V. Crabb, Jr., *American Foreign Policy in the Nuclear Age* (New York: Row, Peterson and Company, 1960), p. 270.

21 L.N. Vatoli na, "The Growth of National Consciousness among the Arab Peoples (1945-55)", in Walter Z. Laqueur, ed., *The Middle East in Transition* (London: Routledge & Kegan Paul, 1958), p. 491.

22 Hitti, n. 20, p. 755.

23 Marlowe, n. 5, p. 13.

24 R.M. Burrel and Alvin J. Cottrell, *Iran: The Arabian Peninsula and the Indian Ocean* (New York: National Information Centre, Inc., 1972), p. 8. In this study it is argued that there was no local pressure adequate to compel the British to 'withdraw' from the Gulf region.

25 Crabb, n. 20, p. 270.

26 Preface by Nasser to a work sponsored by the Liberation Movement, entitled, *North Africa, Past, Present and Future* (Cairo, 1954), pp. 5-6, quoted in Laqueur, n. 21, p. 137.

27 For a brief historical analysis of the Suez crisls which brought an end to the British and French influence in the Middle East, see Robert H. Ferrell, *American Diplomacy: A History* (New York: W.W. Norton, 1959), pp. 523-28.

28 Abdullah, n. 16, p. 74.

29 Philip Windsor, *Oil* (London: Maurice Temple Smith, 1975), p. 17.

30 Crabb, n. 20, p. 270.

31 Marlowe, n. 5, p. 122.

32 *Indian Express* (Cochin), 5 January 1982.

33 Vatolina, n. 21, p. 489.

34 B. Ponmaryov, A. Gromyko, V. Khvostov, eds., *History of Soviet Foreign Policy 1947-1970* (Moscow: Progressive Publishers, 1974), p. 320.

35 House of Commons, 16 January 1968, *British Information Services*, "Economic and Overseas Policy: Cuts in Public Expenditure," p. 2.

36 John C. Campbell, *Defense of the Middle East* (New York: Harper and Brothers, 1960), pp. 29-31.

37 Bruce R. Kuniholm, *The Origins of the Cold War in the Near East* (New Jersey: Princeton University Press, 1980), p. 180.

38 Crabb, n. 20, p. 258.

39 Shwadran, n. 6, p. 310.

40 R.K. Karanjia, *The Arab Dawn* (Bombay: Blitz Publications, 1958), p. 282.

41 Marlowe, n. 5, p. 160.

42 William Luce, "Britains Withdrawal", *The Royal United Service Institution Journal*, March 1969. Reprinted in *Survival* (London), Vol. XI, No. 6, June 1969, p. 188.

43 R.M. Burrell, "Politics and Participation where Britania once Ruled", *New Middle East*, No. 51, December 1972, p. 34.

44 Rouhollah K. Ramazani, "Iran's search for Regional Cooperation", *Middle East Journal* (Washington, D.C.), Vol. 30. No. 2, Spring 1976, p. 181.

45 One view was that the power vacuum in the Gulf became a *fait accompli* and that Iran had warned the US and the Soviet Union not to fill it. See Rouhollah K. Ramazani, *The Persian Gulf: Iran's Role* (Charlottesville: University Press of Virginia, 1972), p. 89. A second view was that the steady erosion of British power in the Persian Gulf area left a vacuum which the US found it hard to fill and which it would have been hard for the Soviet Union not to fill. And "as the Soviet Union gradually filled this vacuum so too it assumed the role of the Champion of the Arab cause". See Robin Edmonds, *Soviet Foreign Policy 1962-73* (London: Oxford University Press, 1975), p. 57.

46 Robert R. Sullivan, "The Architecture of Western Security in the Persian Gulf", *Orbis* (Philadelphia), Vol. 14, no. 1, Spring 1970, p. 71.

47 Dean G. Pruitt and Richard C. Snyder, eds., *Theory and Research on the Causes of War* (Englewood Cliffs: Prentice Hall, Inc., 1969), p. 20.

48 D.C. Watt, "The Persian Gulf—Cradle of Conflicts", *Problems of Communism* (Washington D.C.), May-June 1972, p. 33.

49 Peter Mansfield, *The Middle East: A Political and Economic Survey* (London: Oxford University Press, 1973), pp. 186-90.

50 Marlowe, n. 5, p. 62.

51 The Iran-Iraq conflict has not dampened the initiatives of other Gulf States to ensure stability and security in the region through peaceful cooperation.

52 A.B. Zahlan, "The Acquisition of Scientific and Technological Capabilities by Arab Countries", *Bulletin of the Atomic Scientists* (Chicago), Vov. 25, No. 9, November 1969, pp. 7-10.

53 "Federation of Arab Emirates Agreement of 27 February 1968", *Arab Report and Record* (London), Issue 5, 1-5 March 1968, p. 59, quoted in Robert G. Landen, *The Emergence of the Modern Middle East* (New York: Van Nostrand Reinhold Company, 1970), p. 319.

54 *The Middle East in Crisis: Problems and Prospects*, Report of the Subcommittee on the Near East of the Committee on Foreign Affairs, House of Representatives, 92nd Congress, 1st Session, 21 December 1971, p. 27.

55 *The Defense Monitor* (Washington D.C.), Vol. 4, no. 3, May 1975, p. 1.

56 *Ibid.*

57 United Nations, *Treaty Series*, Vol. 313, p. 347.

58 Faris Glubb, "Backdoor to Arabia", *Middle East International* (London). no. 45, March 1975, p. 12.

59 Burrell and Cottrell, n. 24, pp. 36-37.

60 The other two maritime powers which imposed hegemony on the Gulf waters were Portugal in the 16th century and Britain in the 19th, see J.B. Kelley, n. 2, p. 1.

61 Peter Avery, "The Many Faccs of Iran's Foreign Policy", *New Middle East*, no. 47, August 1972, p. 19.

62 *New Perspectives on the Persian Gulf*, Hearings before the subcommittee on the Near East and South Asia of the Committee on Foreign Affairs, House of Representatives, 93rd Congress, 1st Sess., 6 June, 17, 23, 24 July and 28 November 1973 (Washington, D.C.), US Government Printing Office, 1973), p. 7.

63 Khalifa, n. 4, p. 169.

64 Mohammed Said-Ahmed, *After the Guns Fall Silent* (London: Croom Helm, 1976), p. 90.

65 While nationalisation in some oil producing countries has been for economic reasons, in others, the nationalisation has been for political reasons, See *Baghdad Observer* (Baghdad) 1 March 1976, p. 3; See also Editorial, "Development and Developing", *The Round Table* (London), Vol. LXIV, no. 253, January 1974, p. 6.

66 Jane Perry Clark Carrey, "Iran and Control of Its Oil Resources", *Political Science Quarterly* (New York), Vol. 89, no. 1, March 1974, p. 157.

67 J. Thomas, "Battle for an EEC Energy Policy", *New Scientist* (London), 1, November 1973, pp. 330-33. For the Arabs' decision to use oil weapon in the context of 1973 Arab-Israeli conflict, see *Arab Report and Record* (London), Issue 20, 16-31 October 1973, p. 470.

68 *New Perspectives on the Persian Gulf*, n. 62, p. 7.

69 I. Hijazi, "Saudi Warning to US on Continued Aid to Israel", *Financial Times* (London), 12 July, 1973; R. Beeston, "US Faces Saudi Arabia Oil Cutback over Arms for Israel", *Daily Telegraph* (London), 6 September 1973.

70 *Congressional Quarterly Weekly Report*, Vol. XXXI, no. 49, 8 December 1973.

71 Kissinger's interview to *Business Week Magazine*, quoted in *Congressional Quarterly Almanac*, 93rd Congress, 2nd Sess. 1974, p. 514.

72 Maxwell D. Taylor, "The Legitimate Claims of National Security", *Foreign Affairs*, Vol. 52, no. 3, April 1974, pp. 592-93.

73 David Holden, "Peace or Southern Arabia's Hundred Year War", *New Middle East* no. 50, November 1972, p. 32; See also "US Leaning Heavier than Ever on Foreign Oil", *US News and World Report* (Washington D.C.), 5 April 1976, pp. 36-37.

74 Faisal Alhegelan, "The Economic Policy of Saudi Arbia", *Vital Speeches of the Day* (New York), Vol. XLVII, no. 5, 15 December 1980, p. 159.

75 *Ibid.*, p. 158.

76 *National Herald* (Delhi), 25 July 1981.

77 *New York Times*, 21 February 1981.

78 David D. Newsom, "America Engulfed", *Foreign Policy* (Washington, D.C.), no. 43, Summer 1981, p. 25.

79 Roger Makins, "The World Since the War: The Third Phase", *Foreign Affairs*, Vol. 33, no. 1, October 1954, p. 3.

80 James D. Theberge, *The Soviet Presence in Latin America* (New York: Crane, Russak, 1974), p. 5.

81 O.M. Smolansky, "Moscow and the Persian Gulf: An Analysis of Soviet Ambitions and Potential", *Orbis*, Vol. XIV, no. 1, Spring 1970, p. 92.

82 Bertram D. Wolfe, "A New Look at the Soviet 'New Look", *Foreign Affairs*, Vol. 33, no. 2, January 1955, p. 187.

83 Chester Bowles, "America and Russia in India", *Foreign Affairs*, Vol. 49, no. 4, July 1971, p. 636.

84 V. Solodovnikov, "The Soviet Union and the Underdeveloped Countries," *New Times*, no. 52, December 1954, p. 13.

85 Robert Jaster, "Foreign Aid and Economic Development: The Shifting Soviet View," *International Affairs* (London), Vol. 45, no. 1, July 1969, p. 455.

86 Herbert Dinerstein, "Moscow and the Third World: Power Politics and Revolution?" *Problems of Communism* (Washington), January-February 1968, p. 52.

87 "Middle East Trends: The Dangers of Recolonisation" (Editorial), *New Middle East*, no. 16, January 1970.

88 Arthur Jay Klinghoffer, "Pretext and Context: Evaluating the Soviet Role in the Middle East," *Mizan* (London), Vol. X, no. 3, May/June 1978, p. 86.

89 The total extent of known or probable oil and gas bearing territory in the world is 32 million square kilometers, according to Soviet estimates. Of this total 11.8 miliion square kilometers lie in the Soviet Union, with the United States accounting for 6.4 million square kilometers and the rest of the world for 13.8. The inference is that USSR will be able to meet in full her oil requirements. See S. Orudjev, "Soviet Oil", *New Times*, no. 50, December 1968, pp. 5-7; See also R.M. Burrell and Alvin J. Cottrell, n. 24, p. 39; and "Soviet Interest in Middle East Oil," *Mizan*, Vol. X, no. 3, May/June 1968, pp. 79-84.

90 *The Straits Times* (Singapore), 23 December 1974.

91 Smolansky, n. 81, p. 97.

92 *Patriot* (New Delhi), 26 February 1975.

93 Udo Steinbach, "The Arab World—Where is it Going?" *Aussen Politik*, 1/76. Reprinted in the *Strategic Digest*, Institute for Defence Studies and Analysis (New Delhi), July 1976, p. 41.

94 T.B. Millar, *Soviet Politics in the Indian Ocean Area* (Canberra: Australian National University Press, 1970), pp. 20-21; See also

Lord Chalfont, "Russia and the Indian Ocean: New Attitudes to Sea Power", *New Middle East,* no. 44, May 1972, pp. 4-6.

95 Alvin Z. Rubinstein, "Soviet-American Rivalry in the Middle East", *Middle East Review* (New York), Vol. IX, no. 3, Spring 1977, p. 34; See also John C. Campbell, "The Superpowers in the Persian Gulf Region", in Abbas Amirie, *The Persian Gulf and Indian Ocean in International Politics* (Tehran: Institute for International, Political and Economic Studies, 1975), p. 54.

3

The Dynamics of Armamentism in the Gulf Region

In the first chapter an attempt was made to identify three categories of forces-domestic, regional and extra-regional—responsible for the initiation, intensification and continuance of the phenomenon of regional arms races. Do these forces operate in the Gulf region where there is a great spurt in weapon acquisition which has set in motion a multilateral arms race? It is necessary to examine the dynamics of this arms race or in other words, to determine those domestic, regional and extra-regional forces which directly or indirectly, singly or cumulatively, influence the arms policy of each of the Gulf States.

A. DOMESTIC FACTORS

There are three predominant domestic factors influencing the Gulf States to acquire sophisticated weapons. They are : (i) threat perceptions of Gulf States; (ii) petro-dollar boom of the Gulf region; and (iii) need for modernisation of the armed forces.

i) Threat Perceptions

States, whether big or small tend to procure weapons, based on perceptions of insecurity arising from forces within themselves or form without. These threat perceptions need not necessarily be absolutely real and imminent; very often, they happen to be reflections of the belligerent attitude or justifications for future arms build-up. Apparently, the Gulf States are no exception to the general concern of States for national security. The very fact that none of the Gulf States is self-sufficient in arms provided the alibi for a security conscious State to work out scenarios which would justify an arms build-up. What is the nature of the threat perception of each Gulf State?

Iran

From the early 1950s to 1978, the late Mohammed Reza Shah Pahlavi had been relentlessly engaged in a weapon-building programme to ensure the security of his country. In this process, he was more guided by his own security perceptions drawn from his historical experience than from the actuality of the situation in the Gulf.

Historically, Iran has been under pressure during the course of several centuries form the North as well as from the South. Insecurity for Iran arose from the fear of Soviet Union[1] as its 2500 kilometre northern border lies along that great land power which in the earlier centuries was known to have entertained plans of expansion towards the south or at least sought an access to the Gulf waters through Iran.[2] It should be noted that British policy, since the development of the Indian empire, regarded the Persian Gulf region as the lifeline to the empire, and strenuously attempted to control all possible approaches to the area and deny the penetration of other great powers.[3] Russia too having ambitions to control events in its southern neighbourhood repeatedly clashed with Britain and ultimately in 1907 both agreed to a *modus vivendi* according to which Persia was divided between Britain and Russia. Britain controlled the South and Russia the North.[4]

Iran's experiance[5] in World War I and II reinforced its

fear and seems to have all the more influenced its policies to obtain more arms. The late Shah once commented : "In World War I the country was trampled by alien forces because of the central government's weakness and lack of organisation. In World War II, we were resting peacefully, credulously thinking that mutual respect would hold sway in our golden age of so-called neutrality, until those enjoying power taught us what neutrality meant".[6] He almost vowed when he said : "we have decided to destroy our country ourselves, before allowing it to be occupied by the enemy. But before we do that we will fight. And to fight we need weapons. That is our policy".[7]

The major threat to Iran's security was said to be from the Soviet Union. The Shah's strategic and political thinking therefore, was diametrically opposed to Soviet security interests. One of his basic assumptions was that Iran's fate, its chances of survival as an independent nation, and the maintenance of its territorial integrity were intrinsically associated with the fate of the western alliance system.[8] Hence, he became an active promoter of the military activities of Central Treaty Organisation (CENTO) and in turn succeeded for many years in securing a good deal of military hardware and economic assistance from the United States.

However, with the game of *detente* between the United States and the Soviet Union, Iran's historical memories of the Anglo-Russian partition agreements (1907 and 1941) were vivid in the political psychology of the Iranian leadership. An important, implied aspect of the superpower *detente* was that the superpowers in their competitive co-existence could as well exercise a supervisory role and control over regional conflicts where regional compulsions force the combatants into belligerent postures.[9] As early as 1962, the Shah had recognised that if he were to avoid a permanent state of tension with Moscow, he had to carry out his own *detente* by not allowing US missiles on Iranian soil.

Further, the Shah began to foster close economic cooperation with the Soviet Union,[10] and derived much advantages from it. Hence, the fears and apprehensions about the big neighbour on the North diminished to a considerable extent, if not altogether disappeared, with the *detente* between that country and Iran, so much so that the northern border was known to be a "frontier of peace and understanding" by both sides. This situation has led Marlowe to comment that neither did the Soviet Union really apprehend any real danger from Iran nor did Iran really apprehend any danger of being invaded by the Soviet Union.[11] However, the Shah appeared to have remained suspicious of Soviet designs in the region. This was evident from the distinction the Shah was accustomed to draw at public speeches between his aim of securing good neighbourly relations with the Soviet Union while maintaining unwavering opposition to communism, which he thought was determined to destroy his rule.[12]

An improvement in the relationship with the Soviet Union however, became a strategic necessity for Iran as the Shah began to focus more attention to the South[13] where Iran's security interests were perceived to be more vulnerable especially because of a series of political developments in the late sixties which led to a scramble for power among great powers.

Iran had to encounter security threats often from the South in the past. The power that dominated the Gulf waters wielded influence and control over all the surrounding region, including Iran. In the southern sector, therefore, the Shah did not want to see any superpower gaining total control of the Gulf waters in the wake of the British decision in 1968 to withdraw from the Gulf. Since then the Shah had advocated the principle that the security of the Persian Gulf should be maintained primarily by the littoral States and that great powers should keep out of the Gulf area.[14] In the meanwhile, the Shah's aim was to strengthen Iran's southern flank by building a strong navy that could be commissioned to function in the way the British navy did during the heyday of British power in the Gulf.

Potential threats to Iran's security seemed to have been perceived by the Shah in his regional relationship with the neighbouring Arab States as well. There were several reasons for it. From ancient times, the Iranians and Arabs were traditional rivals. The Iranians are said to be Aryans and hold no cultural or ethnical association with the Arabs; whereas the Arabs trace their lineage to the semitic roots. Besides the Arabs are predominantly Sunni Muslims and the Iranians are Shia Muslims. According to Hermann Eilts, "both are vantage

conflicts in the sense that they have afflicted the Gulf peoples
for centuries; both are rooted in age old religious—cultural
disparities; both are hegemonial in objective; and both have in
the past been characterised by a high level of mutual intole-
rance and distrust".[15] Such sectarian [and ethnic differences
are also deeply reflected in their mutual political relationship.
Even the naming of the Gulf is shrouded in political controversy. No Arab calls the Gulf, the Persian Gulf; to Arabs it is
the Arab Gulf.[16]

While the Arabs were relentlessly set against Israel's ultimate defeat, the Shah's political overtures were more favourable
to Israel and its western allies. He feared that once the Arabs
closed their western front with Israel, they would eventually
open the northern front against Iran. This might have influenced the Shah to structure Iran's defence forces in such a way
as to be a match against the military capability of all the countries in the region combined.[17]

If the fears of an overt aggression arising from the northern
neighbour did somewhat decrease by the diplomatic understanding and economic cooperation with the Soviet Union, the
Shah still felt that the major threat to his power would come
from Moscow through Baghdad. After the Soviet·Iraqi friendship treaty was concluded in 1972, the Shah was reported to
have said that the Soviet friendship with Iraq, Afghanistan and
India was meant to encircle Iran.[18] The Shah always suspected
Moscow's hand in every anti-Iranian sentiments in Iraq and
hostile left-wing movements in the Arabian Peninsula.[19]

Besides, the Shah was well aware that it was not so much
an overt aggression from Iraq that posed a serious threat to his
power as the insurrectionary movements in the region encouraged and supported by the Baath Socialist regime. The Shah's
decision to launch a heavy weapon building programme should,
therefore, be viewed against insecurity alleged to be arising
from the revolutionary regime of Iraq and its proselytising
activities in the Gulf.[20]

Iraq

The most pressing domestic problem that for long threatened
Iraq's security was the consistent pressure of the Kurds in their
demand for autonomy. It should be noted that throughout

history the Kurds were kept divided and always were the subjects of the empires that dominated the area. Their aspiration for an autonomous state, has been crushed by the central government. As elsewhere with post-colonial frontiers, tribes were split, traditional migration routes bisected. From a position of loose autonomy within the Ottoman empire the Kurds were suddenly reduced to minority communities within militantly Arab or Turk States, and stringently controlled and kept in place. But there has been considerable freedom of crossing as the wild mountain frontiers could not possibly be kept well-guarded.[21] By the treaty of Lausanne, the Kurds were divided between Turkey, Iran, Iraq, Syria and the USSR. Excepting Iraq where the Kurds could have a meaningful political movement, all other countries forcefully suppressed Kurdish nationalism.[22]

The demand for Kurdistan autonomy in Iraq was initiated as early as 1961 by the Kurdish Democratic Party (KDP), headed by the late Mullah Mustafa Barzani. Diplomatic negotiations for a number of years between the Iraqi government and KDP did not result in any acceptable solution to both sides, but this problem continued to endanger the security of Iraq as such. There were attempts to grant the Kurds a semi-autonomous status but these were foiled by the failures of the two sides in defining the area of an autonomous Kurdistan.[23] The major hurdle for an amicable settlement was the Kurdish insistence to include Kirkuk within the area of Kurdistan, a proposition to which Iraq could not possibly agree because of the suspicions that "its political hold over the whole country would be somewhat insecure if the government of the Kurdish autonomous region effectively controlled the revenues derived from the Kirkuk oil fields".[24]

The problem reached its climax in 1974-75 and regular war started between the government forces and that of Barzani's. Iran's support of the Kurds added a further dimension to the whole Kurdish problem.[25] Iran's intrusion into the war theatre, at least indirectly by providing arms to the Kurds, had all the potentials of a war of escalation with Iraq. For, there had been already sporadic border clashes between Iran and Iraq, especially since 1970, when each government accused the other of backing an attempted *coup* against the regime across the border.[26]

Iran, not only supplied the Kurdish guerrillas with artillery and anti-tank weapons which helped them to hit at various Iraqi positions,[27] but also provided asylum to the Kurdish people fleeing under the pressure of Iraqi attack.

In a bid to control the Kurds, Iraq used Soviet supplied bomber, fighter and strike aircraft including Mig-17, 19 and 21, Su-7 and Tu-16 and also relied heavily on mechanised units and on Soviet supplied T-54/55 and T-7-62 tanks.[28]

The Kurdish problem was settled following a rapprochement between Iran and Iraq in 1975 by which Iranian support for the Kurdish rebellion came to an end.[29] Thus the 14 year old struggle for regional autonomy for the Kurds also collapsed with it.[30] One of the major thrusts, therefore, in the arms procurement policy of Iraq was closely associated with the offensive strategy of quelling the Kurdish revolt which often demonstrably posed threats to its internal security.

The collapse of Barzani's rebellion in 1975 opened the way for a leftward shift of the Kurdish movement as a whole. There are now a number of small, clandestine parties which tend to advocate socialist or marxist solutions.[31] In Iraq, the guerrilla war against the government had been resumed but looks ineffectual, and possibly even irrelevant to the cause of Kurds. In Iran the ideological and factional disputes seriously weakened the strong position the Kurds had achieved by force of arms, since the revolution in Iran.[32]

OTHER STATES

The problem of internal insecurity regarding Saudi Arabia, Kuwait, Bahrain, Qatar, United Arab Emirates and Oman was centred mainly on two fears : (a) the fear of Arab revolutionary forces at work throughout the Gulf region, on the one hand, and (b) the fear of a communist takeover of the region as a whole on the other.[33] The fundamentalist fervour of the Islamic regime to export the fruits of the Iranian revolution to the neighbouring Arab countries has become a third source of fear since 1979.

The Popular Front for the Liberation of Oman and the

Arabian Gulf (PFLOAG) have the declared aim of overthrowing all the rulers of the Arab littoral States except Iraq and replacing them with revolutionary regimes.[34] PFLOAG cells were discovered in Abu Dhabi, Bahrain and Kuwait.[35]

Threats to Saudi Arabia's internal security chiefly come from the revolutionary regimes of Iraq and South Yemen. Of late, though there has been a rapprochement between Saudi Arabia and Iraq, based on common interests since the commencement of the Iran-Iraq war of 1980,[36] the socialist regime in Baghdad cannot be expected to give up its mission of radicalisation of the Arab Gulf.

South Yemen is posing a great threat to Saudi Arabia by way of subversion as well as open hostilities. Many incursions directed against Saudi frontier posts in the Rub al-Kahli desert and a still larger number of attempts at subversion by mercenaries operating from Aden along the 3,000 km. south coast of the Arab peninsula towards Muscat in the east, were reported in 1974.[37]

Similarly, the feudalistic regime in Kuwait feared that Iraq would influence the radicals to overthrow the ruling clan. With the termination of the defence obligations by Britain, Kuwait had to manage its own security.

The United Arab Emirates feels insecure because of its smallness in size as compared to the neighbouring States which are bigger in size, having more population. The efforts of the smaller Sheikhdoms to federate in 1971, demonstrated their decision to be strong and secure against any potential threats internal as well as external. Constrained by the politics of the region, it has since long taken measures to build-up its own defence forces against any threat to its security.

Oman's insecurity chiefly arises from a perpetual internal problem localised in the Dhofar region where for some years the Sultan was in direct confrontation with armed guerrillas who were alleged to be supported by South Yemen.[38]

A radical movement that started in 1965 in the southern province of Dhofar had as its objective both to end British domination and Omani feudalism in Oman. The leftist challenge to the Omani regime gathered momentum between 1966 and 1969 when Sultan Qaboos took over from his father, Said bin Taimur, in a *coup* in 1970. The back of the Dhofar rebellion was broken in 1975 with the assistance and support of the late Shah of Iran.[39]

Although that war culminated in the defeat of the rebels, relations between Oman and South Yemen remain strained. The guerrillas were originally believed to have been supported by the Chinese guerrilla experts but later were reportedly financed and helped by European communist states.[40] For a time, the Sultan of Oman kept an Iranian force of 4,000 equipped with American-made tanks and F-4 Phantom jets as he entertained suspicions about the intentions of South Yemen, of the Cubans and the East Germans there.[41] With the Shah's exit from Iran in 1979, Egypt has undertaken to station 7,000 soldiers to help Oman. In this, Egypt has Washington's full approval "to protect the west's interests in that country."[42]

The fear of the communist threat to all the Gulf States has been a constant theme of rationalisation for the West to conveniently establish their own military presence in the area.[43] As far as Oman is concerned, Sultan Qaboos has said that Communists have no chances of penetration into Oman now that those who originally joined the rebels realise that the Sultanate is providing every opportunity for progress and welfare to the Omani people.[44] Whether the Sultan would prove right or wrong is a different matter. However, now the West seems to have shifted its emphasis from the Soviet threat to the Gulf States themselves.[45] What had happened in Iran in 1979 could as well happen elsewhere in the region, with catastrophic consequences to Western interests.[46] Iran-Iraq war again is pointed out as another dreaded spectre which has nothing to do with communism.[47]

A new threat to the internal security of the Arab Gulf kingdoms has arisen from the installation of an Islamic regime in Tehran following the Iranian revolution. Already, we have noted that ethnic differences have long been playing an obnoxious role in deeply stifling good neighbourly relations between the Arabs and Iranians. Now the Islamic fundamentalists, backed by the revolutionary regime in Tehran are keen on exporting the Iranian revolution to other Gulf countries.

In an effort to help propagate the Iranian revolution, the Islamic regime in Tehran is said to be actively encouraging the Shiite communities and peoples of Iranian origin in the various

Gulf States. The Shiites claim majority in Iraq. Shia grievances manifested in disturbances in the Shia holy cities of Karbala and Najaf. The restiveness among Shiites of Iraq, who acknowledge Imam Khomeini as their leader, forced the Iraqi authorities to expel about 35,000 of them in 1979.[48]

Elsewhere in the Gulf, tradesmen and merchants of Iranian origin account for between 30 to 40 per cent Shiites in Kuwait, close to 75 per cent in Bahrain, 20 per cent in Abu Dhabi, 30 per cent in Dubai, 20 per cent in Qatar and 50 per cent in Oman.[49] Indeed, the non-Sunni religio-ethnic groups can provide ample opportunities for the Islamic regime in Iran to exploit Shia grievances in these countries to its own advantage. As for example, there were disturbances in Saihat and Qatif among Saudi Arabia's 400,000-strong Shia community reflecting the increased confidence of Shiites following the Iranian revolution of 1979.[50] The Iran-backed terrorist plan to stage a coup on Bahrain's National Day on December 16, 1981 was described to be an Iranian attempt to undermine the security and stability of all the Gulf States from Oman to Kuwait.[51] Security of the smaller Sheikhdoms is proposed to be taken care of by particularly Saudi Arabia through security pacts.[52]

ii) *Petro-dollar Boom*

The weapon-building programmes of the various Gulf countries are stimulated by the petro-dollar boom in the region. These countries have substantial gold and currency reserves. Massive supplies of arms are used by the industrially developed countries to pursue a special strategy aimed at protecting the international oil monopolies in the region.[53]

Price per barrel of oil was one dollar until 1970. It rose to $ 3.44 by the end of 1973 and reached $ 10 by the end of 1974.[54] Oil price now stands at over $ 36 per barrel. In 1970 OPEC produced 1.16 billion tons of crude oil of which 1.12 billion were exported and the revenues totaled $ 7.8 billion. In 1979 OPEC exported 1.43 billion tons and their export revenues totalled $ 199 billion.[55] A large part of it has been used for arms purchases. The arms race in the Gulf region as in other parts of the developing world is nourished primarily by arms deliveries from the US, France and Britain.[56]

The highly industrialised nations of the West, whose commercial productions and exports of weapons are essential to maintain in turn their industrial economies, are not only involved in a rivalry among themselves to export their weapons but also engaged in a keen competition with the United States to sell arms in the Gulf area. It was only after the October 1973 war and the ensuing Arab oil boycott of the West coupled with the European energy crisis, that a new type of weapons spiral began—the so-called oil—for—arms deals.[57] Therefore, if the States of Gulf region are able to procure large quantities of highly sophisticated weapons from weapon producing countries, it is because they have enough oil deposits to bring immense revenues, more than what they can absorb in domestic developmental projects.

Until the 1970s the world oil was controlled by a number of internatioal oil companies which produced, transported, refined and distributed the bulk of internationally traded oil and they held the technical and commercial know-how needed to explore and market oil.[58] Their oligopolistic position was effectively broken by the Yom Kippur war. As far as the Gulf countries are concerned they asserted full control over their oil reserves, production levels and depletion rates, relegating the oil companies to the background. It meant, the producer governments could legitimately save billions of dollars which otherwise would go into the coffers of the oil middle men.

As both domestic and regional security are major concerns of the Gulf kingdoms, a large portion of oil revenues is allocated for defence purposes. According to some observers, the small number of oil exporting countries, being swamped with increased oil revenues within a short time, could afford to purchase most modern armaments in hitherto unknown quantities from the United States and Western Europe.[59] It was observed that if the Sheikh of Dubai wanted he could have just bought up Britain's entire arms production for a few years.[60] Iran, for example, increased its military spending five-fold between 1970 and 1976 to over $ 12 billions.[61] In fact, it is the petro-dollar boom that has made possible the potentially most dangerous assemblage of conventional weaponry in the Gulf region. The part of the oil money that is being invested in armaments can fit in very well with the strategic interests of the Western world.[62]

iii) Modernisation of Armed Forces

Despite the fact that some of the Gulf States such as the United Arab Emirates and Kuwait have the highest GNP and deal in multi-billion dollar petroleum business, they are all developing countries; nay, most of them are in their pre-industrial stages of development. Indigenous scientific progress is the basis of all development. What Thabet has observed in 1970 regarding the development of science in the Arab world remains generally true even today. According to him, countries where science is flourishing can be divided into two classes; firstly, those where the priorities are laid by the States and where science development occupies a prominent place for various reasons; economic, military or prestige; and secondly, those where science development is determined by scientific and technological needs, economic prosperity and demands of the private sector.[63]

According to Thabet, none of these conditions are present in the Arab world at present. No government is strong or stable enough to place the development of science on top of the priority list. The economic structure of the Arab countries and the absence of large and important industries precludes the development of science by private sector impulse.[64]

A substantial socio-economic development in terms of an independent programme of national development by the people and for the people with exclusively indigenous personnel and expertise, is yet to take place in most of the Gulf States. The so-called modernisation programme presently being pursued by these States is not rooted in their native culture and the prevalent socio-economic conditions of the gradually developing Arab societies.

An orderly development of the region is to be the primary concern of the regional powers. This should be left to the regional powers who should plan and execute their development programmes without interference by external agents. In all probability these external agents cannot identify themselves with the national urge and local aspirations. Any attempt to foist external models on them, be it European or American, would only ruin these developing nations and their economies.

When it comes to the question of modernisation of the armed forces of their countries, it remains true that the process of modernisation is nothing but imposing a superstructure on to a very weak indigenous defense infrastructure.

No doubt, the necessity of modernisation of armed forces arises out of the recognition of the qualitative change in the weapon systems of modern warfare. It is this consideration more than any other that motivates all States to modernise their armed forces.

Modernisation of armed forces, in the sense of acquiring the most sophisticated weapons available in the arms market, is made easy because of the newly found enormous wealth from exports of oil. The oil price-hike since 1973 has generated a new impulse for industrialisation along with massive acquisition of arms.

The process of modernisation has set in motion an arms spiral in the region unprecedented in history; unprecedented: because almost none of the countries except Iraq has now the ability to build-up an effective indigenous military capability of any worth within the next fifty years or more. The possession of sophisticated modern weapons does not invest a nation with credibility of defence or offence unless they are coupled with the potentiality to use them in contingencies. This is, indeed, the technological aspect of the weapons systems. In the Gulf, there is a known technological gap. Mastery over the technology, at least in its mechanical aspects of the weapons acquired, is a necessity. This should not pose a serious problem as the weapon suppliers are also ready to provide training to handle the weapons. In any case, there is a general belief that the countries in the Gulf region are able to obtain a fighting capability at comparatively less cost, based on imported modern weapons.

There is another important factor which impels these nations on the road to modernisation of armed forces. The process of socio-political development of the Gulf region has evolved elite pressure groups including army officers whose radical tendencies to revolutionise[65] the political systems have had considerable impact on the monarchical regimes. Being staunch supporters of ancient feudal regimes, its modernisation would be an additional incentive for the armed forces to support the conservative incumbents against the radicals. "As real economic, social, military and other forms of power shifted increasingly to the technically able men of the modern component of society, the traditional government came to rely increasingly upon instruments of repression to keep itself in power. Ultimately, however, the instruments of repression had to be manned by the 'new men' as they came increasingly to rely upon modern tools and techniques".[66]

In Iran, for example, the power of the late Shah depended largely on the army and a massive police apparatus,[67] despite the fact that his white Revolution had made him acceptable to large section of Iranian society. It was well known that the Shah was only following a tradition of his father whose take-over of power in Iran was accomplished by the support of the army in 1922.

When Mussadeq became Prime Minister of Iran in 1951, he restricted the role of the army in domestic politics. He even reduced the size of the armed forces but he could not survive long. He was overthrown in a *coup* in August 1953 and the late Shah Pahlavi established himself firmly on his saddle and to maintain this position, he modernised and expanded the army, with the help of the Unided States.[68] The late Shah initiated various programmes of economic and social reform during the sixties; and given the important role of the army, the purchase of sophisticated weapons formed a part of the policy of modernisation, though the reforms created serious internal problems.[69]

Modernisation of armed forces of some States, at least, of the region is also based on prestige considerations. Frankel has observed that during the "hey-day of French influence even the pettiest of European rulers tried to emulate the court of Versailles and today even the pettiest states show a craving to operate the most sophisticated and expensive modern weapon systems, usually at the cost of operational efficiency".[70]

The late Shah of Iran for example, had taken care to build-up the Iranian forces which were to emerge to match against the combined strength of the forces of all countries in the region.[71] The bulk of the Shah's multi-billion dollar air force included some of the world's most sophisticated gunships and fighter-bombers. When the war with Iraq started, most of them were grounded for lack of maintenance. Iran's reputation as the strongest air power in the region was based on possession of F-4 Phantoms, F-5s and F-14 jet fighters but even under the Shah the Iranians never got these into operation. The Americans only could fly them.[72] Most of the weapons were transferred from the US. However, Iran was denied US spare parts and supplies to maintain its armament. A wonderful array of sophisticated arms is being brought into Saudi Arabia. The problem really is whether the Saudi Arabians can handle them in case of serious contingency. It is one thing to have a wonderful static display of modern weaponry, but it is another to have experienced and trained personnel to operate them.

B. REGIONAL FACTORS

The regional factors which have considerably influenced the Gulf States to increase their arms build-up are chiefly two : rivalry for regional dominance and regional disputes.

i) Rivalry for Regional Dominance

Iran, Iraq and Saudi Arabia were the three regional contestants who vied with one another to assume the role of protector of the Gulf region following the British decision in 1968 to relinquish the special position in the area.[73] Each one of them had its own claims. But the political forces working for each one of them differed in accordance with the interests of external powers. And the external powers, particularly, the United States availed of this opportunity to manipulate the situation and foisted the late Shah of Iran as the surrogate *par excellence* to take care of US interests in the area.[74]

In order to build-up a new relationship with the Gulf region, the US applied the Nixon Doctrine of the late 60s which permitted surrogates to guard American and Western interests in peripheral regions instead of direct involvement as was the case in Vietnam.

The US was willing to assist the Gulf States in the spirit of the Nixon Doctrine. It was the responsibility of the Gulf States to cooperate among themselves and ensure regional peace and stability besides bearing the main burden for their own defence. In the Persian Gulf region, the US expected the leading States —Iran and Saudi Arabia—to cooperate for this purpose.[75] (Iraq was considered a pro-Soviet socialist State and anti-US). Of the two, the US relied heavily on the supposedly stable, pro-western and politically conservative Iran because of its predominant power position and historical record.

As things stood in 1971, Iran was considered the strongest State militarily. The historical record shows, firstly, that as early as 1942 the late Shah had begun to cultivate US friendship both as a means of strengthening his regime through military modernisation and as a counterweight to the Soviet Union. Secondly, the Shah's admiration and support for US only increased when he was brought from exile and was installed on the peacock throne in 1953, after having overthrown the Mussadeq government in Tehran with the support of the CIA. Thirdly, the Shah willingly joined the CENTO pact, designed to contain the so-called Soviet expansionism. Through its membership in the CENTO, Iran succeeded in acquiring a lot of weapons and military assistance and economic aid. In return, the American oil companies acquired a share in Iranian production capacity for the first time in 1954 (40 per cent); and US was accorded an unprecedentedly favourable climate for private investment and commerce in Iran under a treaty in 1957.[76] Fourthly, Iran was not entangled in the complex Arab-Israeli conflict and it showed its readiness to defend the status quo against radical nationalists and leftists who threatened US interests in the area. "Iran offered the best long-term prospect for a conservative regime, hostile to Soviet interests and sympathetic to the US bordering both the Middle East and the Indian sub-continent."[77]

Written into the Nixon Doctrine was the proxy concept. It implied a more indirect US involvement than had been the practice before. This reduced involvement was rationalised by assuming that such US allies as Iran had interests identical to those of the United States and by ensuring that these allies had the wherewithal to carry out policies on America's behalf. Military sales to Iran (after 1973 Iran could afford the bill) ensured that Iran could have a formidable military capability.[78] The late Shah's dream of the Cyrus and Xerxes empires made him over-ambitious. The United States played upon this wild sentiment of the conservative king and deliberately armed him to assume the role of a policeman in the troubled but strategic Persian Gulf area, and boosted him up as a powerful ally in the CENTO to block potential Soviet advances into the area.[79] The Shah seemed to have said once : "what we are buying is a deterrent that will be credible to all our neighbours. . . The Nixon Doctrine says the US will help those who help themselves. That is what we are doing".[80]

However, with the fall of the Shah in 19/9, the American policies received a great set-back in the Persian Gulf. Militarily Iran became a weak nation. The arms acquisition programme was suddenly stopped by the Islamic regime of Ayatollha Khomeini that succeeded the Shah. Even the existing weapons could hardly be operated for want of spare parts and experienced personnel. The Shah's dream of the Cyrus and Zerxes empires was replaced by Khomeini's hegemonic dream of an Islamic empire spread around the Gulf and elsewhere proclaiming the 'good-tidings' of the Iranian revolution. On 21 March 1980 Khomeini said "we should exert all efforts to export our revolution to other parts of the world. Let us abandon the idea of keeping the revolution within our borders".[81] While the Shah was wanting to establish Iranian hegemony through the medium of borrowed weapons from the west, the new regime wanted to establish a Shiite hegemony in the region by the medium of Koranic fundamentalism.

Viewed in terms of US interests in the area, Saudi Arabia had already accumulated many negative points to its credit and hence it could not have merited US preference to allow it to assume the surrogate role in 1971. First, no doubt, Saudi Arabia was extremely conservative and traditional in outlook and nourished an unflinching hostility to left-wing movements and governments—a plus point—but "it lacked the manpower to develop a large strategic force."[82] Secondly, Saudi Arabia's deep hostility to the US protege, Israel, and its active support of the Arab confrontation states was quite evident during the Arab-Israeli wars of 1956 and 1967.[83] In 1956 when Britain, France and Israel launched open aggression against Egypt,

Saudi Aradia came out in support of Egypt breaking off diplomatic relations with Britain and France and giving considerable financial assistance to it.[84] In 1962 the US had to vacate the Dhahran air base in Saudi Arabia as the latter disliked the US policy of helping Israel. The US could never predict in what way Saudi foreign policy would turn particularly when it touched upon US preferences and priorities in the region concerned. Saudi Arabia refused to be a party to the Baghdad pact aimed at involving the Arabs in the Western policies towards the Gulf region. Thirdly, despite its economic and political ties with the West, Saudi Arabia stood for pan-Arabism and pan-Islamism and hence the US could not rely on it as a dependable ally in situations of crises in the Middle East.

However, Saudi Arabia could not be left out from the overall US strategy in the Gulf area because of its preeminent position as the leader of the Muslim world and its pivotal role in the OPEC. It was thought appropriate to assign to Saudi Arabia a subsidiary role just to assuage Saudi susceptibilities. Thus the idea of the twin-pillar theory came into vogue. But what was left undefined was how Iran and Saudi Arabia could co-operate in order to maintain the security and stability of the region when their mutual relationship was bedevilled by numerous problems. What the US wanted was to consolidate its own position by exploiting such problems.

Saudi Arabia entered the arms race in the Gulf following a massive investment for defence forces by Iran with the stated objective of becoming the 'superpower' or policeman of the Gulf.[85] For one thing, Saudi Arabia did not like to see the political and military influence of Iran being gradually spread over to the Arab side of the Gulf,[86] for another, Iran's presence in Oman in the early seventies was a case in point where Saudi Arabia as the leader of the Islamic world had clearly lost its control.

However, Saudi Arabia's unique economic power enabled it to project its influence within and beyond the region. If the Shah had chosen to prepare himself to be the military policeman of the Gulf, the Saudis have attempted to use their tremendous economic influence to achieve the same result.[87] This was evident in 1976 in its diplomacy in the Lebanon crisis and in OPEC pricing decisions.[88]

In order to lessen Soviet influence in the Gulf, Saudi Arabia granted the Yemen Arab Republic $ 200 million in a deal. This resulted in Yemen breaking relations with the Soviet Union. Towards the end of 1976 Saudi Arabia sought to supplant Soviet influence in Somalia and South Yemen by economic means.[89]

Since the Iranian crisis in 1979, the US has been making frantic efforts to resurrect the surrogate model by trying to pack as much military muscle as possible into the 'other pillar'—Saudi Arabia. The presumption after the fall of the Shah is that Saudi Arabia has emerged as the protector and guarantor of the Persian Gulf region and it could be trusted upon to take care of US and western interests in the area. Saudi Arabia has now become the centrepiece of American interest in the area.[90] Through an extensive military relationship the US hopes to ensure the continued supply of Saudi oil—an "arms for oil" deal—and to counter Soviet involvement in the region.[91]

Saudi Arabia is also wary about Iraq's ambition to capture the leadership of the Arab world. There were attempted *coups* against the Saudi regime by Ba'athist and Arab nationalist elements in the armed forces and civil service in 1969.[92] The Iranian revolution of 1979 followed by the stated intention of exporting the revolution to other parts of the Gulf, and the Iran-Iraq war have brought closer understanding between Iraq and Saudi Arabia. The conservative States of the Gulf, led by Saudi Arabia, have been conducting a public information campaign against Iran, which they accuse of sponsoring a network of saboteurs to destabilise the Gulf region by organising pro-Iranian revolution. The campaign reflected increasing expression of support to the Iraqi regime.[93] However, arms are procured with the intention of offsetting any overt challenge that might possibly come from the revolutionary regime of Iraq and South Yemen.

The late Shah's policy in the 1970s was to undermine the influence of Iraq in the Gulf, an Arab influence which the Ba'athist leadership has sought to increase.[94] Despite the 1968 Ba'athist take over of government in Iraq, the main concern of the ruling elite was to organise the army effectively and increase in military capability. No Arab State liked the idea of Iran controlling the destiny of the Gulf.

Besides, they perceived in the Shah's talk of the Aryan renaissance the symptoms of expansionist overtones which unsettled even the most conservative Arabs.[95]

Iraq claims to be the most progressive State of the region and it has been championing radical revolution throughout the Gulf region. From time to time, it supplied arms to revolutionaries and to those engaged in transforming the traditional political systems of the region through guerrilla activities. Iraq was helping the "party for Arab Action" which claimed to work as a progressive party in Ras-al Khaima and Abu Dhabi and the Oman Liberation Front movement.[96] During the political upheavals in Iran, Iraq maintained a semblance of non-interference. However, Iraq's role in lending support to leftist forces in Iran by way of distributing arms and other material help clandestinely, cannot be minimised. With the Shah's exit from the Iranian political scene, Iraq has emerged as the strongest military power in the Gulf region. The revolutionary regime in Tehran is trying to relegate Iraq, if possible, to a secondary place and maintain its own regional hegemony.

The Arabs will now think of building their common defence against two fronts: one against Israel and the other against Khomeini's Iran. Saudi Arabia, Bahrain, Kuwait, the United Arab Emirates, Qatar and Oman have agreed in principle to set up a joint military defence force. Its purpose is to defend the region from external threat, establish a joint air defence system and co-ordinate arms purchases.[97] The agreement to conclude a Gulf security pact enhances Saudi Arabia's growing role and influence in the region.

ii) Regional Disputes

The political history of the Gulf region has been beset with a number of territorial and boundary disputes among the regional powers. This has often led to interestate conflicts such as the ongoing Iran-Iraq war (see Chapter V). Though serious attempts are being made to settle outstanding disputes, they tend to promote inflated budgetary allocations for defence purposes, setting in motion an action-reaction phenomenon.

In the Persian Gulf area, different state boundaries have been established rather arbitrarily by external powers. As

Marlowe observes: at the beginning of the 19th century the Ottoman Empire contained within its dominions most of the territories comprising the former Arab Emirates and nearly all the peoples speaking Arabic as their mother-tongue.[98] The colonial powers particularly Britain, for its own interest, cut and divided the area for administrative purposes and politically exploited their differences and disputes to hold on to its position in the area.

Boundary disputes came into sharp focus after World War II, when oil was discovered in large quantities, and it became the major source of immense revenues for the various Sheikhdoms of the Gulf region. Earlier, there were cases when claims have been advanced for territories far removed from one's own State, as for example, the Saudi's claim (now relinquished) for Buraimi oasis. Buraimi is the name of only one village out of the nine forming the oasis; six belong to the ruler of Abu Dhabi and three to the Sultan of Muscat and Oman. Several hundred miles separate it from the nearest settled part of Saudi Arabia.[99] But Saudi Arabia claimed this oasis tracing its rights to the 18th and 19th centuries. With the intervention of Britain which was directly responsible for the external relations of Abu Dhabi and Oman, the other parties to the dispute, Saudi Arabia came to a compromise. Later in 1974, the king of Saudi Arabia and the President of United Arab Emirates made an agreement which contained three conditions: (a) Saudi Arabia is to renounce its claim to the Buraimi oasis; (b) the Saudis, in return, will get an outlet to the sea fifteen to twenty miles in width encompassing Kaur al-Odaid at the base of the Qatari peninsula; and (c) the Saudi-UAE border will undergo minor adjustments in favour of Saudi Arabia. According to this agreement the rich Zarrarah oil field will now be within Saudi territory.[100]

Iran's seizure of three small islands—the Great Tunb, the Small Tunb and Abu Musa—in 1971,[101] located in the strait of Hormuz, was a test case that established Iran's unchallenged position in the region. Britain recognised the sovereignty of the Sheikh of Sharja over Abu Musa while the other two islands were historically part of Ras-al-Khaimah. Iran reasserted its claim to these islands on a historical basis. However a more serious interest in them arose when Britain's decision to vacate the Gulf was announced in 1968. Iranian troops landed

on the three islands on November 30, 1971. In the case of Abu
Musa, there was some agreement between Iran and Sharja.[102]

It was not however the territorial or historical factors but
the over-riding politico-strategic factor that prevented the late
Shah of Iran from finding a negotiated political settlement with
the Sheikhdoms. According to one view, the reason why
Iranian troops landed on the three islands near the Strait
shortly before the formation of the United Arab Emirates, was
because Iran thought that UAE alone could not provide the
required security around the strategic Strait of Hormuz.[103] It
was estimated that over 230 outward-bound tankers from Iran
were passing through the Strait of Hormuz every week. If
'unfriendly powers' controlled the Straits, the Iranian economy
could be threatened. This was the underlying reason why the
late Shah sought claim to the three strategic islands.[104]

Yet another view was that the take-over of these islands
was strategically significant to the erstwhile CENTO, thereby
indicating a US-Iranian joint policy for the Indian Ocean.[105] It
was reported that the US was collecting intelligence from
an electronic listening post at Abu Musa, at the mouth of the
Gulf.[106]

Iran's strategic moves caused considerable concern in the
Arab world.[107] The President of UAE condemned it as aggression and appealed to other Arab nations to help regain the
rights.[108] South Yemen, Iraq and Libya sharply reacted to it.
Libya accused Britain of collusion in the take-over and nationalised a part of British oil interests in that country. Iraq
severed diplomatic relations with both Iran and Britain as a
protest and further called for a concerted Arab action to block
what has been described as Iranian expansionism.[109]

However, until the ouster of the Shah in 1979, this issue
remained rather at a low level, for, the Arabs could do very
little. Following the Iranian revolution, the Arabs, particularly
Iraq, asked the new regime in Iran to return the islands to
their owners. But Khomeini stated that Iran would demand
the imposition of domination on Baghdad if Iraq persisted in
its efforts to recover the three Arab Gulf islands.[110] Khomeini
also addressed the Iraqi people and the Moslems among the
Iraqi armed forces, inciting them to revolt against the Ba'aths
and instigating them to overthrow the government of Iraq.[111]

Whatever may be the outcome of the present Iraqi-Iranian conflict, the issue of the three islands is bound to come up again and again to stifle the good relations between the two countries. When the Arabs will have mustered enough military strength, Iran would find it difficult to hold on to these islands indefinitely.

Iran's claim to Bahrain was abandoned on UN intervention and a settlement by plebicite.[112] But since the 1979 Iranian revolution, the Khomeini regime has renewed the claim. Sadiq Rouhani, a leader of the conservative religious wing said in April 18, 1980; "Iran may claim Bahrain again if Iraq continues claiming the three islands in the Gulf, ie., Abu Musa, Greater Tunb and Lesser Tunb which were occupied by the Iranian army in 1971". Rouhani added : "the Shah's parliament which abandoned Iran's claim to Bahrain in 1970 was an illegal parliament".[113] An Iran-backed terrorist plan to stage a *coup* on Bahrain's National Day on December 16, 1981, was an indirect attempt by the Islamic regime in Tehran to annex Bahrain.[114]

A border dispute between Iraq and Kuwait goes as far back as the 1960s. Britain terminated the treaty of 1899, and granted independence to Kuwait in June 1961. General Abdul Karim Qasim, Prime Minister of Iraq claimed that Kuwait belonged to the district of Basra under the Ottomans. Kuwait seemed to have remained an independent entity unattractive to fortune seekers, be they the Ottomans who conquered most of the Arab countries or European colonising expeditions which frequented the Arabian Gulf in search of stations and naval bases.[115] At the height of the Iraqi-Kuwait crisis, Kuwait requested military aid from UK in accordance with the agreement concluded between the two countries in 1961. Kuwait also welcomed the Saudi forces. The Arab League acted quickly and made Kuwait a member on 20 July 1961.[116] Quasim was overthrown in 1963 and a conciliatory regime that succeeded Qasim recognised Kuwait's independence.

Though Iraq recognised Kuwait's independence, border demarcation was not fully effected. Troops of both the countries clashed at Kuwait's border post of Sameta.[117] The Iraqi claim seemed to be that there was an Iraqi military position to which access was not possible unless the Iraqi forces passed along a road, lying near a post which Kuwait claimed was within its own territory.[118]

Strategically Sameta is important for Iraq as it lies near the Iraqi naval base at Umm Qsr. Besides, Iraq's immediate objective was to secure the Kuwaiti islands of Bubiyan and Warbah at the mouth of the Umm Qsr inlet to prevent any blockade of its Gulf coast. The two islands also command the narrow straits through which Iraqi ships transport oil from its southern oil fields.

Saudi Arabia has border problems with South Yemen. In the early 1960s, Saudi villages were bombed by the revolutionary regime in South Yemen.[119] About 50,000 Egyptians fought on the side of the Yemeni regime against the royalist elements which were supported by Saudi Arabia. It should be noted that Saudi Arabia built a large military complex near the border area in an effort to defend the south-eastern part of the kingdom. A Saudi military facility was built near the Iraqi-Kuwait borders to counter any incursion from Iraq.[120]

The incessant interstate boundary or territorial disputes appear to be another justification for the ruling elites of these developing nations for acquiring large quantities of sophisticated weapons.

EXTRA-REGIONAL FACTORS

i) *Arab-Israeli Conflict*

The nature and political dimension of what is commonly known as Arab nationalism is not quite relevant here but the concept of Arab nationalism merits some attention in so far as it is "essentially a domestic movement within the Arab world endeavouring to convert and to absorb the various centrifugal forces operating within the Arab world".[121] Indeed, it would not be an exaggeration to say that Arab nationalism happens to be the one single major political force that buries all local differences and prejudices of individual Arab States and rally them all together to fight common dangers, namely Zionism and Israeli militarism.

Whatever may be the weakness of Arab nationalism the very concept is dynamic enough to fire the imagination of all

Arabs. The Arab leaders have made effective use of it for political purposes. The differences in the interpretation of the theory of Arab nationalism have not deprived it of its pragmatic value. For, Arab nationalism acted and still continues to act as a potent factor in uniting all Arabs in West Asia.

Though torn within by various inner contradictions and conflicts, the Arabs saw it as a cementing force against their inveterate enemy, Israel. A more flexible attitude has emerged after the 1973 war, culminating in the Camp David Accord of 17 September 1978 between Israel and Egypt.[122] It is because of this common sentiment and unifying force that even those Arab States which are not directly involved in the Arab-Israeli conflict are encouraged to lend political, economic, and military support to the confrontation states.

Saudi Arabia has been effectively using its oil money to support the Arab countries directly involved in the conflict with Israel. The Saudis are aware that in another war they might very well become a front-line participant since their influence has expanded enormously in the Arab world. Their own military presence has grown on the northern Saudi border, which perhaps may invite Israel to make a direct attack on Saudi territory.[123] After the six day war in 1967 some of the oil revenues went to Egypt and Jordan to restore their war-torn economies. Saudi Arabian forces were also sent to the fighting front in the 1973 Arab-Israeli war. Though Saudi Arabia's participation in a future military operation is proposed to be marginal, there is no doubt the Saudi weapons would probably be made available to the front-line Arab States.[124] In this sense, the arms build-up in Saudi Arabia logically implies possible broadening of the Arab-Israeli conflict through Israeli pre-emption.

In the 1973 October war, Iraq made a substantial contribution of three divisions and three fighter squadrons to fight Israel. There were other Arab States like Morocco and Jordan which also participated actively in the same war on the side of Egypt and Syria.[125]

In October 1974, at an Arab summit conference in Rabat, the Arab oil producers set up for the confrontation States a war chest of $ 2.35 billion. Since that meeting, the Arab oil producers have agreed to pay $ 580 million each to Egypt and

Syria, $ 175 million to Jordan and $ 30 million to the Palestinian guerrillas.[126] Abu Dhabi gave an assistance of $ 600 million to Egypt alone in 1975.[127]

Tremendous efforts are being made by many supporting Arab States to boost up the defence potentials of the confrontation States. Purchase of 36 French Mirage fighters by Kuwait in early 1974 has been indicated as a deal which would ultimately benefit Egypt.[128] It was reported that Saudi Arabia and Abu Dhabi would provide French-built jet fighters to Egypt.[129] It appears rather odd for a small Sheikhdom like Abu Dhabi to possess the most modern Mirage fighter bombers. But there was a clear ring of Arab nationalism when the ruler of that country said: "It is quite possible we may not need them. But if there is another confrontation with Israel, one of the Arab front-line States may need them and we would then be in a position to turn them over. This is a common struggle; during the October war, Kuwait contributed forces. If there is a next time, perhaps we will also contribute forces".[130]

This line of thinking has not been in any way affected by the recent Camp David Accord by which Egypt and Israel went in for a bilateral deal. The accord was condemned by most of the Arab States. As a consequence, much of the aid promised to Egypt, has been cancelled. Denouncing Egypt as a betrayer of Arab interests, every Arab country is contemplating another possible round of conflict with Israel and is deliberately acquiring large quantities of sophisticated weapons. "As the Arabs had to face up to the danger of Zionist Settlement and expansion they would have to divert a good deal of their income to armament. . ."[131] Here precisely, Arab nationalism assumes a dynamic role transcending all barriers of local disputes, feuds and ambitions appealing to the patriotic sentiment of all Arabs and to their collective commitment to meet the challenges of what the Arabs consider as the aggressive encroachments of Zionism in the Middle East.

The trans-shipment of these weapons is not unknown to the supplier countries. However, they would not object to such transactions because they want to deny to other weapon suppliers commercial benefits which would accrue to them in large scale arms deals with these nations. It is evident, therefore, that the arms build-up in the Gulf region derives great incentive because of the Arab solidarity and conformity of thinking vis-a-vis their number one enemy, namely, Israel.

ii) *Superpower Rivlary*

a) *United States.* The supply of sophisticated weapons to the Gulf region by the United States is closely related to its security interests in the Gulf area. In 1975 the US Defence Department sized it up in terms of three main considerations.[132] The first was related to and reminiscent of the Cold War politics, namely the US policy of containment of communism.[133] It was this policy, despite the superpower *detente* in the seventies and the improved relations between the Soviet Union and Iran, that made the US pump in more sophisticated weapons into Iran. The Iranian navy, in fact, had participated on several occasions in joint naval exercises with the British and American vessels in the Gulf of Oman which obviously signified the interests of great powers to involve Iranian participation on wider issues.[134] The military alliance between Iran and the West was considered strategically or politically necessary as part of the West's grand design vis-a-vis the communist bloc.[135]

The second consideration is related to the economics of oil which the US is increasingly trying to link up with US security interests. The projected claim was that by 1980, more than half of US requirements of oil would have to be imported and that half of this would come from the Gulf area.[136] It was said that the US would be vitally dependent on Arab oil in the 1980s unless new or alternative sources of energy[137] were rapidly developed. *Newsweek* reported in 1975: "The US has two main interests in the area: to strengthen the hands of non-radical regimes while assuring the West an uninterrupted flow of oil. Thus for all its apparent paradox the civilian executive mercenaries is a relatively inexpensive way to serve those interests up to and including the opportunity of gathering intelligence on the Gulf military establishments against the unlikely day when the US might feel called upon to intervene."[138]

Successive US Presidents have stated in no uncertain

terms that force would be used if somehow there arose grave difficulties in the flow of oil through the straits of Hormuz. President Carter, for example, said: "we can get along without oil from Iran and Iraq, but we cannot get along without oil, ourselves or the rest of the world, from the rest of the Persian Gulf region. The United Arab Emirates, Kuwait, and Saudi Arabia ship about 12 million barrels of oil every day out of the straits of Hormuz and we will use whatever means is required to keep the straits of Hormuz open".[139]

The argument in favour of arming the non-radical regimes in the Gulf region was that if per chance, radical regimes succeeded in establishing their hegemony in the Gulf region, US interests there would be greatly threatened. US military assistance to Iran and Iran's oil exports to the US were the most significant elements in US-Iranian relations even just before the Iranian revolution of 1979. US policy objectives for Iran centred on assuring the continued availability of Iranian oil at reasonable prices. In addition, US aims included strengthening Iran as a deterrent to possible Iraqi and Soviet aggression and supporting Iran in its determination to provide political stability, economic development and regional co-operation throughout the area.[140]

After the fall of the Shah of Iran, the US has turned to Saudi Arabia. Highly sophisticated weapons are being transferred to Saudi Arabia. In this, US policy objectives are very clear: *a*) Saudi Arabia should maintain a freeze in the OPEC price of oil which is an objective consistent with US domestic and foreign policy objectives; *b*) US trade deficit should be reduced by Saudi Arabian reliance on and encouragement of US investments and services to assist in its internal economic development thereby offering an extensive export market for US business;[141] *c*) Saudi Arabian preference to satisy its legitimate national security defence requirements by purchasing US military equipment complements US foreign policy objectives in the area. The Reagan administration, for example, seeking to improve ties with anti-Soviet Saudi Arabia sought approval to sell fuel tanks and other equipment to Riyadh to enhance the range and firepower of 62 F-15 jet fighters purchased by the Saudis since 1978;[142] *d*) Saudis' firm opposition to the spread of communism and Soviet influence complements US policy in the area.[143]

Another argument for the continued arms supply to the region is that it greatly improves the US balance of payments. This thesis is rather controverted, for, as against this it is argued that if the US were to lose its entire arms market to the underdeveloped world the impact on its overall balance of payments would be very small.[144] It was further argued that if the US does not sell arms to the Gulf States, the British and French would do it on a competitive basis and this would mean a lessening of US influence in the area. "Preventing the influx of military equipment of other nations, a sort of pre-emptive selling" has been considered a strong motive in selling arms to the Gulf region.[145]

The third security interest is related to the US military strategy in the Gulf. It is claimed that the US security interest demands continued free movement of the US ships and aircraft into and out of the area, and continued access to logistic support facilities at Bahrain.[146]

The concept of Rapid Deployment Force (RDF) in the Indian Ocean has been developed in the context of the Iranian crisis of 1979 with potential threats to the oil supply lines followed by the Iran-Iraq war. The RDF has an intervention capability in the Persian Gulf.

The Eisenhower Doctrine of 1957 stipulated that the US would come to the aid of nations requesting assistance when attacked by countries "controlled by international communism". The Carter Doctrine in the wake of the Iranian revolution went further and decided when to intervene, with or without request. Of course, President Reagan agrees with the view that military force is a key element in any global strategy.[147]

The Reagan administration's obsession with the Gulf security has several facets. These are: a quick—fix force for the region, a role for the Gulf States in its deployment, integration of a willing Pakistan into its grand strategy, raising the level of American arms assistance to Afghan rebels and last, but not least, a collective western strategy, including a multinational naval fleet.[148] The ostensible purpose of all this is to pose a challenge to Moscow which has now attained a strategically advantageous position in Afghanistan to attack the West's economic life-line in the neighbouring Gulf region.

b) *Soviet Union.* Unlike the United States and West European countries, the Soviet Union is rather selective in supplying arms to developing nations in general. The arms transfers are usually politically motivated. The Soviets also sell arms to acquire hard currency. Payments in goods and commodities are also acceptable to the Soviets. Since 1976 the USSR has increased sales of weapons to the developing world and 1979 was a record year. The average annual transfer figure for the year 1977 through 1979 was estimated at $ 7.2 billion compared to a $ 5.1 billion average for the 1974-76 period.[149]

In the Gulf region, most of the Soviet supply of arms has gone to Iraq. The motivations of this restricted policy of arms supplies are rather mixed and in some ways influenced by the global policies of the Soviet Union. The Soviets have been successful in befriending some Arab countries which, while denouncing imperialism and colonialism, were attempting to follow a socialistic pattern of economy.[150] "The Soviet Union has supported the most 'progressive' of the regional powers against the others".[151]

The main motive of the Soviet Union in supplying arms was to give support to the revolutionary and radical regimes such as Iraq and South Yemen and through them to encourage and build-up revolutionary movements in the Gulf area. In doing so, the Soviet Union expects to further her influence in the region and at the same time deny it to the United States and West European countries.

Another motive of Soviet supplies of arms is related to the Arab-Israeli conflict. Deeply committed to the defence of Israel, the United States knows no restraint in its policy of supplying enormous quantities of weapons to that country. In their dire need for weapons, the Arab confrontation States have turned to the Soviet Union and they have not been refused military hardware to offset the Israeli build-up. Broadly, it was admitted in the seventies that in West Asia and North Africa, the Soviets had succeeded in assembling an impressive military, economic and political presence by identifying themselves with the Arab cause against Israel.[152] The supply of arms was the manifest expression of such an identification with that cause.

Iraq was in open confrontation with Israel in 1967 and 1973 and it has been equipped with large quantities of Soviet weapons. In the sporadic conflicts between the Arabs and Israel, the arms which played the defensive and offensive role on either side, were supplied by their respective patrons.

c) *Other Arms suppliers : United Kingdom, France, Federal Republic of Germany and Japan*: Western Europe's arms exports are a political and economic necessity, according to Price.[153] West European countries, especially UK, France and Federal Republic of Germany are highly industrialised nations whose commercial productions and exports of weapons are essential to maintain in turn their industrial economies. Hence, these countries are not only involved in a rivalry among themselves to export their weapons but also engaged in a keen competition with the United States to sell arms to the Gulf Area. An important factor, according to Freedman, originating in the mid-60s, has been the commercial desire of Western countries to improve their balance of payments.[154]

The British government feels that arms sales have two advantages; first, they will be a major booster for Britain's ailing manufacturing industries; and second, sales will give Britain an edge in strategic areas like the Gulf, Southern Africa and even South America.[155] As Britain became unable to accept direct responsibility for the security of former dependencies 'East of Suez', arms sales became a substitute for a British presence.[156]

Only the increased exports of weapons can help to finance the fast growing requirements of R and D as being determined by the United States who pattern the vertical dimension of the armaments dynamics. Without exports, France, for example, would never be able to procure the technologies, prerequisite to the *"force de frappe"*.[157]

France and Britain went along with the United States in imposing an arms embargo on Iran on 28 January 1981, but that did not prevent France from delivering to Iraq—the other party in the Iran-Iraq conflict—60 Mirage F-1 supersonic fighter aircraft ordered by Iraq in 1977 and 1979. France also supplied helicopters to Iraq to make up its war losses and agreed to sell SAMS to shore up Iraq's air defence. UK also is reported to have agreed to sell Iraq 200 Crusader tank-towing vehicles.[158] These arms transactions were economically profit-oriented, despite the fact that the arms flow would certainly escalate the conflict in the region.

In some cases, the Gulf States are themselves ready to finance part of the research and development of the weapons systems ordered by them. This is because firstly, the Gulf States are eager to augment their armouries in the shortest period of time and secondly, they have more money than can perhaps be assimilated into their socio-economic development. These two factors are being heavily exploited by the arms suppliers. F-14 Tomcat, the air superiority fighter was one such example which the US navy found too expensive to afford and which for that reason would have gone out of production, had the late Shah of Iran not come to the rescue of Grumman Corporation by ordering as many as 80 aircraft against liberal advances.[159]

The Gulf countries are also interested in diversifying their arms deals. This is because: first, they have enough money to purchase the best quality weapons in the arms market; second, political considerations at times may induce them to have more than one arms supplier. Despite his pro-US policies in the Gulf area, the late Shah of Iran used to threaten to go elsewhere if the US did not meet his specific requirements. He once said: "I am afraid that today American credibility is not too high. You look rather a crippled giant". He added : "we have ten other markets to provide us with what we need. There are people just waiting for that moment".[160]

When there was opposition in the Senate to the sale of F-15 aircraft to Saudi Arabia, it entered into separate negotiations with the French to fund the Mirage 4000 as an alternative to F-15. There is an increasing awareness of the weak ties with US and some have begun to advocate that Saudi Arabia must as early as possible try to decouple its military development from the US.[161] In 1980 Saudi Arabia made an informal pro-posal to West Germany for the purchase of 300 Leopard II tanks and 2000 armoured personnel carriers. The decision of the Saudis was influenced by two considerations : (i) Saudis regard Leopard II as the latest tank for the desert warfare, and

(ii) to diversify their arms purchases. It was in pursuance of this policy that Saudi Arabia also signed a $ 4 billion agreement with France for naval equipment.[162]

The Kuwaiti efforts in purchasing Soviet arms also must be seen as: *a*) an indication of diversifying sources of arms supplies; *b*) a strategy to lessen the dependency on the West; and *c*) a means to obtain counter-weapons to respond effectively to Iraqi arms build-up. Under an agreement signed with a Kuwait military delegation in Moscow at the beginning of 1975, it was reported that Kuwait had obtained modern military weapons from the Soviet Union.[163]

Oil of the Gulf region was another important factor which has drawn the attention of the West European countries and Japan.

The West European countries and Japan depend heavily on the Gulf States for the major import of their oil requirements which alone can guarantee their economic growth and stability. After the 1973 Arab-Israeli war, the oil policy of the Middle Eastern oil producing countries have seriously and dangerously challenged the economic system of the West and Japan.[164] Next to the United States, West Europeans are the largest oil consumers.

There is a close correlation between France's arms sales and its oil imports.[165] France must import over 98 per cent of the oil which supplies approximately two-third of its energy needs. In 1977, about 83 per cent of these imports came from the Middle Eastern Arab States and Iran. Over 36.4 per cent of France's supply is derived from Saudi Arabia and 15.3 per cent from Iraq. France has signed its largest contracts for arms with these countries since 1974.[166] In return for commitments of assured supplies of oil, France has provided arms and a nuclear reactor to Iraq.[167]

Japan was the fourth largest oil consumer in 1973 using nearly 5.4 million barrels daily or 267.2 million tons a year. Japan is convinced that oil imports from the Middle East producers, particularly the Arabs, will remain fundamental to Japan's economic prosperity for the foreseeable future.[168] Japan's dependence on foreign oil is put at 99.7 per cent of which roughly four fifths come from the Middle East[169]

The increased dependence of these industrialised nations on

oil imports for the maintenance and progress of their economy has provided an advantageous leverage which the oil exporting nations are utilising to their own benefit.[170] The oil exporting countries' inherent capability to cause serious crises in the industrial economy of the advanced nations of the West and the East has been to a considerable extent demonstrated when in 1973 the Gulf States hiked the oil price simultaneously cutting back production.[171]

The use of oil as a political weapon in the context of the Arab-Israeli conflict of 1973 provided many lessons to the allies of the United States in Europe.[172] They significantly changed their pro-Israeli attitudes and approach which were generally in tune with the American policy of active support for Israel. The first lesson was the sombre realisation on the part of these nations that their industrial economy could be equally vulnerable by another oil embargo which could vitally affect even their national security.[173] Secondly the vulnerability of the NATO powers, ensuing from a future oil embargo emerged more sharply and the inability of the United States to suggest alternative sources of oil supplies indicates the patent weakness of the American or Atlantic alliance. "On the international front the oil situation will be an even greater disaster to her NATO allies, Japan and many developing countries caught in the power play of the oil producers. Without prompt relief, the plight of the European and Japanese economies may bring about runaway inflation and a global recession which could easily involve us. A military consequence would be a further decline in the effectiveness of the NATO alliance and an added reason, the shortage of oil, to doubt the capability of NATO for prolonged self-defence."[174]

In a major crisis, if the oil kings shut off the oil flow to the Western powers, the US will not be in a position to help them. The Western powers are reminded of their experience during the Suez crisis in which the United States failed to support the Anglo-French interests of controlling the Suez waters which seemed to have been vitally important to them.[175] The basic structure of western or Atlantic alliance remained unaffected (i.e, the Soviet-American cooperation instead of confrontation) despite the Suez crisis. As no nation would like to negotiate about its own survival, the West European nations and Japan indicated a major shift of policy by delinking their Israeli connection and adopting a pro-Arab policy however embarrassing it was to the United States. The oil weapon proved Japan's basic politico-economic vulnerability. From a position of political neutrality, Japan soon changed to follow EEC's example and appealed to Israel to withdraw to the 22 October ceasefire line as a first step toward total withdrawal from occupied Arab territories.[176]

After the 1973 Arab-Israeli war, the West European countries, "not only suppressed whatever sympathy or scruples they may have had toward Israel and hurried to subcribe to political formulations demanded by the Arabs, but they also blamed the United States for their plight and scrambled to make whatever bilateral or multilateral deals they could with the Arab states".[177] Besides, most of them prefer to negotiate with the oil exporting Gulf States on a bilateral basis, independently of any action contemplated or views expressed in Washington.[178] It was only after the October 1973 war and the ensuing Arab oil boycott of the West coupled with the European energy crisis that a new type of weapons spiral began—the so-called oil-for-arms deals.[179]

In the final analysis of the dynamics of arms race in the Gulf region, the following observations may be made; the unprecedented efforts of the Gulf States to build-up first rate military forces must be viewed against the imbroglio following the decision of Britain in 1968 to discontinue its role as protector of the Gulf area. But it is not to be construed as a consequence of the exit of the British or as a result of the 'power vacuum' that was supposed to have followed it which gave a sudden spurt to the arms business in the Gulf region. There does not exist any correlation between the two. For, backward nations whose national identities have long been overshadowed by the oppressive presence of imperial and colonial powers, have always made such efforts to build their defence with a view to reasserting their identities in a world of unambiguous power struggles and conflicts. It was, therefore, a simple logical response to a new situation that demanded the Gulf States to fulfil a requirement of their own needs of security and national interests by restructuring their own defence system.

It should be further remembered that military power is not the same as military force.[180] The latter may be available and at times be borrowed but the former cannot be made available unless a country already possesses it. What could be easily converted into military power, as applied to the Gulf States is oil which they have in abundance. Oil as a cheap source of energy is constantly in demand specially in the industrialised nations of the West and East whose economies may grind to a halt if the Gulf States refuse to sell them oil.

The ability to manipulate oil as a political weapon has already brought significant political gains and prestige to the Arab States. The increase in price of oil, though extremely unpalatable to the industrialised nations and rather burdensome to developing countries, is mainly aimed at drawing an equation with the highly priced industrial goods, imported from western countries, particularly the highly sophisticated weapon systems which the Gulf States covet most.

The Arab-Israeli conflict, though a potent cause, is not the only one energising the Arabs to expend their resources on military weapons. "Sporadic but intense inter-Arab wars and near wars at times have overshadowed the conflict between them and Israel".[181] There are so many seething unseen stresses and strains within the regional system itself which are quite unrelated to the xenophobic Zionism,[182] but closely related to the sharply divided political conservatism and radicalism, the continued survival of each of which is based on the premise of procuring more weapons—one trying to outdo the other.

Though the Gulf States are determined to build up their own defences, nevertheless they are conditioned by the arms suppliers, especially the superpowers. For one thing, the Gulf States do not have weapons of their own, for another, they do not have the technical skill and defence infrastructure so essential to structure modern defence system. As a result of the lack of these basic factors the arms recipients would have to accept men in support capacity whose presence is necessary to operate the weapons transferred.

Though the weapons transactions appear quite legal and the presence of men in support capacity justifiable according to business stipulation, it is a matter for strategic rethinking

whether or not the Gulf States are creating their own Franken-
steins as it recently turned out to be in the case of Iran.

REFERENCES

1 For a brief discussion on the evolution of Iran's military policies over
   the past decade, see Alvin J. Cottrell, "Iran, The Arabs and the
   Persian Gulf", *Orbis*, Vol. 17, no. 3, Fall 1973, pp. 978-88.

2 Sepehr Zabih, "Iran Today," *Current History*, Vol. 66, no. 390,
   February 1974, p. 66.

3 Benjamin Shwadran, *The Middle East, Oil and the Great Powers*
   (London : Atlantic Press, 1955), p. 7.

4 *Ibid.*

5 For an account of Iran's experience during and after the two great
   wars see Tareq Y. Ismael, *Governments and Politics of the Contemporary Middle East* (Illinois: The Dorsey Press, 1970), pp. 156-61.

6 *Kayhan International* (Tehran), 9 November 1974.

7 *Kayhan International*, 26 July 1975.

8 Yair P. Hirschfeld, "Moscow and Khomeini: Soviet-Iranian Relations in Historical Perspective," *Orbis*, Vol. 24, no. 2, Summer 1980,
   p. 221.

9 B.K. Narayan, *Lessons and Consequences of the October War* (New
   Delhi: Vikas, 1977), p. 72.

10 Economic cooperation between Iran and the Soviet Union was at its
   peak just before the ouster of Shah in 1979, see Hirschfeld, n. 8,
   p. 234.

11 John Marlowe, *Iran: A Short Political Guide* (New York; Praeger,
   1963), p. 132; see also *Pravda*, 29 October 1971, pp. 1-4.

12 *New Perspectives on the Persian Gulf*: Hearings, Subcommittee on
   the Near East and South Asia,Committee on Foreign Affairs, House of
   Representatives, 93rd Congress, First Session, June 6, July 17, 23, 24
   and November 28, 1973 (Washington, D.C., US Government Printing
   Office, 1973), p. 122.

13 Muhammad Morsy Abdullah, *The United Arab Emirates: A Modern
   History* (London, 1978), p. 201.

14 Rouhollah K. Ramazani, "Iran's Search for Regional Co-operation",
   Middle East Journal (Washington, D.C.), Vol. 30, no. 2, Spring 1976,
   p. 181.

15 Hermann F. Eilts, "Security Considerations in the Persian Gulf,"
   International Security (Cambridge), Vol. 5, no. 2, Fall 1980, p. 89.

16 *The Observer* (London), 5, August 1973.

17 *The Times* (London), 6 March 1973.

18 R.M. Burrell, "Iranian Foreign Policy: Strategic Location, Economic
   Ambition and Dynastic Determination", *Journal of International
   Affairs* (London), vol. 29, no. 2, Fall 1975, p. 137.

19 *The Hindu* (Madras), 10 April 1973.

20 *The Observer*, 5 August 1973.

21 Andrew Whitley, "The Kurds: Pressures and Prospects," *The Round Table* (London), no. 279, July 1980, p. 247.

22 Sa'ad N. Jawad, "The Kurdish Problem in Iraq," in Abbas Kelidar, ed., *The Integration of Modern Iraq* (London: Croom Helm, 1979), p. 171.

23 Edgar O' Ballance, "The Kurdish Factor in the Gulf," *The Army Quarterly and Defence Journal* (London), Vol. 104, no. 5, October 1974, p. 570.

24 *Strategic Survey 1974*, 1975, p. 82; see also Sa'ad N. Jawad, n. 22, p. 180.

25 Edgar O' Ballance, "The Kurdish Factor in the Gulf War," *Military Review* (Leavenworth, K.S.), Vol. LXI, no. 6, June 1981, p. 15.

26 *The Hindustan Times* (New Delhi), 8 March 1975.

27 *Strategic Survey 1974*, 1975, p. 83.

28 *Ibid*.

29 *Ibid*.

30 *International Herald Tribune* (Paris), 12 March 1975.

31 Whitley, n. 21, p. 247.

32 *Ibid*.

33 It should be noted that some countries like Saudi Arabia and Qatar do not have any dealings with communist states, not even recognize them. See *Qatar MEED Special Report* (London), April 1977, p. 25.

34 *Strategic Survey 1973*, 1974, p. 44; See also Ralph Joseph, "Iraq: The Baath Settles in", *The Middle East* (London), no. 22, August 1976, p. 12.

35 *Ibid.*, p. 44.

36 Iraq and Saudi Arabia signed a frontier delimitation treaty on 26 December 1981. See *The Hindu* (Madurai), 28 December 1981.

37 Christoph Von Imhoff, "From the Persian Gulf to the Indian Ocean", *Aussen Politik* (Bremen-Nord), Vol. 26, no. 1, 1st Quarter, 1975, p. 47.

38 For a brief account of the origins of Dhofar revolt and its gradual development, see R.M. Burrell, "Rebellion in Dhofar", *New Middle East*, March 1972, pp. 55-58; see also *Strategic Survey 1973*, 1974, p. 44.

39 B.K. Narayan, *Oman and Gulf Security* (New Delhi: Lancers Publishers, 1979), p. 118.

40 In 1979, China established diplomatic relations with Oman. See A. Stepanov, "New Fit of Pactomania," *New Times* (Moscow), no. 42, October 1979, p. 12.

41 V.R. Bhatt, "Politics of British Defence", *The Hindustan Times*, 13 December 1974; see also Thomas W. Lippman, "Uneasy Peace in Gulf Area," *Sunday Standard* (New Delhi), 27 March 1977.

42 K. Kudryavtsev, "Oman: Looking for a New Prop," *New Times* (Moscow), no. 11, March 1979, p. 12.

43 *Arab Report and Record*, 16-31 March 1973, p. 141.

44 *Washington Post*, 17 January 1976.

45 David R. Griffiths, "Congress Probes Yemeni Arms Policy," *Aviation Week & Space Technology* (New York), Vol. 112, no. 21, 26 May 1980, p. 79; see also Ferdinand Hurni, "The Complex Middle East," *Swiss Review of World Affairs* (Zurich), Vol. XXXI, no. 3, June 1981, p. 6.

46 Harold H. Saunders, "The Middle East 1978-79 : Forces of Change," *Current Policy No. 77* (Washington, D.C.), 26 July 1979.

47 *The New Republic* (Washington, D.C.), 24 January 1981.

48 *Kayhan International*, 2 October 1979.

49 John K. Cooley, "Iran, the Palestinians, And the Gulf", *Foreign Affairs* (New York), Vol. 57, no. 5, Summer 1979, p. 1019.

50 Valerie Yorke, "Security in the Gulf: A Strategy of Pre-emption", *The World Today* (London), Vol. 36, no. 7, July 1980, p. 242.

51 *The Hindu* (Madurai), 23 December 1981; also see *Indian Express* (Cochin), 22 December 1981.

52 Harish Chandola, "Six Nations Enter into Gulf Security Pact", *Indian Express* (Cochin), 29 January 1982.

53 E. Tarabrin, "The Developing Countries and Disarmament", *International Affairs* (Moscow), no. 6, June 1977, p. 38.

54 Mohamed Sid-Ahmed, *After the Guns Fall Silent* (London: Croom Helm, 1976), p. 86.

55 Hanns W. Maull, "The Control of Oil," *International Journal* (Toronto), Vol. XXXVI, no. 2, Spring 1981, p. 275.

56 A. Kislow, "The Arms Race in the Middle East", *International Affairs* (Moscow), no. 7, July 1978, p. 91.

57 Stockholm International Peace Research, *World Armaments and Disarmament, SIPRI Yearbook 1975* (Stockholm: Almqvist and Wiksell, 1975), p. 198.

58 Maull, n. 55, p. 275.

59 U. Albrecht, D. Ernst, P. Lock and H. Wulf, "Militarization, Arms Transfer and Arms Production in Peripheral Countries", *Journal of Peace Research* (Oslo), Vol. 12, no. 3, 1975, p. 197; see also *Current Foreign Policy: US Relations with Arabian Peninsula/Persian Gulf Countries*, 17 April 1975, p. 7.

60 *The Observer*, 5 August 1973.

61 Tarabrin, n. 53, p. 38.

62 Brian Beedham, "Look Beyond the Oil", *The Economist* (London), 17-23, May 1975, p. 11.

63 S.K. Thabet, "Can Science Flourish in the Arab Middle East", *Scientific World* (London), Vol. XIV, no. 1, 1970, p. 16.

64 *Ibid.*

65 An interesting attempt to define the role of the army officers in the unfolding of Arab history, i.e. to what extent are they revolutionaries, or simply opportunists, See Eliezer Be'eri, *Army Officers in Arab Politics and Society* (New York: Praeger, 1970); see also Gabriel Ben-Dor, "Civilization of Military Regimes in the Arab World", *Armed Forces and Society*, Vol. 1, No. 3, Spring 1975, p. 317.

66 William R. Polk, "The Middle East: Analysing Social Change", *Bulletin of the Atomic Scientists*, January 1967, p. 17.

67 "The Arming of the Oil Kings," *The Observer*, 5 August 1973.

68 *The Arms Trade with the Third World*, SIPRI (Stockholm : Almqvist and Wiksell, 1971), p. 575.

69 *Ibid.*

70 Joseph Frankel, *National Interest* (London: Pall Mall, 1970), p. 145.

71 *The Times* (London), 6 March 1973.

72 T.V. Parasuram, "Iran's Armed Forces now Ineffective", *Indian Express* (Cochin), 20 November 1979; see also, "Air Force Grounded", *Kayhan International*, 19 March 1979.

73 Arnold Hottinger, "Iran: An Empire Flexes Its Muscles", *Swiss Review of World Affairs*, Vol. 24, no. 9, December 1974, pp. 14-17.

74 Ali Mohammed Khalifa, *The United Arab Emirates: Unity in Fragmentation* (Colorado: Westview Press, 1979), p. 169. According to Burrell the Shah had recognized the importance of the Gulf and had determined to achieve local hegemony there even before the announcement of British withdrawal was made in January 1968. See R.M. Burrell, "Iranian Foreign Policy during the Last Decade", *Asian Affairs*, Vol. 61, pt. 1, February 1974, pp. 8-10.

75 *New Perspectives on the Persian Gulf*, Hearings before the Sub-committee on the Near-East and South Asia of the Committee on Foreign Affairs, House of Representatives (Washington, D.C.: US Government Printing Office, 1973), p. 39.

76 Rouhollah K. Ramazani, "Iran's Foreign Policy: Perspectives and Projections", *Economic Consequences of the Revolution in Iran*: A Compendium of papers submitted to the Joint Economic Committee, Congress of the US, 96th Congress, 1st Session, November 19, 1979 (Washington, D.C.: US Government Printing Office, 1980), p. 72.

77 Brian B. Beckett, "Giants in the Gulf", *Middle East International* (London), no. 69, March 1977, p. 27.

78 Shirin Tahir-Kheli, "Proxies and Allies: The Case of Iran and Pakistan", *Orbis* (Philadelphia), Vol. 24, no. 2, Summer 1980, p. 343.

79 Peter Duignan, Alvin Rabushka, eds., *The United States in the 1980s* (New Delhi: Kalyani Publishers, 1980), p. 768.

80 Arnaud de Borchgrave, "Colossus of the Oil Lanes", *Newsweek*, 21 May 1973, p. 44.

81 Quoted in the Iraqi-Iranian Conflict: *Documentary* Dossier (Ministry of Foreign Affairs, Republic of Iraq, January 1981), p. 5.

82 Beckett, n. 77, p. 27.

83 *International Herald Tribune* (Paris), 15 January 1975; see also *News Review on Science and Technology* (New Delhi), February 1977, p. 85.

84 A. Feoktistov, "Saudi Arabia and the Arab World", *International Affairs* (Moscow), no. 7, July 1977, p. 101.

85 *Newsweek*, 21 May 1973, p. 14; see also *The Hindustan Times*, 12 June 1973.

86 Arnold Hottinger, "King Feisal, Oil and Arab Politics", *Swiss Review of World Affairs*, Vol. 23, no. 7, October 1973, p. 9.

87 Beckett, n. 77, p. 28.

88 *Strategic Survey 1976*, p. 90.

89 James M. Bedore, "Saudi Arabia: Greatness Thrust Upon Them", *Middle East International*, no. 79, January 1978, pp. 14-15.

90 David D. Newsom, "US-Persian Gulf Relationship," *Department of State Bulletin* (Washington, D.C.), Vol. 80 no. 2041, August 1980, p. 62.

91 *The Defense Monitor* (Washington, D.C.), Vol. X, no. 4, 1981, p. 1.

92 Peter Mansfield, *The Middle East: A Political and Economic Survey* (London: Oxford University Press, 1973), p. 141.

93 Chandola, n. 52. Saudi Arabia is to finance rebuilding the Iraqi nuclear reactor that Israel attacked on 7 June 1982 following Israeli fears that it was to be used to make nuclear bombs, see *The Hindustan Times* (New Delhi), 17 July 1981. Further, Iraq and Saudi Arabia signed a frontier delimtation treaty in December 1981. See *The Hindu* (Maduari), 28 December 1981.

94 Robert Graham, "Iraq and Iran: Gulf Power Struggle Sharpens", *New Middle East*, no. 45, June 1972, p. 15.

95 *The Observer*, 5 August 1972; See also Barry Rubin, "Sub-Empires in the Persian Gulf", *The Progressive* (Madison), Vol. 39, no. 1, January 1975, p. 30.

96 B K. Narayan, *Lessons and Consequences of the October War* (New Delhi: Vikas, 1977), p. 72.

97 Chandola, n. 52.

98 John Marlowe, *Arab Nationalism and British Imperialism* (London: The Cresset Press, 1961), p. 6.

99 Donald Hawley, *The Trucial States* (London: George Allen & Unwin Ltd., 1970), p. 186; See also "Buraimi Settlement: A Factor of Stability", *An Nahar Arab Report*, Vol. 5, no. 31, 5 August 1974, pp. 3-4.

100 For more details on the background and events of the Buraimi dispute, See Alexander Melamid, "The Buraimi Oasis Dispute", *Middle Eastern Affairs* (London), Vol. 7, no. 1, February 1956, pp. 56-63; George Lenczowski, *Oil and State in the Middle East* (New York: Cornell University Press, 1966), pp. 141-52; and Husain M. Albaharna, *The Legal Status of the Arabian Gulf States* (Manchester: Manchester University Press, 1968), Chapter 13.

101 *Daily Report, Middle East and Africa*, V, no. 230, 20 November 1971.

102 Khalifa, n. 74, pp. 153-54.

103 Rouhollah K. Ramazani, *The Persian Gulf: Iran's Role* (Charlottesville: University Press of Virgina, 1972), p. 89.

104 "Three Islands that Could Strangle Iran's Oil Artery," *Middle East International*, no. 5, August 1971, p. 30.

105 *Indian Express*, 10 April 1973. The late Shah supported the US naval facility at Diego Garcia in the Indian Ocean. See *Strategic Survey 1975*, 1976, p. 89.

106 Brigadier F.W. Speed, "Indian Ocean Rivalry," *The Army Quarterly and Defence Journal*, Vol. 104, no. 4, October 1975, p. 459.

107 D.K. Palit, "Britain's Defence Cut: II; The Indian Ocean Region". *The Hindustan Times* (New Delhi), 1 February 1975.

108 Roy E. Thoman, "Iraq and the Persian Gulf", *Current History*, 4 January 1973, p. 25.

109 Khalifa, n. 74, p. 154.

110 *The Iraqi-Iranian Conflict: Documentary Dossier* (Ministry of Foreign Affairs; Republic of Iraq) January 1981, p. 5.

111 *Ibid.*

112 United Nations, Security Council, *Draft Resolutions* Docs. S/9792, 11 May 1970; See also S/9726, p. 2, and S/9772, Para 57.

113 Quoted in *The Iraqi-Iranian Conflict: Documentary Dossier*, n. 110, p. 10.

114 *The Hindu* (Madurai), 23 December 1981.

115 *The Kuwait-Iraqi Crisis* (Government of Kuwait: Printing and Publishing Department, August 1961), p. 4·

116 *Ibid.*; see also *The Truth about the Crisis between Kuwait and Iraq* (Government of Kuwait: Printing and Publishing Department, March 1961).

117 For details see R.M. Burrell, "The Gulf Pot Begins to Boil Once More", *New Middle East*, no. 56, May 1973, pp. 37-38; See also *Arab Report and Record*, 16-31, March 1973, pp. 127-28.

118 *Indian Express*, 10 April 1973.

119 Joseph J. Malone, *The Arab Lands of Western Asia* (New Jersey: Prentice-Hall, 1973), p. 161.

120 Dale R. Tahtinen, *National Security Challenges to Saudi Arabia* (Washington, D.C. : American Enterprise Institute for Public Policy Research, 1978). p. 6.

121 Marlowe, n. 98, p. 4.

122 Most of the Arab States have opposed Camp David Accord and agreed to impose a series of sanctions on Egypt, see *Review of Recent Developments in the Middle East, 1979*. Hearings before the Sub-committee on Europe and the Middle East of Committee on Foreign Affairs, House of Representatives, 96th Congress, 1st Session, July 26, 1979 (Washington: US Government Printing Office, 1979), p. 50; see also Michael Rubner, *Camp David Aftermath* (Los Angeles: Centre for the Study of Armament and Disarmament, Occasional Papers Series, No. 7, 1977), p. 20.

123 Louis Turner and James Bedore, "Saudi Arabia: The Power of the Purse-Strings," *International Affairs* (London), Vol. 54, no. 1, July 1978, p. 408.

124 John Waterbury, Ragaei El Mallakh, *The Middle East in the Coming Decade* (New York: McGraw-Hill, 1978), p. 15.

125 *Strategic Survey 1973*, 1974, p. 25; see also *News Review on Science and Technology*, 15 April 1970, p. 40; and *The Hindustan Times*, 14 January 1975.

126 *International Herald Tribune,* 14 January 1975.

127 *Newsweek,* 10 March 1975, p. 15.

128 *The Hindustan Times,* 10 November 1974.

129 *International Herald Tribune,* 15 January 1975; see also *News Review on Science and Technology,* February 1977, p. 85.

130 *Newsweek,* 10 March 1975, p 15.

131 Editorial, *Iraq Today* (Baghdad), Vol. II, no. 27, 16-31 October 1976.

132 *New Perspectives on the Persian Gulf,* n. 75, p. 39; see also "US Statement on Middle East/Persian Gulf/South West Asia Strategic Consensus", *USICA, Official Text* (American Center, New Delhi), pp. 4-6.

133 Carl Kaysen, "American Military Policy", *Survival,* Vol. XI, No. 2, February 1969, p. 51.

134 R.M. Burrell, "Iran in Search of Greater Responsibilities", *New Middle East,* no. 49, October 1972, p. 28.

135 John Marlowe, *Iran* (London: Pall Mall Press, 1963), p. 130.

136 *New Perspectives on the Persian Gulf,* n. 75, p. 39.

137 David G. Nes, "The US Energy Crisis and Middle East," *Military Review* (Leavenworth, K.S.), Vol. LIII, no. 3, March 1973, pp. 3-7. The US constituting only six per cent of the world's population, uses one-third of the world energy. *Ibid.,* p. 4; see also D. Penzin, "Oil and Independence," *International Affairs* (Moscow), no. 10, October 1972, pp. 34-40.

138 *Newsweek,* 24 February 1975, p. 20.

139 *Weekly Compilations of Presidential Documents,* Vol. 16, no. 40, October 1980, p. 2025; see also *Department of State Bulletin* (Washington, D.C.), Vol. 80, no. 2044, November 1980, p. 53.

140 *Peace in the Middle East: A Delicate Balance*: Report of a Study Mission to the Middle East and Ireland, January 2 to January 20, 1978 to the Committee on International Relations, US House of Representatives, 95th Congress, 2nd Session (Washington: US Government Printing Office, 1978), p. 23.

141 *Ibid.,* p. 17.

142 *New York Times,* 1 March 1981.

143 *Ibid.,* p. 17; see also *Weekly Compilations of of Presidential Documents,* Vol. 15, no. 36, September 1979, p. 1585.

144 "Arms Sales and Foreign Policy", *Bulletin of the Atomic Scientists,* Vol. 23, no. 7, September 1967, p. 45.

145 *Congressional Quarterly, Weekly Report,* Vol. XXXIII, no. 13, March 29, 1975, p. 659.

146 *New Perspectives on the Gulf,* n. 75, p. 39.

147 David D. Newsom, "America EnGulfed", *Foreign Policy* (Washington, D.C.), no. 43, Summer 1981, p. 18; The motives for the US intervention policy "in large parts of the third world are economic, political and also strategic-military in nature". See Helmut Kramer and Helfried Bauer, "Imperialism, Intervention Capacity and Foreign Policy Making", *Journal of Peace Research,* 1972, p. 283.

148 S.P. Seth, "Gulf Security and the US: How Real is the Soviet Threat?", *The Times of India* (Bombay), 23 March 1981.

149 *US Conventional Arms Transfer Policy*: A Report to the Senate from the Committee on Foreign Relations, United States Senate, 96th Congress, 2nd Session (Washington: US Government Printing Office, 1980), p. 2.

150 For the main stages in the development of Soviet-Arab Friendship, see R. Petrov, "The Soviet Union and Arab Countries", *International Affairs* (Moscow), no. 11, November 1972, pp. 22-29.

151 Leonard Binder, "The Middle East Crisis: A Trial Balance", *Bulletin of the Atomic Scientists*, Vol. 23, no. 7, September 1967, p. 7.

152 Bhabani Sen Gupta, "Soviet Foreign Policy Strategic Thinking for the Seventies", *India Quarterly* (New Delhi), Vol. XXXI, no. 4, October-December 1975, p. 331.

153 D.L. Price, "Building Bridges in the Gulf," *Middle East International* (London), no. 59, May 1976, p. 25.

154 Lawrence Freedman, "Britain and the Arms Trade," *International Affairs* (London), Vol. 54, No. 1, July 1978, p. 383.

155 *The Hindu* (Madurai), 29 April 1981.

156 Freedman, n. 154, p. 387.

157 Albrecht, Ernst, Lock and Wulf, n. 59, p. 197; see also *US Conventional Arms Transfer Policy*, n. 149, p. 2.

158 Mohammad Afaf, "The Drives Behind Defence Spending", *Islamic Defence Review* (London), Vol. 6, no. 1, 1981, p. 38.

159 Abdul Rahman Siddiqi, "Western Oil-Strategy, Soviet Geo-politics and Gulf Security", *Defence Journal* (Karachi), Vol. VII, no. 3, 1981, p. 3; see also Robert Graham, *Iran: The Illusion of Power* (London): Croom Helm, 1978), p. 173.

160 *New York Times*, 5 February 1976; see also *Washington Post*, 28 January 1976.

161 Abdul Kasim Mansur, "The American Threat to Saudi Arabia", *Survival*, Vol. XXIII, no, 1, January-February 1981, p. 39.

162 Afaf, n. 158, p. 38,

163 *Aviation Week and Space Technology* (McGraw-Hill), Vol. 106, no. 15, April 1977, p. 17; see also *USSR and Third World* (London), Vol. V, nos. 6-8, 7 July, 31 December 1975, p. 374; and the *Indian Express* 4 April 1977.

164 Benjamin Shwadran, "Middle East Oil", *Current History*, Vol. 66, no. 390, February 1974, p. 80.

165 Edward A. Kolodziej, "France and the Arms Trade", *International Affairs* (London), Vol. 56, no. 1, January 1980, p. 63.

166 *Prospect for Multilateral Arms Export Restraint*, US Senate, Committee on Foreign Relations, 96th Congress, Ist Session (Washington, D.C.; Government Printing Office, 1979), p. 11; see also Organization for Economic Cooperation and Development, *Quarterly Oil Statistics*, Second Quarter, 1978 (Paris).

167 Shahram Chubin, "US Security Interests in the Persian Gulf in the 1980s", *Daedalus* (Boston), Vol. 109, no. 4, Fall 1980, p. 61.

168 Antony McDermott, "Japan and the Arabs," *Middle East International* (London), no. 63, September 1976, p. 13.

169 *Ibid.*, p. 12.

170 For an elaborate discussion on this view, see Edward Friedland, Paul Seabury and Aaron Wildavsky, "Oil and the Decline of Western Power," *Political Science Quarterly* (New York), Vol. 90, no. 3, Fall 1975, pp. 437-50.

171 Jane Perry Clark Carey, ["Iran and Control of its Oil Resources," *Political Science Quarterly*, Vol. 89, no. 1, March 1974, p. 157.

172 For a short analysis of the aftermath of the use of oil weapon, see Willy Linder, "The Price of Oil: A Political Time Bomb," *Swiss Review of World Affairs*, Vol. 24, no. 11, February 1975, pp. 4-6.

173 V.R. Bhatt, "Oil Threat to World Peace," *The Hindustan Times*, 27 November 1974.

174 Maxwell D. Taylor, "The Legitimate Claims of National Security," *Foreign Affairs*, Vol. 52, no. 3, April 1974. p. 593; see also Geoffrey Kemp, "East-West Strategy and the Middle East—Persian Gulf," in Kenneth A. Myers, ed., *NATO, The Next Thirty Years* (Colorado: Westview Press, 1980), pp. 207-21.

175 "Suez: An Inside Story," *Observer*, 3 October 1976.

176 Willard A. Beling, ed., *King Faisal and the Modernization of Saudi Arabia* (London: Croom Helm Ltd., 1980), p. 215; see also Yuan-Li Wu, *Japan's Search for Oil* (Stanford: Hoover Institution Press, 1977), p. 3.

177 Nadav Safran, "Engagements in the Middle East," *Foreign Affairs*, Vol. 53, no. 1, October 1974, p. 56.

178 Immediately in 1974, Japan and Iraq signed an agreement providing for $1 billion Japanese credits to Iraq for economic development projects in exchange for crude oil and oil products. See *New York Times*, 17 August 1974; Iraq and Italy signed a 10 years agreement for about $3 billion worth of Italian aid in exchange for Iraqi crude oil, see *Arab Report and Record*, 16-31, July 1974.

179 Stockholm International Peace Research, *World Armaments and Disarmament, Year Book 1975* (Stockholm: Almqvist and Wiksell, 1975), p. 198.

180 Military force consists of concrete things such as tanks, airplanes, rockets, ships, submarines, etc. These are means for generating military power, *not military power itself*. See Fred C. Weyand and Harry G. Summers, Jr., "The Need for Military Power", *Military Review*, Vol. LVI, no. 12, December 1976, pp. 8-18. For a deeper analysis of the distinction between armed forces and military power, see Klaus Knorr, *The Power of Nations* (New York: Basic Books, 1975).

181 Fred M. Gotthel, "An Economic Assessment of the Military Burden in the Middle East, 1960-1980", *The Journal of Conflict Resolution*, Vol. XVIII, no. 3, September 1974, p. 504.

182 It should be noted that there have been 25 revolutions and at least 45 others that have been attempted between 1945 and 1971. *Ibid.*

4

Arms Race in the Gulf Region

Diverse domestic, regional and extra-regional pressures and incentives have influenced the Gulf States to assemble an impressive array of weapons and military equipment within a short period of time. Some of the most modern combat aircraft such as F-14 Tomcat, Mirage F-1 and AWACS (Air borne Warning and Control System) have already entered the arsenals of some of the States in the region.[1] Deliveries will continue of (a) MIG-23, MIG-21, F-4E, A-4E, F-5E and Mirage III combat aircraft (b) T-62, M-60, AMX-30 and Chieftain main battle tanks and scorpion light tanks (c) Missile systems of nearly all varieties—surface-to-surface, surface-to-air, air-to-surface, ship-to-ship, air-to-air and antitank, and (d) a large assortment of helicopters, trainers, transport aircraft and light strike COIN aircraft. (For military establishment of the Gulf States, see Table 4).

The competitive nature of the arms build-up becomes evident while carefully examining the defence budgets and the quantum of weapons already acquired by each of the Gulf States. Therefore, in this chapter it is proposed to deal with: (A) an analysis of the military budgets and other relevant data along with a quantification of the weapons acquired by each Gulf State; and (B) an examination of the consequences of the arms race in the Gulf region.

TABLE 4

Military Establishments of the Gulf States

	Iran	Saudi Arabia	Iraq	Kuwait	Oman	Qatar	Bahrain	UAE
Total armed forces	2,000,000 reported incl. active paramilitary	51,500	517,250	12,400	23,550	6000	2,700	49,000
Army	150,000	35,000	475,000	10,000	19,550	5000	2,300	46,000
Navy	20,000	2,500	4,250	500	2,000	700	300	1,500
Air force	35,000	14,000	38,000	1,900	2,000	300	100	1,500
Tanks	1,735MBT	350MBT	1,800MBT	280MBT	—	12MBT	—	30Lt.
Combat Aircraft	447	178	339	50	35	4	—	52
Major craft	28	4 (+120)	48	28	13	6	9	9

Source: Adapted from *The Military Balance 1979; 1983-1984* (London, 1983).

DEFENCE EXPENDITURE OF THE GULF STATES

For the purpose of a comparative study of annual military expenditure of the Gulf States, 1968 has been taken as the base year as that year foreshadowed the impending collapse of a so-called British security system that was said to be existing in the Gulf region. We would also consider 1978 as the cut off year as that year paved the way for the Iranian revolution which brought to an end the rule of the Shah whose philosophy was to buy the most up-to-date weapons systems in great quantities, thus accentuating the multilateral arms race in the region. That the arms acquisition competition is multilateral is evident from the political dynamics of the Gulf region where Iran, Iraq Saudi Arabia and Kuwait are presumably caught up in a quadrilateral contest with the other States—Bahrain, Qatar, UAE and Oman—subsequently contributing to the arms race.

IRAN

During the 1970s Iran became the largest buyer of military equipment in the developing world. Defence accounted for nearly 27 per cent of the government spending and this budget quadrupled in size between 1974 and 1977. Over one-third of US foreign military purchases during that period were made by Iran.[2]

In 1968, the military expenditure of Iran totalled $2119 million, when its Gross National Product (GNP) was reckoned at $28501 million.[3] It was 7.4 per cent of the GNP or 25.7 per cent of the Central Government Expenditure (CGE). The military expenditure went on spiralling through the subsequent years when it touched a ceiling of $3927 million in 1973 and the GNP for that year stood at $47327 million.[4] It means that 8.3 per cent and 30.2 per cent of the GNP and CGE respectively were spent on defence that year.

A sharp increase in defence spending became inevitable with the sudden hike in oil prices by the OPEC countries since the Arab-Israeli conflict of 1973. The increase from 7.4 per cent of the GNP in 1968 to 14.3 per cent in 1975 reflects the staggering rise in military expenditure by Iran. On the eve of the Khomeini revolution, Iran's GNP increased to $79513 million and the amount set apart for defence expenditure for 1977 came to $9242 million[5] (Table 5).

A sizeable portion of the budgetary allocation every year for military purpose was set apart for imports of sophisticated weapons and hardware such as hovercraft with surface to surface missiles, mine-laying helicopters, small aircraft carriers, with vertical take off planes for anti-submarine warfare, etc.

If in 1968 the arms imports cost $135 million, it rose to $295 million in 1971 and further increased to $455 million in 1973. In 1974, Iran purchased US weapons costing $3.8 billion and in 1975 it contracted for $1.7 billion worth of arms supplies, chiefly 80 navy F-14 jet fighters.[6] What was most astounding was the announcement of a $15 billion five year trade deal between the United States and Iran that was expected to include the delivery of $5 billion worth of US arms.[7] By the end of December 1976 it was reported that the pending US foreign military orders to Iran came to a total of $4,400 million for 160 F-16 fighters with spares, training and construction, (b) $241 million for 350 AIM-9 sidewinder, 350 AIM-7 sparrow and (c) $25 million for support of six RH-53D mine-clearing helicopters.[8] The proposed sale of 250 Northrop F-18 L aircraft to Iran would alone account for $4000 million.[9] (For US military sales to Iran, see Table 6).

According to a report in 1973, the overall operational combat readiness of the Iranian air force was considered the best of its kind available in the world.[10] However the recent Iran-Iraq war has proved the shallowness of that report. Iran had acquired about 80 F-14 A Tomcats by mid-1978. Of these 50 were based at Khatami AFB at Isfahan and 30 aircraft at Shiraz.[11] The primary reason for Iran ordering the F-14A Tomcats was to counteract the Russian MIG-25 Foxbats which regularly overfly the country.[12] Besides, the Iranian strike-intercepter force consisted of ten squadrons of Phantoms equipped with 32F-4Ds, 141 F-4Es and 4 RF-4Es; a further 12FR-4Es and 36 F-4Es were delivered between May 1976 and July 1977.[13]

TABLE 5

GNP and Military Expenditures of Iran, 1968-1980 (in million US dollars)

Year	Military Expenditure		GNP		Central Govt. Expenditures (CGE) million dollars	Milex GNP %	Milex CGE %
	Current	Constant	Current	Constant			
1968	2119	1313	28501	17653	8237	7.4	25.7
1969	2600	1692	31459	20468	9149	8.3	28.4
1970	2766	1892	35323	24167	10727	7.8	25.8
1971	2644	4524	31652	54143	17134	8.4	26.4
1972	3266	5365	38269	62870	19349	8.5	27.7
1973	3927	6103	47327	73545	20200	8.3	30.2
1974	6654	9447	56322	79965	32433	11.8	29.1
1975	9128	11828	63651	82483	36840	14.3	32.1
1976	10038	12377	74337	91657	38412	13.5	32.2
1977	9242	10747	79513	92461	43337	11.6	24.8
1978	11342	12320	77448	84131	45097	14.6	27.4
1979	NA	NA	73203	73203	39937	NA	NA
1980	NA	NA	72660	65875	NA	NA	NA

Notes: 1 The constant figures for the years 1971-1980 regarding Military Expenditures, GNP and Central Government Expenditures are in constant 1979 figures.

Source: Adapted from US Arms Control and Disarmament Agency, World Military Expenditures and Arms Transfers, 1968-1977 (Washington, D.C., 1979), p. 46; ibid., 1971-1980 (Washington, D.C., 1981), p. 52.

TABLE 6

US Military Sales and Services to Iran, 1969-1978 (in thousands of dollars; fiscal years)

Year	Foreign military sales agreements	Foreign military sales deliveries	Military assistance program deliveries expenditures including military assistance service funded and excluding training	International military education & training program deliveries including military assistance service funded	Summary of students trained under International military education and training programme, including military assistance service funded
1969	235,821	94,881	45,343	3,247	765
1970	134,929	127,717	12,791	2,447	504
1971	363,884	78,566	4,290	2,230	354
1972	472,611	214,807	6,277	885	186
1973	2,171,355	248,391	2,621	—	—
1974	4,325,357	648,641	191	—	—
1975	2,447,140	1,006,131	2	—	—
1976	1,794,487	1,927,860	—	—	—
1977	5,713,769	2,433,050	—	—	—
1978	2,586,890	1,792,892	—	—	—
1955-78	20,751,656	8,715,810	766,733	67,445	11,025

Source: Foreign Military Sales and Military Assistance Facts (December 1978), Department of Defense, Security Assistance Agency quoted in *Economic Consequences of the Revolution in Iran*; A Compendium of Papers Submitted to the Joint Economic Committee, Congress of the United States, 96th Congress, 1st Session, November 19, 1979 (Washington: US Government Printing Office, 1980), p. 16.

Iran's expansion of the helicopter force exceeded the total of Iraq and Saudi Arabia put together,[14] and larger than many of the world's air arms with a total of some 700 machines. Similarly the navy air arms too underwent fast expansion. It began to operate ten Augusta SH-3D Seakings for ASW work, AB. 205s, 14 AB. 206s, six AB-212s, six strike commanders for liaison and two F. 27MK 400 Ms and two Mk 600s for transport duties.[15] It was reported that Iran had developed undoubtedly the largest operational hovercraft fleet in the world.[16]

As regards the navy, Iran had developed the largest navy in the Gulf. It possessed six ocean-going submarines, four 7,800-ton 'Spruance'—class destroyers and 12 missile armed patrol boats together with two 2,500 ton logistical support ships and one 11,000-ton fleet replenishment vessel.[17]

However, as far as Iran is concerned, it has, by sheer force of the exigencies of a popular revolution in 1978-79, opted out of the arms race in the Gulf region, at least for the time being. The military weakness, ensuing the drastic alienation of one-time allies and the weapon suppliers, has cost the Iranians dearly in its war with Iraq about which will be discussed later.

IRAQ

As compared to Iran's military expenditure, Iraq's was almost just the half, amounting to $590 million in 1968. But it should be observed that it constituted 11.4 per cent of the GNP that totalled $5192 million in the same year. The annual rise in military expenditure after 1968 has been significant. With the increase in GNP, the corresponding increase in military expenditure has been kept up to a steady average of 12.8 per cent of the GNP.[18] If in 1972 the total military expenditure was to the tune of $816 million, in 1975-76 it was almost double, $1684 million; Iraq's GNP in 1975 was $13154 million.[19] It may be noted that in 1968 the arms imports to Iraq alone cost $133 million but the cost of imports in 1973 increased nearly three-fold to the tune of $306 million. (Table 7).

Since the withdrawal of Iraq from the Baghdad Pact (later

CENTO) in 1959, the Western countries were not quite inclined to favour weapon transfers to that country. Iraq had to depend, therefore, on socialist countries especially the Soviet Union for its major arms requirements. The Soviet policy also has been rather selective in transferring weapons to the region. Iraq has been the beneficiary of most of the Soviet arms supplies to the Gulf.

However, the West now realises that despite its heavy dependence on the USSR as a source of military supply, Iraq is not a satellite of the Soviet Union.[20] Its relationship with other countries have been broadened. Bilateral contacts between Iraq and many of the European countries have increased in recent years as a result of a number of factors: *i*) Iraq's desire to maintain a correct non-aligned policy; *ii*) its desire to broaden its sources of military supply; and *iii*) its efforts to secure advanced technology to meet development needs.[21] Iraq has, for example, developed a very good arms-relationship with France since 1974.[22] France has obliged Iraq in setting up even a nuclear reactor at Osirak.[23] Iraq got further commitments to strengthen its potential for air and naval as well as ground-launched missile attacks.[24] Recently, France delivered 60 Mirage F-1 supersonic fighter aircraft and also an unspecified number of helicopters to Iraq to make up its war losses and agreed to sell SAMs to shore up Iraq's air defence. UK also is reported to have agreed to sell Iraq 200 Crusader tank-towing vehicles.[25]

Iraq's relations with US has also, to some extent, improved recently and it is evident from the US Defence Department's approval of the sale of two L-1000 Hercules to Iraq.[26] The most modern type in Iraq's air force inventory is the MIG-23 Flogger of which two strike squadrons are equipped with a total of 40 aircraft, besides the other types in service which include more than 50 Hunter FGA.9/FR. 10s in three strike squadrons, 30-plus MIG-17s in three fighter-bomber units, nine Tu-16s in a bomber squadron and a further unit with ten Il-28s.[27] It is to be noted that 3 strike squadrons fly 50 Su-7Bs, and an interceptor unit consists of five squadrons, with 90 MIG-21s and 20 MIG-19s.[28]

Iraqi navy is yet to be developed with destroyers, logistical support ships, frigates, etc., to match the Iranian naval build-

TABLE 7

GNP and Military Expenditures of Iraq, 1968-1980 (in million US dollars)

Year	Military expenditures		GNP		Central Govt. Expenditures (CGE) million dollars	Milex GNP %	Milex CGE %
	Current	Constant	Current	Constant			
1968	590	953	5192	8383	3220	11.4	29.6
1969	785	1207	5668	8712	3161	13.8	38.2
1970	781	1142	6072	8876	3033	12.9	37.6
1971	762	1303	6220	10640	4214	12.3	30.9
1972	816	1340	7121	11699	4142	11.5	32.4
1973	1168	1816	8623	13401	5920	13.6	30.7
1974	1510	2144	9645	13694	6541	15.7	32.8
1975	1555	2015	13154	17046	9955	11.8	20.2
1976	1684	2076	15343	18918	8690	11.0	23.9
1977	1891	2199	17641	20514	9130	10.7	24.1
1978	2148	2334	21747	23623	16231	9.9	14.4
1979	2671	2671	33475	33475	19996	8.0	13.4
1980	NA	NA	39139	35484	NA	NA	NA

Note: 1 The constant figures for the years 1971-1980 for Military Expenditures, GNP and Central Government Expenditures are in constant 1979 figures.

Source: Adapted from US Arms Control and Disarmament Agency, *World Military Expenditures and Arms transfers, 1968-1977* (Washington D.C., 1979), p. 47; ibid., *1971-1980* (Washington D.C., 1981), p. 52.

up. At present Iraq has 3 submarine chasers, and a number of patrol and missile boats.[29]

SAUDI ARABIA

Saudi Arabia's GNP for the year 1968 was $10318 million, 6.4 per cent of which amounting to $655 million was set apart for military expenditure. The percentage of GNP for military expenditure for the following years up to 1971 remained almost constant; but statistics have shown that there was considerable decrease in the total GNP which came to $9739 million in 1971 and the military expenditure for that year remained $981 million. The year 1974 saw a major departure in Saudi defence expenditure in terms of percentage of GNP set apart for that purpose. 10.9 per cent of the GNP of $34860 million, i.e., about $3792 million, was utilised for military purposes. It may be noted that in 1975, the GNP of Saudi Arabia was $48449 million and the military expenditure was $8448 million. The GNP for the year 1976 was $60801 million and the military expenditure for that year reached an all-time peak of $11623 million, forming roughly 19.1 per cent.[30] (Table 8)

Saudi Arabia's inventory too is full of imported armaments. From 1968 to 1973, on an average, $65.6 million have been spent for weapon imports. The trend towards spending more on imports in the 1970s was induced by Iran's pursuit in a similar fashion to acquire more arms from abroad. Saudi Arabia's arms deal of 1976, in which it spent $62.9 million for 650 Maverick air-launched anti-tank missiles, 1000 Two antitank missiles and 850 AIM-9 Sidewinders, $23.3 million for 4F-5E fighters, and $12.4 million for Vulcan AA Cannon systems, should be seen against a similar deal in 1975 in which the late Shah of Iran spent $1.7 billion for arms supplies, chiefly 80 navy E-14 jet fighters.[31]

Again, the $17 billion contract for goods and services entered into by Saudi Arabia with American firms in 1977 must have been induced by the $15 billion five year trade deal between the United States and Iran that was expected to include the delivery of $5 billion worth of US arms.[32]

Saudi Arabia is able to acquire the most uptodate weapons.[33] In the early sixties, Saudi Arabia's air force had to

TABLE 8

GNP and Military Expenditures of Saudi Arabia, 1968-1980 (in million US dollars)

Year	Military expenditures		GNP		Central Govt. Expenditures (CGE) million dollars	Milex GNP %	Milex CGE %
	Current	Constant	Current	Constant			
1968	655	1058	10318	16657	6979	6.4	15.2
1969	801	1230	11738	18041	7914	6.8	15.5
1970	840	1228	13725	20061	8769	6.1	14.0
1971	573	981	5693	9739	3209	10.1	30.6
1972	792	1301	7162	11767	3811	11.1	34.1
1973	1187	1845	8972	13943	10568	13.2	17.5
1974	2670	3792	24552	34860	10929	10.9	34.7
1975	6519	8448	37387	48449	24741	17.4	34.1
1976	9426	11623	49312	60801	32771	19.1	35.5
1977	9505	11053	61932	72018	43743	15.3	25.3
1978	10751	11678	67734	73579	40312	15.9	29.0
1979	13831	13831	76380	76380	50632	18.1	27.3
1980	16740	15176	116636	105744	56764	14.4	26.7

Note: 1. The constant figures for the years 1971-1980 for Military Expenditures, GNP and Central Government Expenditures are in constant 1979 figures.

Source: Adapted from US Arms Control and Disarmament Agency, *World Military Expenditures and Arms Transfers, 1968-1977* (Washington, D.C., 1979), p. 59; *ibid*, *1971-1980* (Washington, D.C., 1981), p. 65.

be contented with old US B-26s, and some Korean war Vintage F-86s. But now, Saudi Arabia can boast of Mirage III EEs, F-5Es and AWACs. It is hoped that when the entire F-5Es fleet is operative, Saudi Arabia will be owner of 2,400 side-winders for 110 aircraft each of which can carry two of the air-to-air missiles.[34] The 40 F-5Es and 20 F-5Fs ordered (most of them have been already received by the Saudi Air Force) are destined to equip two new fighter-bomber squadrons based at Taif and Tabuk which are partially equipped with 30 F-5Es delivered earlier, while on air defence duties are six squadrons at Khamis Mushayt near the Yemen border and 2 squadrons at Dahran.[35]

Two training units with a secondary strike potential are squadron Nos. 9 and 11 at Riyadh, which form part of the King Faisal Air Academy. A total of 35 BAC strike master MK 80/80 have been delivered to the RSAF. No. 9 squadron is tasked as a purely basic jet training unit, while sq. 11 operates as a weapon training unit. No. 7 squadron at Dahran has retired its Sabres and is phasing in most of the 20 North-rop F-5F two-seat combat trainers. Its companion squadron No. 15 flies 20 older F-513 trainers. Two transport squadrons, Nos. 4 and 16 are based at Jeddah and equipped with ten C-130E Hercules, 14C 130 Hs, four KC-130 Hs (for F-5 air fuelling), plus a further 11 C-130 Hs. on order. Based at Taif are squadrons 12 and 14 flying 16 AB. 206 Jet-Rangers and 24 AB. 205s on liaison and light transport/assault duties. No. 8 sqn. at Riyadh, a part of the KFAA, is a primary training unit with an establishment of four Cessna 172 Gs, four 172 Hs and four 172 Ls. Also in use are two Alouette IIIs and a Royal Flight equipped with a single Boeing 702-320 two Lockheed Jetstars and an AB. 206 helicopters.[36]

Saudi Arabia has virtually no naval forces, but has already contracted for the construction of two naval bases and was negotiating with the United States for the acquisition of 19 naval vessels, including destroyers, frigates and missile-armed patrol boats.[37] This naval initiative was considered as a reaction against the development of an Iranian naval complex at Chah Bahar on the Arabian sea to support Iran's existing and prospective fleet.[38]

The focus of US military planning in the Persian Gulf area

has shifted to Saudi Arabia since the 1979 Islamic revolution which washed out the American presence in Iran lock, stock and barrel. Saudi Arabia now ranks as the biggest buyer of US arms with a total of about 40 billion dollars in such purchases dating back 24 years.[39]

The US military sales to Saudi Arabia have skyrocketed from $300 million in 1972 to $6.5 billion in 1979. Saudi Arabia has accounted for 36 per cent of all US foreign military sales since 1975 or $34 billion. From the establishment of diplomatic relations in 1947 through 1979, Saudi Arabia purchased US products worth $56 billion of which 55 per cent was spent on military arms and services.[40] Saudi-American military cooperation has assumed massive proportions in the mid-1970s. An example of this military cooperation is provided by the projects worth $18 billion, entrusted to the American Corps of Engineers. The three largest of these projects are the so-called "Cities of the Kings", major Saudi military complexes named after Saudi Kings: at Al-Baten (The King Khaled City), close to Saudi-Iraqi-Kuwaiti border junction; at Tabuk (the King Abdulaziz City), close to the Jordanian and Israeli borders; and at Khemis Misheyt (The King Feisal City) located near the border with Yemen on the Red Sea.[41]

According to the *Defense Monitor*: *1*) Saudi Arabia is the number one US arms customer in the Persian Gulf. *2*) The sale of five AWACs aircraft, several tanker aircraft and armaments for 60 previously purchased F-15 fighter aircraft would add to Saudi Arabia's offensive military capability and would not meet any new Saudi defense need. *3*) Saudi Arabia has hired the US Army Corps of Engineers to build a vast array of military and civilian projects at a cost of $24 billion. *4*) The US-Saudi "arms for oil" relationship accelerates the Middle East arms race and increases the likelihood and destructiveness of war in the area. *5*) Saudi Arabia ranks sixth in the world military expenditures and spends more on per capita military expenditure than any other country.

Saudi Arabia, by its size, wealth and history is one of the most important countries in the Gulf today. But its 93,500 strong military force is not adequate. Saudi Arabia is modernising its forces with the help of US advisers. Four battalions, modernised in weapons and doctrine, are to be turned out shortly to guard the oil fields.[42] Other regular forces are being equipped with US and French armaments and trained in US tactical doctrine to take the weight off the Kingdom's defence.[43]

Saudi Arabia has very recently ordered a large stock of advanced weapons, including Marder infantry combat vehicles from West Germany, 170 US M-60 tanks and Dragon anti-tank missiles, Vulcan anti-aircraft guns and six batteries of Hawk surface-to air-missiles.[44] It is all set to launch an intensive programme of modernisation of the army, navy and air force.

KUWAIT

Kuwait's military expenditure in 1968 was rather moderate compared to other countries in the region and it amounted to $202 million, though its GNP for that year was $6204 million. On an average over 3 per cent of the GNP was being spent up to 1973 for defence purposes by Kuwait; however, the trend to increase budgetary allocations for defence is not decreasing. If the military expenditure in 1968 was only $202 million, in 1974 it rose to $568 million and for the year 1976 it shot up to $1086 million.[45] (Table 9) It should be noted that in 1975 alone Kuwait ordered for new military equipment costing $333.1 million from the United States.[46] In 1979, there were more than half a dozen FMS cases for a total value of more than $100 million.[47] Kuwait also has purchased SA-7 and Frog missiles from the Soviet Union.[48]

Kuwait remains the world's richest nation with a per capita income of $20250 according to the recent World Bank Atlas.[49] Its efforts for modernising defence forces are, therefore, made practical in view of the availability of resources.

Kuwait is fast modernising its air force. The first McDonnell Douglas Skyhawks have been delivered to two strike squadrons. A total of 36A-4KUs and Six TA-4 Kus are involved and the aircraft are being based at one of two new fields constructed to the south and west of the KAF's present main fighter base.[50] Eighteen Mirage F. ICK strike-fighters and two F-IBK two-seat combat trainers which will eventually replace the squadron of the F-53 Lightning interceptors and two T-67 two-seat trainers are also being delivered.[51] A ground attack squadron of 12 BAC MK 83 strikemasters is complemented by

TABLE 9

GNP and Military Expenditures of Kuwait, 1968-1980 (in million US dollars)

Year	Military expenditures		GNP		Central Govt. Expenditure (CGE) million dollars constant (1979)	Milex GNP %	Milex CGE %
	Current	Constant	Current	Constant			
1968	202	326	6204	10016	3864	3.3	8.4
1969	224	345	6780	10421	4116	3.3	8.4
1970	225	329	7376	10780	4246	3.1	7.7
1971	185	317	3882	6641	2071	4.8	15.3
1972	210	345	3778	6206	2428	5.6	14.2
1973	234	364	4032	6266	2844	5.8	12.8
1974	568	807	11481	16301	5460	5.0	14.8
1975	731	948	13438	17414	5023	5.4	18.9
1976	1086	1340	15509	19122	6785	7.0	19.7
1977	1043	1213	16562	19259	8253	6.3	14.7
1978	1076	1168	17856	19397	7651	6.0	15.3
1979	1181	1181	26663	26663	8887	4.4	13.3
1980	1315	1192	30969	28077	8482	4.2	14.1

Note: 1. The constant figures for the years 1971-1980 regarding Military Expenditures, GNP, and Central Government Expenditures, are in constant 1979 figures.

Source: Adapted from US Arms Control and Disarmament Agency, *World Military Expenditures and Arms Transfers, 1968-1977* (Washington, D.C., 1979), p. 49; *ibid*, 1971-1980 (Washington, D.C.), p. 55.

another unit flying four Hunter FGA-57s and five T-67s.[52] A helicopter force has also been expanded and now operates 20 SA-342 Gazelle AOP and liaison aircraft, some equipped for anti-tank duties with Hot missiles.[53]

Kuwait does not have a navy for the present. However, the provisional contract signed by Kuwait with Japan for maritime work at the Kuwaiti naval base appears to be in the direction of developing its naval capability.[54]

UNITED ARAB EMIRATES

Since 1971 the United Arab Emirates has been showing continuous interest in acquiring advanced types of weapons.[55] In 1972 UAE's GNP was $1979 million and in 1974 it rose to $10678 million. It has been reported that the UAE earned $74 billion from oil exports in the decade 1970-80. Most of the revenue came following the oil price-hike in 1973. The state income from oil exports reached 64.5 billion dollars as against 9.3 billion dollars between 1970 and 1975.[56] Corresponding to the huge revenues derived from oil export, expenditure on various development programmes, particularly defence projects also increased. The amount spent on weapons imports to UAE, begining in 1969, is a clear indication of a gathering momentum in the military expenditure. From 1975 onwards military expenditure increased. The GNP for 1975 was $12041 million and the military expenditure stood at $42 million. But with a GNP of $17344 million in 1977, UAE spent $587 million on defence. While the percentage of GNP for defence expenditure in 1972 was only 1.4, in 1977 it shot up to 3.4[57] (Table 10).

In 1969, $1 million was spent on arms imports, but in 1973 it increased to $10 million. The most salient feature of the military expenditure is that UAE has, together with the collaboration of Egypt, Saudi Arabia and Qatar, established a 4 billion Arab Arms Consortium[58] and it was reported that France would supply the Consortium Mirage F-1 jet fighter-bombers in a major new West Asia arms deal.[59]

British, German and American equipment was to be produced under licence. Production was to have been in Egypt, at least

TABLE 10

GNP and Military Expenditures of UAE, 1971-1980 (in million US dollars)

Year	Military Expenditures		GNP		Central Govt. Expenditures (CGE) million dollars	Milex GNP %	Milex CGE %
	Current	Constant	Current	Constant			
1971	NA	NA	NA	NA	NA	NA	NA
1972	16	27	1204	1979	64	1.4	43.0
1973	13	21	2384	3705	158	0.6	13.2
1974	20	29	7521	10678	274	0.3	10.8
1975	32	42	9292	12041	401	0.4	10.5
1976	81	100	11905	14679	809	0.7	12.5
1977	505	587	14915	17344	1891	3.4	31.1
1978	791	859	14404	15647	2131	5.5	40.3
1979	1151	1151	18987	18987	2269	6.1	50.7
1980	1658	1503	26035	23604	3636	6.4	41.4

Note: Until 1971 the Sheikhdoms were under the British protection.

Source: Adapted from US Arms Control and Disarmament Agency, *World Military Expenditures 1968-1977* (Washington, D.C., 1979), p. 65; ibid., 1971-1980 (Washington, D.C., 1981), p. 70.

in the first instance, but, in protest against Egypt's policies towards Israel, Saudi Arabia, Qatar and the UAE have withdrawn their promises of financial support and the Arab Military Industrial Organisation must be regarded now as defunct.[60]

The nucleus of UAE's combat force, an interceptor-strike wing of some 24 French supplied Mirages is stationed at Abu Dhabi and eventually 32 Mirages of all versions are expected to be in service.[61] A ground-attack squadron based at Sharjah operates 8 Hunter FGA. 76s and two T. 77 trainers. UAE has a small counter-insurgency force based at Dubai equipped with three armed single-seat Aermaechi MB. 326 KDs and a two-seat MB. 326 LD,[62] in view of the contingencies that may arise of local insurgencies.

OMAN

Oman occupies a strategic position in the Arabian peninsula at the straits of Hormuz through which much of the World's oil supply moves. The United States and the West have taken keen interest, therefore, in assisting the Sultan of Oman to sufficiently strengthen his defence forces in view of the supposed threats to his regime emanating from South Yemen as well as from the guerrillas of Dhofar. Oil revenues, have provided incentives for modernising the defence forces.

In 1970 the GNP of Oman was $977 million, 15.2 per cent of which ($148 million) was set apart for military expenditure which was almost 60.2 per cent of the total government expenditure that year. In 1974 the GNP stood at $1713 million and military expenditure soared to $485 million, forming 28.3 per cent of the GNP. Oman spent 40.9 per cent of the GNP of $2213 million for defence in 1975. As the oil revenues increased, the defence expenditure also increased but at the cost of other socio-economic development. In 1977, 31.6 per cent of the GNP of $2527 miliion was spent on defence[63] (See Table 11).

In 1974 an order worth £47 million for Rapier low level SAMs was placed with BAC, together with an order of 12 Jaguar International strike aircraft made up of ten single-seaters and two trainers.[64] Also was on order worth £25 million for an air-defence radar communications system to be

TABLE 11

GNP and Military Expenditures of Oman, 1968-1980 (in million US dollars)

Year	Military Expenditures		GNP		Central Govt. Expenditures (CGE) million dollars	Milex GNP %	Milex CGE %
	Current	Constant	Current	Constant			
1968	n.a.	n.a.	460	743	n.a.	n.a.	n.a.
1969	n.a.	n.a.	616	947	n.a.	n.a.	n.a.
1970	10	148	668	977	246	15.2	60.2
1971	46	79	293	501	228	15.9	35.0
1972	77	127	308	507	338	25.0	37.6
1973	121	189	324	504	412	37.5	45.8
1974	342	485	1207	1713	1547	28.3	31.4
1975	698	905	1708	2213	1889	40.9	47.9
1976	785	968	1968	2427	2126	39.9	45.5
1977	686	798	2173	2527	1803	31.6	44.3
1978	768	834	2247	2440	1763	34.2	47.3
1979	779	779	2998	2998	1884	26.0	41.4
1980	1179	1069	4786	4339	2430	24.6	44.0

Note: The constant figures for years 1971-1980 regarding Military Expenditures, GNP and Central Government Expenditures are in constant 1979 figures

Source: Adapted from US Arms Control and Disarmament Agency, *World Military Expenditures and Arms Transfers, 1968-1977* (Washington, D.C., 1979), p. 46; ibid, *1971-1980*, (Washington, D.C., 1981), p. 62.

integrated with the Jaguars and Rapiers and to be based on Marconi S600 radars and a Marconi troposcatter Comms. system.[65] The first two Jaguars were delivered in March 1977[66] and the 12 aircraft will replace the 29 ex-Jordanian Hunters currently equipping 6 squadrons at the Thumryat main strike base. However, it must be remembered that these aircraft are operated by the RAF personnel and not Omanis.[67]

No. 1 sqn. at Salalah has 12 BAC strikemasters operating in the ground attack role. At the same base 3 sqn. flies 20 AB-205s, three AB-206s, and five Bell 214B heavy lift machines. Based at Seeb are 2 sqn. with 15 short skyvan 3 Ms, 4 sqn. with two Viscounts and three BAC One-Eleven 475s, and 5 sqn. with eight B-N Defenders. Detachments of Skyvans and Defenders are maintained at Salalah.[68]

In 1980 the United States initiated a foreign military sales financing programme of $15 million for Oman.[69]

BAHRAIN

From a mere $10 million military expenditure in 1974, Bahrain stepped up its defence expenditure to $45 million in 1977 while the corresponding GNP for 1974 was $1001 million and for 1977, $1660 million respectively (Table 12). The weapon systems of Bahrain are all imported, mainly from UK. The US has entered into a 180 million dollar deal with Bahrain to sell Bahrain two-seater Northrop F5F fighters and F5G Tigershark jet fighters in order to create an airforce for Bahrain.[70]

QATAR

In 1973 Qatar's GNP was $932 million of which $177 million went for defence expenditure, forming about 19 per cent of the GNP. The trend towards increased defence expenditure was visible from 1973 to 1977. Of the GNP of $3026 in 1976, Qatar allocated $205 million for defence. But with increased GNP in 1978, military expenditure for the same year came to $286 million [71] (Table 13).

The Qatar Emiri Air Force flies a small strike force of three Hunter FGA. 78s and a single two-seat T. 79 from its main base at Doha. Two whirlwind IIIs and a B-N Islander

TABLE 12

GNP and Military Expenditures of Bahrain, 1971-1980 (in million US dollars)

| Year | Military expenditures | | GNP | | Central Govt. Expenditures (CGE) | Milex GNP | Milex CGE |
	Current	Constant	Current	Constant	million dollars	%	%
1971	NA	NA	NA	NA	NA	NA	NA
1972	NA	NA	NA	NA	NA	NA	NA
1973	4	7	356	554	171	1.3	4.3
1974	7	10	705	1001	290	1.0	3.6
1975	14	19	740	960	414	2.0	4.6
1976	28	35	1060	1307	657	2.7	5.4
1977	39	45	1427	1960	790	2.8	5.8
1978	49	54	1687	1832	812	3.0	6.7
1979	57	57	2048	2048	666	2.8	8.7
1980	55	50	2899	2628	754	1.9	6.6

Note: Data for the years 1968-70 not available.

Source: Adapted from US Arms Control and Disarmament Agency, *World Military Expenditures and Arms Transfers, 1968-1977* (Washington D.C., 1979), p. 33; ibid., *1971-1980* (Washington, D.C., 1981), p. 39.

TABLE 13

GNP and Military Expenditures of Qatar, 1972-1980 (in million US dollars)

Year	Military expenditures		GNP		Central Govt. Expenditures (CGE) million dollars	Milex GNP %	Milex CGE %
	Current	Constant	Current	Constant			
1972	52	85	461	758	895	11.3	9.5
1973	114	177	600	932	1249	19.0	14.2
1974	104	147	2020	2839	1306	5.2	11.3
1975	124	160	2170	2812	2118	5.7	7.6
1976	167	205	2454	3026	2323	6.8	8.9
1977	230	267	2490	2896	2542	9.2	10.5
1978	264	286	2966	3222	1956	8.9	14.7
1979	458	458	4709	4709	2192	9.7	20.9
1980	555	503	6644	6024	2498	8.4	20.1

Source: Adapted from US Arms Control and Disarmament Agency, *World Military Expenditures and Arms Transfers, 1971-1980* (Washington, D.C., 1981), p. 64.

are used for transport duties together with three Westland
MK 2A Commandos.[72]

CONSEQUENCES OF THE ARMS RACE IN THE GULF REGION

The Gulf States are increasingly allocating substantial resources
for their defence build-up. Their present rate of acquisition
of weapons is rather alarming. They are competing among
themselves to purchase the most modern weapons systems
to add to their inventories. The reasons for such a sudden
spurt of arms acquisition by the Gulf States have been examined
at length earlier in the study. The magnitude and intensity of
the arms race reflected in the defence expenditure and weapon
purchases of the Gulf States obviously raise an important
question. What are the consequences of such an arms race? Or
what impact these weapons will have on the security and
stability of the region in general and each State in particular?

i) *Institutionalisation of Foreign Presence*

Dependence on a foreign power for assistance, whether economic or military generally constitutes a source of weakness
which often tends to undermine the security of developing
nations.

The policies underlying the military assistance programme
or arms sales programme of developed nations do not ostensi-
bly reveal any sinister motives or intentions. But there is more
to it than can meet the eye. It is a programme of intervention
in the recipient countries. As William Fulbright has observed:
"a meaningful and effective aid programme far from avoiding
intervention in the affairs of a recipient, in fact, constitutes
intervention of a most profound character".[73] These programmes have provisions, along with the despatch of military hardware to send a number of military officers, advisers and
technicians in support capacity in order to assume duties
particularly related to the training of indigenous forces to
operate the sophisticated military systems they have been
supplied with.[74] What counts is that the military of the weaker
State becomes equipped with and trained to handle the hardware

of the supplying power, creating a high degree of dependence on the supplier for training, parts and replacements.[75]

There are several other functions these foreign personnel are supposed to perform in the host country, the most significant among them are: one, they are supposed to "further the sale of US-produced military equipment,"[76] and two, they are to "provide the points of contact for the exchange of information on forces, budgets, weapons and capabilities."[77]

The conclusion to be inferred from this is that the military advisory and training programme exerts a significant influence over both the quantity and quality of arms transferred to developing countries. Further, it should be realised that one of the dominant aims of the military sales programme or military assistance programme is to extend and preserve the military influence of the big powers in the regions concerned. An observer has aptly said that if weapons have to be imported, then an amount of foreign involvement (interference?) in the form of foreign expertise has got to be accepted as a part of foreign weapon systems. Foreign weapon systems can be as deadly and effective as establishing foreign presence and holding a foreign ideology.[78]

In other words, through military assistance and weapon sales programmes, the supplier country has the chance to institutionalise its presence in the recipient country. Institutionalisation of foreign presence through an arms race in a region is an overall intervention of a foreign power in the region concerned.

Insecurity has been created through the policy of armamentism. Insecurity for the states in the Gulf region has risen not so much by the existence of innumerable local disputes and interstate rivalries as by the institutionalisation of foreign presence, concreticised in the arms race of the Gulf region. For, institutionalisation of such foreign presence through an arms race is a form of interventionism, which is likely to lead the host country to political instability and economic chaos.

We shall illustrate how Iran's military relationship with the United States has caused the present instability and political chaos in that country. The US institutionalised its presence in Iran through the stimulation of a steady arms build-up that began in the early 1950s. The massive infusion of sophisticated weapons into Iran created great imbalances, weakening the entire socio-economico-political structure.

Through military assistance programmes and arms sales agreements, US presence in Iran came to be operationalised. In other words, the US could easily intervene in Iran's internal affairs and manipulate foreign policy decisions in favour of its own interests.[79]

The greater the increase in the supply of modern weapons, the more will be the likelihood of the increase in foreign military personnel. On the eve of the Khomeini revolution in Iran, there were over 70,000 US personnel. A sizeable section of this came in "support capacity", tied to the arms sales programme. There were also 40 US companies in Iran executing military contracts.[80] Social unrest and political upheavals in Iran intensified in the 70s not merely from excessive armaments but from the presence of military personnel in 'support capacity', and this ultimately led to strong anti-Americanism.[81] The people in Iran generally came to recognise that the oppressive rule of the late Shah was being strongly supported by the United States. In doing so, the US did not respect the genuine aspirations and desires of the people of Iran, but the whims and fancies of an individual—the Shah—were being constantly manipulated to maintain its own interest in the country. In the eyes of the Muslim fundamentalists, the cultural and social values of the West, especially, the United States were equal to decadence and immorality and were seen as an imminent danger to any traditional, pious Muslim society.[82] "Anti-Americanism has thus been one of the main themes of Khomeini's political agitation since the 1960s".[83] The late Shah of Iran put his faith in imported arms and foreign military personnel in order to maintain his dominance in the Gulf region as well as for his political survival against domestic uprisings. The United States too bolstered up the Shah to police and intervene in the Gulf at will. Khomeini's strategy was to get popular support by fanning up anti-US sentiments and depicting the US-military personnel as agents of Satan, trying to corrupt the society in league with the Shah who was termed a heretic. The revolution succeeded in making the Shah flee the country. Along with him crumbled the institutionalisation of US presence symbolised dramatically in the complete stoppage of US arms flow and the exit of all US personnel from Iran. Iran, which seemed to have acquired an intervention capability anywhere in the Gulf region with the support of Washington, withered away. Iranian predominance in the region abruptly ended. US no more backed Iran in the area. "The fall of Shah closed an era when proxies would act to preserve US interest in the Persian Gulf."[84]

Military relations have been the cutting edge of US involvement with Saudi Arabia. With the fall of Iran, US now attempts to make Saudi Arabia an important ally in the Persian Gulf and it views weapons transfers as one of the most important and effective instruments for gaining influence in Saudi Arabia. The US has institutionalised its presence in Saudi Arabia already by the massive infusion of sophisticated weapons. Military and civilian personnel numbering over 30,000, tied to the weapons sales programme, are presently at work in the country. For, Saudi Arabia does not have the man power or the know-how to maintain and operate most of the US military systems already provided.[85] In this context, the US is in an advantageous position to manipulate situations in Saudi Arabia to maintain its interests, especially its energy needs. In 1978 when there occurred a global oil shortage, Saudi Arabia raised its production by over three million barrels a day. At the behest of US, Saudi Arabia has become the moderator of oil prices in the OPEC.[86] The Iran-Iraq war diminished oil exports from these countries to the West. But with a steady output of 10.3 million barrels a day, Saudi Arabia accounts for nearly half of all OPEC exports. The *Washington Post* observed in July last that "despite the risk of a backlash, Saudi Arabia is continuing its campaign to keep the world awash in oil until OPEC opponents bow to its long-term pricing strategy, which is designed to lower prices and preserve oil as the West's main energy source."[87]

However, the Saudis now feel that a continued close relationship with the US may prove to be a liability in the long run rather than a gain in terms of the security and stability of their political system, controlled by the royal family. This point has been well driven home due to the Iranian revolution astride the Gulf, where the US proved very weak and ineffective in the political crisis which engulfed the Shah and the US. The weakness of US was further demonstrated by its failure to rescue the American hostages and US inability to do no more than protest against the Soviet drive into Afghanistan.[88] "The American image has suffered in the eyes of the people of Middle East not just from misunderstanding but from the uncertainties and weakness of American policies."[89]

Though the development of Saudi armed forces is totally dependent on US equipment, military advisers and contractors, Saudi Arabia is reluctant to identify itself with American interest lest it should become the key target for anti-US interest in the Gulf.[90] With a deep military relationship, the Saudis now view the US as the most serious threat to their own security. As it happened in Iran before, during and after the revolution, radical forces could easily whip up anti-American feelings and undermine the stability of the royal family and bring to an end the Saudi-US military relationship once and for all.

Even other Gulf countries do not want the United States to be involved in the affairs of the region. The UAE president, Shaikh Zayed for example said: "The presence of US forces in the area is not something we expect from a friendly country like US. The peoples of the world would cooperate and live in peace if it were not for the intervention of the big powers; so these powers must work to keep the Gulf region clear of their rivalry."[91] Strong protests have been raised against the design of the United States to acquire bases and facilities in the region for the Rapid Deployment Force which many feel is a device to grab Saudi oil fields in case of another oil embargo.

The other Gulf States which have imported large quantities of sophisticated weapons from US, UK and France are also placed in similar predicaments. The vigorous activation of the Mutual Assistance Programme and military sales programmes are designed to create instability and insecurity in the Gulf region by stimulating an arms race which may be profitably exploited by the military industrial complex of the weapon supplying countries.[92] They are likely to manipulate political problems, conflict situations and regional rivalries with which the Gulf region is known to be infested and they are likely to create artificial crises in order to entrench their positions and make these developing nations depend more and more on the "arms merchants". The army and the arms industry, due to their tendency to become practically autonomous, also provide the incentive to intensify international tensions for military interventions, and for military solutions of conflicts in general.[93]

ii) *Arms in the Arab-Israeli Context*

The arms build-up in various Arab Gulf countries has wider implications viewed in the context of the endemic Arab-Israeli antagonism. During the 1967 and 1973 Arab-Israeli conflicts, men, money and weapons were transferred to the Arab confrontation States from various Gulf States. As we have earlier noted, some of the rulers of the Gulf States have made no secret of their intentions to transfer much of the sophisticated weapons they have acquired to the frontline Arab States in case of another round of Arab-Israeli conflict.

Israel, too, is aware of the weapons-transfer game of the Arabs in the region. Hence, Israel has not been negligent in obtaining counter-weapons to offset any advantage the Arab countries may gain by the transfer of a new weapon system to the Gulf area. Despite Israel's objections the US approved the sale of 62 F-15 jet fighters to Saudi Arabia in 1978.[94] The former Secretary of State, Alexander Haig said to Israeli Foreign Minister, Yitzhak Shamir that the strategic situation in the Persian Gulf was the most crucial problem in the region and that a strong Saudi Arabia was in Israel's interest. But the Israelis fear that arms given to Saudi Arabia might be used against them.[95] The Israeli fear was reinforced when Edward Kennedy said that the sale of bomb racks, missiles, fuel tanks etc., would enable Saudi F-15s to attack and devastate foreign territory, including that of Israel.[96] Hence Israel also decided to have almost an equal number of US made F-15s on preferential financial terms.[97]

Whenever the US decides to sell weapons for its own economic interest in the area, it raises the bogey of its own security. For example, the US decision to sell additional military equipment to Saudi Arabia is shown as a part of a policy of halting a "serious deterioration" in Western security interests in the Middle-East and Persian Gulf. The sale of 62

F-15 jet fighters to Saudi Arabia was justified against the "growing threat" in the area from the USSR.[98]

The Israelis are as unpredictable as the Arabs. They are surviving in an extremely hostile environment. They have their own military strategy and survival doctrines like the Arabs. When the Israelis perceive that their survival as a nation is at stake, they do not hesitate to pre-empt the enemy. The Iraqi nuclear reactor at Osirak was incapacitated by an Israeli pre-emptive strike because Israel feared that Iraq was on the verge of producing a nuclear bomb with which it could possibly destroy Israel. Likewise, if the arms build-up in Saudi Arabia or in any other country around is perceived as a potential threat, a pre-emptive strike by the Israelis may become a distinct possibility. Therefore, the arms build-up in the Gulf region has the dangerous implication of potentially inducing the Israelis to strike the non-confrontation States as well in any future round of Arab-Israeli conflict.

iii) Commercial Rivalry

The giantic arms build-up in the Gulf region has been made possible through the active involvement of arms suppliers. A sharp increase in the sale of weapons was caused by the sudden hike in oil prices by the OPEC countries since the Arab-Israeli conflict of 1973. The major arms suppliers to the Gulf region are the United States, the Soviet Union, Britain and France. Evidence shows that a number of small suppliers, such as Canada, Federal Republic of Germany, Netherlands, Italy and Czechoslovakia have also energetic sales programme and are providing limited categories of weapons to the Gulf littoral States.[99]

The arms transactions between the Gulf countries and developed countries cannot be merely considered as activities engendering innocent impacts. Unlike other commercial commodities, the weapons transferred to one country in the region would have the effect of deterrence. The presence of large-scale weapons in a country, whose motives of possessing them remain concealed, creates in others a conjectural frame of mind and in turn encourages them to acquire more arms to strike a possible balance. The weapon suppliers would do all that they can to foster a competitive arms build-up based on the age-old theory of regional balance.

The arms sellers' competition to deliver their war goods is a dynamic activity, generating its own momentum. This competitive process leads to unexpected changes, for the intrinsic nature of competition is essentially unpredictability. Depending on their political and economic interests in the area, the weapon suppliers would try to boost one country or the other, pitting it against others. This was what the United States did in the case of Iran from the fifties to the fall of Mohammed Reza Shah Pahlavi in 1979. American interest in the area was maintained by the Shah and in turn, he received the most sophisticated weapons on a preferential basis. But the consequence of accepting such weapons was disastrous for him as well as for the supplier.

Saudi Arabia now gets the preferential treatment from the United States. Sophisticated weapons are now being transferred to this undeveloped country, for, the US wants that Saudi Arabia should maintain the Wests' interest in the area. For the moment, Saudi Arabia could very well take care of foreign interest in the region. But what would be the impact of the weapons acquired on the body-politic of Saudi Arabia in the decade to come is another matter. How long the US will be able to influence Saudi Arabia by dangling weapons, is a crucial question. As a matter of fact all the destabilising elements one witnessed in the US-Iranian military relationship prior to the revolution are already present in the Saudi Arabian context too. Even if Saudi Arabia goes the way Iran had gone in 1979, the Gulf region would still remain a covetous arms sellers market, for war business is a real 'big business' and the Arabs would continue to purchase arms so long as their oil does not run out.

iv) *Regional Instability and Tension*

The existing level of armaments has not only destabilised the Gulf region but also has diminished the security of the entire region.

It has been always a favourite argument with the arms vendors to the region that weapons supplies to various countries in the Gulf would create a balance among the States. Any regional stability or balance of power equation should normally preclude further arms race but it is not the case with most of the Gulf States. Maintaining a balance means a freezing of weapons production or arms acquisition at a minimum or optimum level, agreed upon by the balancing powers. The problem of balancing the forces of many nations, engaged in a multilateral arms race, as in the Gulf region, becomes extremely difficult. The complexity of the issues, regional security problems and above all great power interests and interventionism make it almost impossible for anyone to work for such a balancing of forces.

The more a region comes under the influence of outside powers, the greater will be the chances of destabilisation in that region. Latin America, South Asia, Far East, Southern Africa and other regions are under the influence of Great Powers whose presence is steadily maintained through large scale weapon supplies to rival nations. The history of the Middle East itself is one of great power politics. The occurrence of many interstate disputes was exploited by big powers to build-up artificial pressure points and encourage local arms race. As a consequence, the assured availability of weapons from their respective patrons have often induced the developing countries to settle political issues or local problems by the strength of arms. The Indo-Pakistan wars, the sporadic Iran-Iraqi border clashes and Arab-Israeli wars reveal the same pattern of peripheral wars which were virtually the weapon suppliers' proxy wars, to put it very crudely. The weapons used in the ongoing Iraqi-Iran war had come from various arms suppliers over the years. Despite the Iraqi-Iran war and its destabilising effects on the region, what sounds paradoxical is that the regional powers are being encouraged by the Western powers to continue to stockpile armaments. In doing so, what the weapon suppliers may probably want is the continuance of instability and tension in the region. For, instability and tension would provide the necessary psychological background for them to step up the arms sales in the area.

The application of military force in extremely volatile situations has been tried ever since the arms flow into the Gulf region began. It only confirms the fact that wars have increased in scope, seriousness and frequency in proportion to the availability of sophisticated weapons.[100] The Iraqi-Iran war is another major consequence of the arms race. The next chapter would deal with it in some detail.

REFERENCES

1 *Flight International* (London), Vol. 112, no. 3564, 2 July 1977, p. 52.
2 Barry Rubin, *Paved with Good Intentions* (New York: Oxford University Press, 1980), p. 158.
3 *World Military Expenditures and Arms Transfers, 1968-77* (Washington, D.C.: US Arms Control and Disarmament Agency, 1979), p. 46.
4 *Ibid.*
5 *World Military Expenditures and Arms Transfers*, n. 3. p. 46; see also *The Military Balance 1976-77*, 1976, p. 33. The two sources slightly differ in furnishing figures of military expenditure by various States in the Gulf region.
6 *Congressional Quarterly, Weekly Report*, Vol. XXXIII, no. 13, 24 March 1975, p. 656.
7 *The Defense Monitor*, Vol. 4, no. 3, May 1975, p. 1.; see also *International Herald Tribune*, 11 July 1975, *New York Times*, 25 August 1974 and *International Defense Review* (Geneva), Vol. 8, no. 3, June 1975, p. 317.
8 *International Defense Review*, Vol. 5, no. 6, December 1976, p. 430.
9 *Middle East Economic Digest* (London), Vol. 21, no. 24, June 1977, p. 23; see also *Kayhan International*, 11 June 1977.
10 *Aviation Week and Space Technology* (McGraw-Hill), 7 May 1973, p. 14.
11 *Flight International*, n. 1, p. 52.
12 The F-14 Tomcat with Phoenix missiles must be rated the West's most effective interceptor. With its AN/AWG-9 weapons control system, it has the ability to guide six phoenix missiles simultaneously against six targets. See *Air Force Magazine* (Washington, D.C.), Vol.60, no. 1, January 1977, p. 33.
13 *Flight International*, n.1.
14 *Armed Forces Journal*, 1973, p. 18.
15 *Flight International*, n.1.
16 *Jane's All the World Aircraft, 1972-73 and 1973-74* (London), p. 18.
17 *World Armaments and Disarmament, SIPRI Yearbook 1976* (Stockholm: Almqvist & Wiksell, 1976), p. 71.
18 *World Military Expenditures and Arms Transfers, 1968-77*, n. 3, p. 47.
19 *Ibid.*, see also *The Military Balance, 1976-77*, p. 34.
20 *Review of Recent Developments in the Middle East*, 1979. Hearing before the Sub-committee on Europe and the Middle East of the

140   *Arms and Insecurity in the Persian Gulf*

Committee on Foreign Affairs, House of Representatives, 96th Congress, First Session, July 26, 1979 (Washington: US Government Printing Office, 1979), p. 69.

21 *Review of Recent Developments in the Middle East*, 1979, n. 20, p. 69.

22 *Prospect for Multilateral Arms Export Restraint*, US Senate, Committee on Foreign Relations, 96th Congress, Ist Session (Washington, D.C.: Government Printing Office, 1979), p. 11.

23 Claudia Wright, "Iraq—New Power in the Middle East," *Foreign Affairs*, Winter 1979-80, p. 264.

24 *Ibid.* See also Shaharam Chubin, "US Security Interests in the Persian Gulf in the 1980s", *Daedalus* (Boston), Vol.109, no. 4, Fall 1980.

25 Mohammad Afaf, "The Drives Behind Defence Spending", *Islamic Defence Review* (London), Vol.6, no. 1, 1981, p. 38.

26 *Flight International*, n. 1, p. 52.

27 *Ibid.*

28 *Ibid.*

29 SIPRI, *Arms Trade Registers: The Arms Trade with the Third World* (Stockholm: Almqvist and Wiksell, 1975), p. 51.

30 *World Military Expenditures and Arms Transfers 1968-77*, n.3, p. 59.

31 *Congressional Quarterly, Weekly Report*, n. 6, p. 656.

32 *The Defense Monitor*, Vol. 4, no. 3, May 1975, p. 1; see also *Time*, 11 July 1977, p. 33.

33 *International Defence Review*, Vol. 8, no. 3, June 1975, p. 443.

34 Paul Abrams, "Saudis Want US Missiles," *Jewish Observer and Middle East Review* (London), Vol. XXV, no. 26, 25 June 1976, p. 8; also see *Flight International*, August 1976, p. 313.

35 *Flight International*, n. 1, p. 52.

36 *Flight International*, n. 1, p. 73.

37 *World Armaments and Disarmament, SIPRI Yearbook 1976*, n. 17, p. 71.

38 *Ibid.*, Now, Chah Bahar has been turned into a fishing complex since the Iranian Revolution in 1979.

39 *Sunday Standard* (New Delhi), 29 July 1979.

40 *Defense Monitor* (Washington, D.C.), Vol. x, no. 4, 1981, p. 1.

41 For more details regarding these projects see Abdul Lateef, "Riyadh and Washington: A Mutual Reliance", *Middle East International* (London), no. 85, July 1978, pp. 16-18.

42 "US to train, equip Saudi Army," *Sunday Standard* (New Delhi), 29 July 1979.

43 *Indian Express* (Cochin), 4 August 1980.

44 *Ibid.*

45 *World Military Expenditures and Arms Transfers 1968-77*, n. 3, p. 49; also see *The Military Balance 1976-77*, n. 19, p. 35.

46 *Congressional Quarterly, Weekly Report*, n. 6, p. 656.

47 *Review of Recent Developments in the Middle East 1979*, n. 20, p. 75.

48 *Ibid.*, also see *USSR and Third World*, Vol. V. no. 6-8, July 7-December 31, 1975, p. 374.

49 "Kuwait is the Richest Nation," *Indian Express* (Cochin), 27 March 1982.
50 *Flight International*, n. 1, p. 64.
51 *Ibid.*
52 *Ibid.*
53 *Ibid.*
53 *Ibid.*
54 Radio Kuwait, February 20, 1977, quoted in *News on West Asia* (New Delhi: The Institute for Defence Studies and Analysis, April 1977), p. 12.
55 *Newsweek*, 10 March 1975, p. 15.
56 "Oil Export gives UAE $74 billion", *Indian Express*, 27 March 1982.
57 *World Military Expenditures and Arms Transfers, 1968-77*, n. 3, p. 65.
58 *The Hindu* (Madras), 14 January 1977.
59 *News Review on Science and Technology* (New Delhi), Institute for Defence Studies and Analysis, February 1977, p. 85.
60 *The Military Balance, 1979-1980* (IISS: London), 1979, p. 37.
61 *Flight International*, n. 1, p. 81.
62 *Ibid.*
63 *World Military Expenditures and Arms Transfers, 1968-1977*, n. 3, p. 56.
64 *Flight International*, n. 1, p. 69.
65 *Ibid.*
66 "Oman Gets Most Powerful Jaguar," *Asian Defence Journal*, March/April 1977, p. 69.
67 B.K. Narayan, *Oman and Gulf Security* (New Delhi: Lancers Publishers, 1979), p. 119.
68 *Flight International*, n. 1, p. 69.
69 *Review of Recent Developments in the Middle East*, 1979, n. 20, p. 73.
70 *World Military Expenditures and Arms Transfers, 1968-77*, n. 3, p. 33; see also *Indian Express* (Cochin), 25 September 1982.
71 *World Military Expenditures and Arms Transfers, 1968-77*, n. 3, p. 58.
72 *Flight International*, n. 1, p. 72.
73 J. William Fulbright, *Prospects of the West* (Cambridge, Mass: Harvard University Press, 1963), p. 67; "All Aid Means Some Degree of Intervention. . .", see Frank M. Coffin, *Witness for Aid* (Boston, Mass: Houghton, Mifflin Co., 1964), p. 18.
74 For an elaborate consideration of this aspect of the Military Assistance Programme of the United States, see Jacob S. Refson, *US Military Training and Advice: Implications for Arms Transfer Policies* (Cambridge: MIT, C-170-R, February 1970); see also K. Subrahmanyam, "Military Aid and Foreign Policy," *Foreign Affairs Report* (New Delhi), Vol. 17, no. 11, November 1968, p. 109.

75 Marshall R. Singer, *Weak States in a World of Powers* (New York: The Free Press, 1972), p. 289; see also Harry Magdoff, *The Age of Imperialism: The Economics of US Foreign Policy* (New York: Monthly Press, 1969), pp. 132-33.

76 Military Assistance Institute, Memorandum, Subject: MAAG Duties, 3 December 1964, quoted in Refson, n. 74, pp. 10-11.

77 *Ibid.*

78 Abdul Rahman Siddiqi, "Western Oil-Strategy, Soviet Geo-Politics and Gulf Security," *Defence Journal* (Karachi), Vol. VII, no. 3, 1981, p. 5.

79 M. V. Kamath, "Invisible Strings of US Arms Aid to Iran," *Times of India* (New Delhi), 3 August 1976.

80 Rubin, n. 2, p. 335.

81 Edward M. Kennedy, "The Persian Gulf: Arms Race or Arms Control?" *Foreign Affairs* (New York), Vol. 54, no. 1, October 1975, p. 19.

82 Yair P. Hirschfeld, "Moscow and Khomeini: Soviet Iranian Relations in Historical Perspective," *Orbis*, Vol. 24, no. 2, Summer 1980, p. 228.

83 *Ibid.*

84 Shirin Tahir-Kheli, "Proxies and Allies: The Case of Iran and Pakistan", *Orbis*, Vol. 24, no. 2, Summer 1980, p. 352.

85 *Defense Monitor*, Vol. X, no. 4, 1981, p. 1.

86 Faisal Alhegelan, "The Economic Policy of Saudi Arabia," *Vital Speeches of the Day* (New York), Vol. XLVII, no. 5, 15 December 1980, p. 158.

87 *Washington Post*, 12 July 1981.

88 The US does not wish the insurgency to end in Afghanistan. For details see S.P. Seth, "Afghanistan in Global Politics," *IDSA Journal* (New Delhi), Vol. XIII, no. 2, October-December 1980, pp. 189-201.

89 The Atlantic Council of the United States, *Oil and Turmoil: Western Choices in the Middle East* (Washington, D.C.: Westview Press, September 1979), p. 32.

90 Abdul Kasim Mansur, "The American Threat to Saudi Arabia," *Survival* (London), Vol. XXIII, no 1, January-February 1981, p. 37.

91 Quoted in Robert Bailey, "Superpower War Games Muddy Gulf Waters," *Middle East Economic Digest* (London), 28 March 1980, p. 8.

92 *Bulletin of the Atomic Scientists* (Chicago), Vol. 23, no. 7, September 1967, p. 44. It is a well-known fact that various military firms use questionable means to promote the sale of weapons in developing countries. In the United States, for example, the Securities and Exchange Commission identified thirty-five such firms in 1976. For the list of names, see *Congressional Quarterly, Weekly Report*, Vol. XXXIV, no. 35, 28 August 1976, pp. 2334-35.

93 Helmut Kramer and Helfried Bauer, "Imperialism, Intervention Capacity and Foreign Policy Making," *Journal of Peace Research*, 1972, p. 228.

94 *New York Times*, 7 March 1981.

95 *Ibid.*

96 *Ibid.*, 20 February 1981.

97 *Ibid.*, 26 February 1981.

98 *Ibid.*, 8 March 1981.

99 *Asian Defence Journal* (Kuala Lumpur), no. 3, June 1976, p. 69. For details of weapons transfers by various European countries, see SIPRI *Arms Trade Registers: The Arms Trade with the Third World* (Stockholm: Almqvist & Wiksell International, 1975) and Dale R. Tahtinen, *Arms in the Persian Gulf* (Washington: American Enterprise Institute of Public Policy Research, 1974).

100 Donald A. Wells, *The War Myth* (New York: Western Publishing Company, 1967), p. 191.

5

Iran-Iraq Conflict

REGIONAL BALANCE TILTED

Arms races among nations in the developing regions of the
world have often led to local wars. It is relevant to examine
whether or not the ongoing Iran-Iraq war that commenced
in September 1980 is a direct consequence of the arms race
between the two countries since the withdrawal of British presence from the Gulf in 1971.

Indeed, Iran had built up a formidable military might over
the years and it was leading in arms race in the region. In
strategic terms, Iran lost the lead in the arms race following
the change of regime in that country in January 1979.[1]

The late Shah's removal from the Iranian political scene
foredoomed the very basis on which he built up Iran's military
superiority in the region.

Changes in policies, especially in Iran's external relations
and defence, were brought in by the new regime in Tehran.
The effected changes apparently looked radical in the sense
that they were diametrically opposed to what the Shah had
pursued for several decades with considerable success. However, the new policies of Iran only helped Iraq to gain the
lead in the arms race leaving Iran militarily weak and strategically vulnerable.

What were those changes of policies responsible for a tilt in the balance of power that provided Iraq with an excellent opportunity to achieve certain of its political goals by resorting to an armed conflict?

i) The hasty political decision of the caretaker government of Shahpour Bhaktiar to withdraw Iran's membership from the Central Treaty Organisation (CENTO) was a radical departure from the country's traditional policy of reliance on military pacts to ensure its security. The opposition in Iran had always felt that the CENTO was an ineffective and unreliable guarantor of the independence and interests of the regional States. It was looked upon as an instrument guaranteeing the interests of the superpowers. Bhaktiar's government decided that Iran should not remain a supporter of an agreement that did not preserve and protect the interests of the people of Iran. Consequently, Iran pulled out of CENTO and declared its intention to follow a policy of nonalignment.[2]

However, this political decision seemed to have been arrived at without adequately weighing the strategic implications of a change of *status quo* in the context of a political crisis that enveloped Iran at that time. The Islamic regime headed by Khomeini, followed this policy uncritically because the prevailing mood in the country after the ouster of the Shah was to look at anything associated with America as something profane and therefore had to be avoided.

In the context of the strategic position of the Gulf, the Shah's adherence to the CENTO did provide a degree of local deterrence apart from the fact that it was solely conceived rightly or wrongly as a bulwark against Soviet expansionism. As has already been explained in Chapter III the CENTO provided the basis for the Shah to press his demands for increased militarisation and modernisation of Iran. Britain and the United States helped the Shah build-up the most powerful army in the Middle East with billions of petro-dollars. The United States supported the Shah's ambition to police the Gulf in the 70s because he was considered to be a trusted ally willing to maintain US interests in the area. Under the Nixon Doctrine, he exercised a surrogate role; nonetheless, he succeeded in building up his armed forces into the strongest in the region with the help of no less than 20,000 American advisers.[3] It was acknowledged however, that in the event of a war, Iran would be unable to fight on a day-to-day basis without US support. This variable constituted the strength as well as the weakness of the Shah's armed forces. While the US military presence served as a deterrence to the local would-be-aggressors, its expulsion left a structural gap in the defence infrastructure, weakening the overall fighting capabilities of the Iranian forces. As for example, after having expelled all the American personnel, Iran found it difficult to operate the sophisticated weapons when the war started with Iraq.

ii) The policy of defence cuts reflected in the cancellation of all earlier defence contracts with the United States and West European countries had a debilitating effect on the balance of forces between Iran and Iraq.

The biggest orders cancelled were: 160 General Dynamics Corporation F-16 fighters for $3.2 billion, seven sophisticated AWACS (Airborne Warning and Control Systems) and flying radar units worth $1,300 million, two destroyers worth $1,400 million, 400 Phoenix missiles (about $1,000 million) and about 20 F-4 reconnaissance aircraft totalling some $500 million.[4]

Not only did Iran slash the US arms deal but it also scrapped major UK arms deal as well. British military involvement in Iran covered tanks, communications, guided missiles and ordnance. Britain's biggest contract was for the supply of 2,250 chieftain tanks with Rolls Royce engines. 900 of them had already been supplied at a cost of over $1 billion, but the delivery of the rest has been suspended. The biggest loss caused by the Iranian crisis came in January when the government suspended plans to build a $1.6 billion ordnance complex at Isfahan in which Britain hoped to obtain the lion's share.

There were economic reasons for cancelling such major defence contracts and projects. Shahpour Bhaktiar's government had cancelled many of the orders because of economic difficulties caused by the nation-wide strike halting oil exports.[5] The Islamic regime of Khomeini felt that the Shah's regime drained much government money on all kinds of defence contracts and projects which did not serve any useful purpose for the Iranian people.[6] Iran's new rulers also decided to reverse

the Shah's "gendarme of the Persian Gulf policy" and said
that they no longer need such sophisticated western weaponry.[7]

This policy was in the first instance a total rejection of the
Shah's tested defence policies without replacing them with
credible alternatives to hold the regional balance. Secondly,
it revealed the reduced capability of the armed forces along
with the debility of the regime's political will to continue the
arms race with Iraq. Thirdly, it served to expose incoherent
structural gaps in defence planning. Lastly, it exhibited
economic bankruptcy.

iii) The policy of the late Shah was to pamper the armed
forces for, his political survival depended on their active
support.[8] Whereas, Khomeini's policy is to witch-hunt them
for, he believes that his political survival is under constant
threat from the pro-Shah elements in the armed forces.

Khomeini's policy brought about a great crisis of leadership
and organisation within the ranks of the armed forces. The
entire elite group of senior officers, suspected of being pro-
Shah were ruthlessly executed or jailed as a result of the purge
in the armed forces ordered by Khomeini. The officers and
armed forces personnel untouched by the revolutionary purge
were thoroughly demoralised and could hardly be organised
into an effective fighting force. It has been observed that
Iranian army desertions were well over 50 per cent since the
new regime came into power. To put it simply, the formidable
armed might of Iran was considerably reduced by the Islamic
regime through the so-called law of retribution. It was obvious
that Khomeini operated in a strategic vacuum, allowing the
pendulum of military balance to swing automatically in favour
of Iraq.

iv) The capture of US hostages from the embassy in
Tehran added another dimension to the waning military capability of the Islamic regime. Iran was denied US spare parts
and supplies to maintain its armaments in retaliation for the
seizure of the US embassy personnel. Iran's ties with other
arms suppliers were also strained as a result of Khomeini's
anti-Western stance.

All these policies and actions, no doubt, cumulatively
affected the operational capability and military credibility of
the Iranian armed forces. Iraq, whose ambitions in the Gulf

have been often thwarted by the aggressive defence policies of the late Shah, must have viewed these developments with much satisfaction. By an inevitable turn of events, Iraq found itself as the dominant regional power in the area.

SUPERPOWERS' NEUTRALITY

The arms race between Iran and Iraq was made possible by the willingness of the great powers to support and supply arms to them in large quantities. As already explained the United States was the chief arms supplier to Iran. Most of the arms supplies to Iraq came from the Soviet Union.

For once, the superpowers cannot be blamed for what has happened in the Middle East. It is a home-crown tragedy. The redeeming feature of the Iran-Iraq war is that it has not turned out to be a proxy war of the superpowers. Why is it that the superpowers having strategic interests in the Persian Gulf allow the regional powers to sort out their differences on the strength of their arms? Why did the superpowers declare neutrality in the Iran-Iraq conflict—an uncommon virtue seldom practised by both in the long series of over hundred regional conflicts since World War II? Why is it that the superpowers as conflict or[9] crisis managers did not show keen interest in ending the Iran-Iraq war? Why do they remain indifferent to the continuance of the war?

Proxy war presupposes the willingness on the part of the smaller allies and friends to assume the role of proxies to fight for superpower interests. The wars in Korea and Vietnam were clear examples of wars by proxies. By the time the Iran-Iraq war started in 1980, the two conflicting parties had already shifted their orbits away from the superpowers and therefore they could not possibly be influenced or induced to assume the role of proxies. The next best course left to the superpowers was to make a virtue out of necessity by declaring their neutrality in the conflict and wait patiently for the war to end somehow.

IRAQ AND THE SUPERPOWERS

That the US had considerable influence and military presence in Iraq was evinced by the formation of the US sponsored Baghdad pact, designed to contain the so-called Soviet expansionism in the early fifties. However, a violent revolution in 1958 spelt the death-knell of the Baghdad pact and sealed the fate of the Hashemite monarch who was its active supporter for his own political survival. The socialist democratic form of government that came up following the revolution effaced whatever paraphernalia existed of the Western alliance system and jealously guarded Iraq against all western political overtures.

An important consequence of the withdrawal of Iraq from the Baghdad pact (later CENTO) in 1959, was the disinclination of the Western countries to transfer weapons to that country. Iraq had to rely, therefore, on socialist countries, especially the Soviet Union for its major arms requirements. The Soviet policy also has been selective in the matter of arms supplies to the region. Of all the countries in the area, Iraq got the greatest patronage though there appears to be a slight change in Soviet policy recently. In the early stages, the Soviets were training the Iraqi forces to handle sophisticated Russian-made weapons. At one time there were 8000 Soviet military advisers and technicians present in Iraq in connection with the military training programme.[10]

However, Iraq was trying to follow a Baath-socialist path which demanded of its leadership to keep equidistance from both the West and East and adopt more specifically a policy of non-alignment in world politics. Hence it began to diversify its sources of military supplies and increase trade with West European countries in order to reduce over-dependence on the Soviet Union.

The solidarity of OPEC in raising the oil prices following the 1973 Arab-Israeli war added a new dimension to Iraq's ability to purchase goods and hardwares anywhere in the world. Military imports from the USSR fell from 95 per cent in 1972 to 63 per cent in 1979. Iraq has been acquiring weapons from countries like France, Italy, Yugoslavia, Portugal, Brazil and even the US.

France, for example, sold Iraq 24 Mirage F-1 aircraft in 1980. Recently Iraq has acquired from the same source more than 100 AMX-30 medium tanks, scores of light armoured cars equipped with SS-11 anti-tank missiles and large number of helicopters. Iraq's relations with US also improved as evident from the US Defence Department's approval of the sale of two L-100 Hercules to Iraq.[11] Although Iraq has not resumed diplomatic relations with Washington since the ties were broken off in the wake of the 1967 Arab-Israeli war, cooperation in trade with the US has thrived in recent years. The Reagan administration has removed Iraq from the list of countries encouraging international terrorism, thus opening the way for the sale of US goods and strategic products to it.[12]

Neither the arms relationship Iraq has developed with the Soviet Union over the past several years, nor the Treaty of Friendship and Co-operation signed between them in 1972 could make Iraq a proxy or surrogate of Soviet Union in the Gulf region. Asked whether the Soviet Union fulfilled its obligation under the Treaty of Friendship and Co-operation with Iraq, President Saddam Hussain replied that Iraq maintained broad relations with Soviet Union in the military, political, economic and cultural fields. "There is nothing in the Friendship and Co-operation Treaty which we have with the Soviet Union that requires us to defend the Soviet Union when it has a conflict with a foreign power, or requires it to defend us when we have a conflict with a foreign power", he added.[13]

The Soviet Union is maintaining a discreet neutrality in the conflict because: a) Iraq could never have been influenced to act as a Soviet proxy or surrogate in the conflict; b) Iran was miserably lost to the US as a potential proxy in the conflict which probably inhibited Soviet attempts to make Iraq a proxy for itself; c) The Soviets in any case seemed to have been confident that the existing inventory of Soviet supplied weapons in the Iraqi arsenal would be sufficient to keep the enemy at bay and achieve nevertheless political and military objectives it set for itself. Temporary suspension of Soviet military shipments to Iraq could be interpreted in that light. Two Soviet Cargo ships laden with military supplies for Iraq steamed out of the Persian Gulf without unloading when the war started.[14]

There were also other problems which strained Soviet-Iraqi relations and made the Soviet Union less inclined to support Iraq in its conflict with Iran: *i*) Iraq was prompt in joining other Muslim countries to condemn the Soviet invasion of Afghanistan at the Islamic summit in Islamabad in late January 1980. *ii*) Over the past two years, Iraq has been rather critical of Soviet activities in the Horn of Africa, specifically Moscow's support for Ethiopia against Arab Somalia. *iii*) There has been a closer cooperation of Iraq with conservative Saudi Arabia in its efforts to prevent North Yemen from moving closer to the Soviet Union. In fact, Iraq has been leading a campaign to form a united front of all groups opposed to the Soviet Union with the intention of liberating South Yemen from communist agents.[15] Nevertheless, all these developments have not strained altogether the relationship between Iraq and the Soviet Union.

What stands out in bold relief is that both the superpowers have failed to make Iraq a pawn or proxy to serve their interests in the Persian Gulf region.

IRAN AND THE SUPERPOWERS

Iraq's delinking of its association with the Baghdad pact in 1959 forced the reconstitution of the alliance into the now defunct CENTO, the lynchpin of which was Iran. A very close military relationship was established between US and Iran right from the day the late Shah was installed on the peacock throne.

Since Iraq was lost as an alliance partner, the US was over-cautious to arm the Shah both to satisfy its own strategic needs of maintaning its hold and influence in this vital area and to assure the Shah of its support against any internal and external threat to his regime. The elimination of the monarchic system in Iraq, consequent on the violent revolution in 1958 rather unnerved the Shah. Therefore, he adopted deliberately a draconian policy of restricting political freedom and suppressing ruthlessly his political opponents whom he thought might one day prove to be a threat to his position. He was always on the watchout to eradicate any revolutionary movement of the type that led to both the execution of the Hashemite monarch and the complete elimination of US presence in Iraq.

US arms supplies to Iran, apart from the huge American commercial interests involved, bolstered up the Shah making him a surrogate to take care of western interests in the Persian Gulf area. However, a popular revolution in early 1979 terrorised him to flee the country and along with him the US mercenaries who helped him to survive so long. The US experience of revolutionary Iran in 1978-79 is almost parallel to that of its experience in the revolutionary Iraq of 1958-59. In both these instances, the monarchs who were trusted friends of the US were simply liquidated by forces from within their respective countries over which neither the monarchs nor the US had any control. In both cases, the US policy of militarisation proved a failure and subsequently it had to pack up from these countries lock, stock and barrel. The entire northern shores of the Persian Gulf remain out of bounds for US penetration and political manipulation and hence it is now focussing attention on the southern shores.

The vituperative behaviour of the Islamic revolutionary regime in Tehran in trying to humiliate the US in many ways only added poignancy to the American set-back in Iran. In June 1979, Khomeini's regime nationalised all private banks, thereby hitting the interests of several US banks with considerble share in various Iranian banks.[16] More than a year-long captivity of US hostages in Iran, coupled with an unsuccessful attempt to rescue them,[17] eliminated whatever little good will that was left in US-Iranian relations almost driving the US to take punitive action against its one-time close-ally. Under these changed circumstances, the US could hardly make Iran a proxy to fight its interests in the Gulf area.

As for the Soviet Union, the joyful glee of witnessing its archrival being unceremoniously turned out from its underbelly, quickly turned sour when the Islamic regime dropped most of the prestigious projects on Iranian-Soviet economic cooperation undertaken during the Shah's regime.

The Soviets were particularly worried by Iran's decision to abandon contraction of a $2.5 billion additional Trans Iranian

Gas pipe line to the Soviet Union (IGAT II) which would provide more than 12 billion cubic metres of gas annually from Iran in addition to the 10 billion cubic metres supplied by IGAT I.[18]

Besides, the foreign policy of the Islamic republic veered round the concept of "negative equilibrium", originally propounded by the late Mussadeq.[19] Iran abrogated the Iran-Soviet treaty of 1921 in the wake of the revolution and indicated its anti-communist stance in many ways. The invasion of the Soviet embassy by the Islamic revolutionaries in Tehran protesting against the Soviet military presence in Afghanistan did cause some deterioration in Soviet-Iranian relations. The Islamic regime has been always suspicious of insurrectionary movements, especially on the northern borders, with Soviet Union's support. This being so, no stretch of imagination could make one conclude that Iran could become a proxy of the Soviet Union to maintain its interest in the Persian Gulf.

The two superpowers have thus been kept on the sidelines of the ongoing Iran-Iraq war. But how long will they watch and wait with equanimity. So far, their major interests have not been jeopardised by the Iran-Iraq conflict. The US continues to get its required oil supplies from the area; the Soviet Union is able to maintain its composure in Afghanistan. Superpower intervention by proxy or otherwise certainly would have escalated the conflict.

The superpowers themselves must be deriving a measure of comfort with their present positions in the Indian Ocean area. Geoffrey Kemp has made a pertinent observation:

> The USSR might make an agreement with the Western allies, especially the US, to divide the spoils of the Middle East and set up spheres of influence similar to those agreed to by Britain and Russia in 1906 when after years of antagonism over neutral countries such as Iran and Afghanistan, the two imperial powers decided to partition Persia. The analogy today would be a US-Soviet undertaking to partition the Persian Gulf area.[20]

If nothing else, the Iran-Iraq conflict has provided an

opportunity for the superpowers to parcel out this area expeditiously, without even the combatants fully realising this inexorable turn of history.

POLITICAL CAUSE OF THE CONFLICT

The causes which led to the Iran-Iraq war were neither in any way associated with the superpowers global rivalry nor with their unrelenting struggle for preponderance of influence in the Gulf area.

It would also be incorrect to assume that Khomeini's waning popular support and influence at home had induced him to precipitate a war with Iraq in order to divert the attention of the people away from the socio-politico-economic chaos in the country and to bring about at least a semblance of unity among different factions posing a real threat to his authority. This view may be examined in the light of the domestic progress, despite the ongoing war. Centrifugal forces in Iran militating against Khomeini's regime have become stronger since the beginning of the war. Demands for autonomy by various ethnic groups have become more pronounced. Factions within the Iranian Republican Party (IRP) became so manifest that it dismissed its first elected President, (and commander-in-chief of the armed forces by virtue of his being the President) Bani Sadr for holding liberal and independent views; the second elected President, Mohammed Ali Rajai, the Prime Minister, Mohammad Javad Bahonar and a host of other important party officials were killed in a fire-bomb explosion at the Prime Ministry last August. Street clashes and political murders have become the routine order of the day. The increasing split in the Mullah-led regime is evident from the rejection of Ali Akbar Velayati, President Khamanei's first nominee for the country's Prime Ministership by the Iranian Parliament in October 1981. All these indicate that the war with Iraq has not helped Khomeini in any way to consolidate his position. On the contrary challenges to Khomeini have increased since the beginning of the war. "A regime that consolidates itself and seeks to maintain its revolutionary zeal by the dynamic promotion of its ideals abroad oblivious to such mundane details as state frontiers or secular authority, poses immense problems for all the states in the Gulf. By supporting opposition groups, it would aggravate their internal vulnerabilities and embolden indigenous dissidents."[21]

There is also another view which holds that President Saddam Hussain of Iraq, exploiting a weak moment in Iranian politics, declared a war to win a sudden victory to improve his image at home as well as to capture leadership of the Arab World. This view further assumes that President Hussain failed in this attempt because the Iranian defence proved far too strong to achieve the above objectives. The truth of the matter lay elsewhere.

For one thing Iraq had chosen an appropriate time to begin the offensive, for another its scope was a very limited one. Iraq had a specific objective right from the start of the conflict, namely to gain control over the entire Shatt-al Arab and surrounding areas which would ensure a secure boundary for Iraq in the future. This limited objective was easily attained at the initial bout of the conflict and all subsequent engagements were directed towards maintaining a low profile defence against Iranian attacks. Because the Iraqi objectives were limited and the enemy in question possessed limited ability to display effectively its sophisticated weapons on the battle front, Iraq's reactions were said to be controlled responses. Iraq itself did not have to bring out all its sophisticated weapons in a massive show of force to pulverise Tehran into submission and get its demands recognised. Iraq's controlled military action constituted a very important factor in keeping the casualties and destructions on the Iranian side at a very low level.

Historically, the Iran-Iraq conflict is connected with the vestiges of the past.[22] There were several wars fought between the Ottoman State and Safavi State in Iran on the question of their border demarcations.[23] There were as many as sixteen treaties between the two States since 1520 each of which, of course, was concluded after a war.[24]

The peace treaty of Erzarum concluded in July 1823 and a boundary commission established in 1843 with Russia and Great Britain as mediators were considered very important in the sense that Iran and Turkey which was sovereign over what is now Iraq agreed for a negotiated boundary settlement. As a result of this mediation, the second Erzarum Treaty was signed in 1847. This treaty stipulated that the Ottoman State would relinquish the city of Muhammara (Khoramshahr), the isle of Khider (Abadan) and its wharf and port as well as all the lands lying in the eastern bank of Shatt-al Arab controlled by tribes attached to Iran. As far as the Shatt-al Arab was concerned, the two sides agreed that the "border line should continue with the eastern bank of the river upto the sea and that the entire Shatt-al Arab would be attached to the Ottoman State but without prejudice, however, to the Iranian vessels' free navigation in its waters from its mouth in the Arab Gulf up to the point where the two countries' land borders meet."[25]

The Algiers Agreement of 6 March 1975 was last in the series of negotiated settlements which became the immediate casualty of the Iranian revolution, catapulting Iraq-Iranian relations back to square number one.

The immediate political basis of the conflict should, therefore, be traced to the mutual abrogation of the Algier's treaty of 1975 which was considered the foundation of a new relationship of friendly co-existence and cooperation between revolutionary Iraq and monarchic Iran.

The treaty so painstakingly worked out through the good offices of President Houari Boumedienne of Algeria dealt with the State frontier and good neighbourly relations.[26] The three protocols annexed to it concerned with *a*) the redemarcation of the land frontier between Iran and Iraq; *b*) the delimitation of the river frontier between Iran and Iraq; and (*c*) the security on the frontier between Iran and Iraq.

Relations between Iran and Iraq improved with the conclusion of the above treaty. Essentially the rivalry between the two to capture the leadership of the Gulf region was brought down to a relatively low level. Iraq's incessant efforts at exporting its brand of Baath radicalism and revolution since 1968 became more discreet. The late Shah's unstinted support to the separatist Kurdish movement in northern Iraq, purported deliberately to undermine and destabilise Iraqi politics, was also withdrawn in reciprocation. Outstanding boundary disputes, particularly the frontier line in the Shatt-al Arab was agreeably fixed according to the *thalweg*, i.e. "the

median line of the main navigable channel at the lowest
navigable level, starting from the point at which the land
frontier between Iran and Iraq enters the Shatt-al Arab and
continuing to the sea".[27]

The treaty remained in force until the late Shah was forced
to go into exile. The validity of the treaties and agreements
concluded by the Shah with other States was called into
question by the Islamic regime that replaced the Shah after the
revolution. The late General Falahi, Chief of Staff of the
Iranian armed forces, said: "Iran does not recognise the
Algiers Accord signed with Iraq in March 1975".[28] The
Iranian foreign minister told the Iraqi Ambassador in 1979
that his government was not pleased with the 1975 Accord,
adding: "who told you we are satisfied with that Accord? There
is still an open account beween us, and there is a lot we shall
claim from you".[29] Other leaders like Sadiq Rawhani stated:
"The Shah submitted to Iraq large areas in southern Iran
(Shatt-al Arab) through the Algiers Accord of 1975, in
return for Baghdad radio stopping attacks against monarchy
in Iran".[30]

Therefore, the abrogation of the treaty by both sides was
not done in an outright fashion; conditions were gradually
created to achieve the same purpose. Which side exactly was
chiefly responsible for generating those tension-ridden conditions, and to what extent, one cannot demonstrably prove.
But that there were so many underlying disruptive forces at
work for a long time precipitating the two countries to a
collision course, cannot easily be ignored.

Ethnic differences have long been playing an obnoxious
role in deeply stifling good neighbourly relations between Iran
and Iraq. Many conflicts in the past have occurred on the
issue of the superiority of the two races. Arabs are semites
and Iranians are supposed to be of Aryan origin. Iraq believes
that the new Islamic regime in Tehran has adopted the same
racist-expansionist policy of the late Shah manifested in the
occupation of the three Arab islands in the Gulf contrary to
all international laws and conventions, in collusion with the
imperialist forces.[31] Which of the two factors has now contributed more in escalating the conflict is again drowned in the
din of hectic propaganda and counter-propaganda. Seeds of

the conflict were being sown when the Islamic fundamentalists, backed up by the revolutionary regime in Tehran made explicit their intention to export the Iranian revolution into the other Gulf countries, particularly to Iraq. Bani Sadr, the exiled President, for example, stated: "Iran intends to export its Islamic revolution to support any Islamic movement that may arise against any Arab Government".[32] He called upon the Iraqi armed forces "to dissent and follow the Iranian revolution under the leadership of Ayatolla Ruhollah Khomeini, the most powerful leader of the world".[33] Abu Sharef, the commander of Islamic revolutionary guards said: "the Islamic revolutionary guards are determined to continue their struggle until there is a full liberation of Palestine, Lebanon, Afghanistan, Erithrea, the Philippines, Iraq and all the oppressed people".[34]

Mutual antagonism intensified as the Iraqi Baath-ideology and Khomeini's Islamic fundamentalism could never square with each other. In Iraq, politics is divorced of religion. Secularism is an important element holding together other religionists in the political fabric of Iraq. On the other hand, religion and politics are enmeshed in the Islamic Republic of Iran where secularistic tendencies are discouraged and views other than those consonant with Islamic laws and doctrines are not easily tolerated. Bilateral relations between two neighbouring States, when overcharged with emotions based on ethnic, religious, and ideological differences, will inevitably be reduced to all sorts of instigations, hotile acts and violations of each other's rights. Border infiltrations, skrimishes, violation of air space etc., increased following the eruption of those dormant disruptive forces in volcanic proportions, bouncing over all conventional codes of international restraint. War became a psychological compulsion in the case of Iran and Iraq more than an expression of 'politics by other means'.

CONSEQUENCES OF IRAN-IRAQ WAR

Bombing Economic Targets

Inherent in the war by proxy are the potentials of a wider escalation. In a war by proxy, the objectives are defined invariably by the patrons; the quality and quantity of weapons to be used in the conflict are determined by them; and, they would decide under what conditions, how and when the conflict should end and with what results. The prolonged wars in Korea, Vietnam, West Asia, the Horn of Africa, etc., were made more destructive because they were wars by proxy. They were all fought to achieve superpower objectives. All these conflicts ended on terms acceptable to the superpowers.

Iran-Iraq war is a war without punch because it is not a war by proxy, involving either directly or indirectly the superpowers. Excepting for the initial two or three weeks of fierce bombing operations by the two sides, fighting has been narrowed down to smaller, sporadic engagements; these engagements seem to be more symbolic of the hostile relationship between two nations of diverse ethnicity and religious persuasions than any meaningful thrusts to gain any significant military advantage on either side.

As these two countries, for the moment, are not proxies of the superpowers, their ability to fight an intense war of attrition is very much limited because of three reasons: one, they are cautious not to exhaust their existing weapons indiscreetly; two, the sources of supplies of weapons and spares are almost blocked; and three, they do not possess any significant weapon production capability to augment their defence. Iran is much more in a disadvantageous position than Iraq when it comes to the question of an intensification of the war despite the fact that it possessed a grand inventory of weapons, acquired mostly from the US. However, this reflects only the negative aspect of the consequences of the Iran-Iraq war.

The Iran-Iraq war has brought about in the first instance untold losses in men and material to the two countries. The exact number of men killed on both sides so far is not easily available. According to a recent report the toll on the Iranian side has been conservatively estimated at nearly 50,000, just about the same number of persons who became martyrs of the Iranian revolution.[35] The casualties on the Iraqi side would be less because the Iraqi army took the war into the Iranian territory within days of the all round offensive.

Iran's foreign currency reserves which totalled about $12 billion in 1979 are now estimated at less than $500 million. Iraq, which began the war with reserves estimated at $35 billion is now said to have around $10 billion only.[36]

It is very significant to note that both sides were concentrating their attack on oil refineries and other industrial installations with a view to paralyse the oil exports. For instance, gas and oil pipelines and fuel tanks were destroyed by Iraqi troops in Abadan and neighbouring Kohsrowabad, the main supply line to Abadan.[37] There were reported Iranian air attacks on Iraq's oil installations in the vital cities of Basra, Baghdad, Mosul and Kirkuk,[38] forcing Iraq to suspend export of all grades of oil. Losses in damaged facilities is put at $40 billion. An Iraqi attack on the Iranian Kharg oil installations was feared when Iraq obtained from France five super-Etendard fighter bombers equipped with French built Exocet missiles. President Saddam Hussain even warned that Iraq would bombard Kharg island in the light of its national interest prerequisites and in the light of Iranian stance vis-a-vis peace efforts. In response, Iran threatened to blockade the strait of Hormuz by cutting off oil exports from the area, a total of 8.7 million barrels of oil a day, if the planes were used against its oil fields. Without going into the exact nature of the damages caused and the amount of loss in exports of oil on both sides, one should reflect on the harmful effects of such savagely extensive bombing of economic targets. As long as the war continues, the destruction of their oil refineries will impinge on the countries' economy which solely depends on the export of oil. The economic reconstruction and replenishment of war materials which will become necessary after the end of hostilities can only benefit those countries which have a vested interest in accentuating Third World contradictions. Besides, this will lead to a greater degree of dependence of both Iran and Iraq on outside powers.[39]

Naval Build-up Around the Persian Gulf

A second important consequence of the Iran-Iraq war is that the superpowers have seized the conflict as a pretext to emphasize the need to stabilise their massive military presence in the Indian Ocean area. The geopolitical moves of one super-power are soon countered by the other.

The expulsion of US military personnel from Iran following the 1979 revolution, worried the Pentagon planners about the West's oil interest in the Gulf region. The fall of the Shah of Iran and the global energy crisis that ensued encouraged the Pentagon to advocate vociferously the build-up of the Rapid Deployment Force (RDF) in the Indian Ocean, which could easily project an intervention capability not only in the Persian Gulf but also elsewhere in the developing world of Asia and Africa to protect growing US economic interests,[40] besides its function of acting as a countervailing force to check any major Soviet challenge to the Western jugular, the oil lanes.

The Rapid Deployment Force is the quickest and hardest-hitting expeditionary force ever mounted by the US. It is backed by what is known as "Prepositioned Material Configured in Unit Sets (POMCUS)," which means prepositioning as close to the target area as possible enough equipment for one Marine Brigade of 10,000 men.[41] It has been demonstrated that storing seven ships worth of equipment (enough for one 10,000 men Marine Brigade) at Diego Garcia would have roughly a month of airlift in a Persian Gulf crisis.[42]

In early 1980, Carter underscored the US Administration's resolve to ensure the free flow of oil from the region when he said that any attempt by any outside force to gain control of the Persian Gulf region will be repelled by any means necessary including military force. His statement was backed up by sending additional naval forces into the Indian Ocean area. An assault force of 1800 marines and five amphibious warships was ordered to join the aircraft carrier, Constellation, in the Indian Ocean by July 1980. Seven cargo ships with weapons, ammunitions and supplies for a 12000-man marine corps brigade are now prepositioned near Diego Garcia. Those ships will wait for the possible arrival of marines who will be flown there to draw weapons and equipment in the event of an emergency.[43]

The uncertainty of the oil supplies from the region became more pronounced when the Iran-Iraq war started. Iran threatened to close down or mine the 32 km wide strategic straits of Hormuz through which 60 per cent of the world's crude oil supply passes.[44] Whether or not, Iran actually possessed the capability to execute the threat was a different question. But that situation was quickly exploited by the US and its allies to assemble a formidable fleet of about 60 warships in the Indian Ocean area to protect the strait and the oil lanes. In the multinational show of strength, the Australian contribution consisted of an aircraft carrier and at least three destroyer escorts; Britain brought in a destroyer accompanied by an oiler for refuelling; and France forthwith added as many as fifteen ships. Of course, the US had the distinction of leading this fleet with two task forces of two aircraft carriers with 150 fighter planes making a contingent of 34 ships.[45] In mid-October 1980, the US ordered further a guided missile cruiser into the Gulf, strengthening its air defence capability off Saudi Arabia.[46] The cruiser, Leahy, was said to be equipped with systems to contact the four radar-equipped aircraft the US sent to Saudi Arabia soon after the Iran-Iraq war broke out. The US apprehensions regarding the free flow of oil from the Gulf were further aggravated when the Soviets made their visible military presence in Afghanistan, adjoining the area of Iran-Iraq conflict.

The United States has earmarked $4 billion in its current military budget for equipment for the RDF, and has also called for the establishment of a permanent Gulf command.[47] Even the Sinai multinational peace force which will include the first American combat troops stationed in the Gulf, is being viewed in this light. Personnel from the 82nd airborne division (part of the RDF) will be sent to Sinai and possibly they might be deployed in a crisis situation elsewhere in the region.

The unobstrusive induction of increased US naval forces has encouraged the Soviet Union to increase its naval presence in the Indian Ocean area. The rivalry between the two superpowers has intensified in the Indian Ocean since the outbreak of the Iran-Iraq war. They are strenuously engaged in canvassing support from the Indian Ocean littoral States for their respective military policies.

It may be recalled that the US had to abandon one by one those alliances and bases constructed during the cold war period, designed to contain the so-called Soviet expansionism in the Middle East. The US is now engaged in the process of finding friends and 'facilities' in the region to base its forces in order to protect its oil interests. Egypt, Oman, Somalia and Kenya have already agreed to give 'facilities' to the US. Of course, Diego Garcia's harbours have been deepened to accommodate aircraft carriers and nuclear submarines and the runway lengthened to permit the big nuclear weapon carrying bombers to take off and land.[48] The Soviet Union, for its part, is well entrenched in Afghanistan—a strategic point overlooking the Persian Gulf—Indian Ocean area.

Arab Countries Divided

Thirdly, the Iran-Iraq conflict has clearly revealed a polarisation among the Arab countries. Iraq is being supported by half-a-dozen Arab countries in its war with Iran, and Iran is being backed by Libya and Syria.

Kuwait and Jordan, both of which share borders with Iraq were the most outspoken in support of the Iraqi President, Saddam Hussain. North Yemen, South Yemen, Qatar, United Arab Emirates and Morocco are other Arab countries which have expressed their sympathy and support for Iraq. Though the Arab States in the Gulf have extended moral and financial support (the oil-rich States together provided Iraq with $20 billion in soft loans towards the cost of the war) none of them has yet become actively involved in the war on Iraq's side. This is not only because they are not in a position to provide any significant military assistance, but mainly because of the fear of Iranian military reprisal. Iranian leaders have been repeatedly threatening the Gulf countries of dire consequences if they would harbour Iraqi ships and war planes on their territories. The message was effectively conveyed through the three air raids on Kuwaiti targets during the course of the war. However, Jordan despatched about 5000 Jordanian volunteers to help Iraq. On 22 September 1980, the day the war broke out, King Hussain of Jordan ordered a general mobilisation and kept in readiness a mechanised force of 40,000 troops on Jordan's border with Iraq, awaiting word to join the battle against Iran.[49] It has been reported that Iraqi military planes were permitted to use Jordanian air bases.

To the Gulf States, Iraq, the most powerful of them militarily, was a buffer against Iran. The weakening of this buffer increases the vulnerability of the Gulf States. They are spending huge sums of their oil revenue on armament, but their defence capability remains rather limited. Saudi Arabia, the largest among them, was worried from the start. Its anxiety was reflected by the fact that shortly after the Gulf war broke out, it requested the US to deploy four AWACs reconnaissance aircraft in Saudi Arabia to act as an early warning system against possible attacks. The Islamic regime in Tehran had condemned the Saudi regime as a corrupt tool of American imperialism.

Saudi Arabia and its allies in the Gulf Co-operation Council (GCC) are likely to provide Iraq with additional finance, should the war continue. Iran has not only threatened to mine and block the Hormuz Strait if Iraq uses Exocet missiles launched by super-Etendards, but is said to have threatened also to try and disrupt or destroy the oil fields of Iraq's allies in the Persian Gulf, including Saudi Arabia and United Arab Emirates. Facing the Iranian threat of blockade of their oil supply routes, the GCC members staged joint military manoeuvres in mid-October 1983, aimed at demonstrating to the outside world their capability to defend the region. The military exercises underlined the principles of cooperation, coordination and joint efforts of the armies of the GCC states, promotion of their combat capabilities and mobilisation of their military potential to serve the security of the region, which is an integral part of the Arab nation as a whole.[50] Actually a more aggressive policy by the Iranians could sharpen the Sunni-Shia rivalry in the Gulf region and could eventually whip up more Arab support for Iraq.

The Gulf States, in general, lend support to the Iraqi objectives *a*) of rectifying the territorial problems of the Shatt-al Arab, *b*) working toward return of the islands Iran had seized in 1971, and *c*) humbling the Iranian regime. But no one is interested in the escalation of the war.

On the other hand, Col. Ghadafy of Libya was the first Arab leader to declare open support for Iran. Syria also vehemently criticised the Iraqi President for waging the war that weakens the Arab forces in their confrontation with Israel.

Libya and Syria have been involved in supplying Iran with large quantities of arms and ammunition since the early stages of the war. Besides, the Syrian President, Hafez Assad rushed to Moscow in early October 1980 to sign a 20-year friendship treaty that called for strengthening military cooperation at a time when Iraqi-Soviet relations were somewhat bedevilled by minor irritants. The Arab States' hostility to the regime of President Saddam Hussain of Iraq accounts for their support to Iran. Syria shares with Iran a common cause in the endeavour to overthrow Saddam, who, it says has been exporting death to Damascus and other cities by sending saboteurs, carbombs and weapons.[51] To these Arab States, Iraq was the aggressor in the war.

If the Iran-Iraq war is to escalate and intensify, more sophisticated arms have to be pumped into the area of conflict. But arms supplies had been halted totally by the arms merchants even before the war started. The reported transfers of smaller armaments to Iran from third countries such as Syria and Libya do not significantly alter the character or course of the conflict.

The Iran-Iraq war would continue to remain a very limited one provided it could be successfully insulated against the tempting pressures of the "merchants of death" who for the sake of providing benefits to their arms industries, would surreptitiously try to snatch opportunities to supply weapons to the conflicting parties. While the superpowers now abide by their declared neutrality in the Iran-Iraq conflict, one could not be sure how long would they remain in their self-imposed abstinence if it were to continue indefinitely.

PROSPECTS OF CONFLICT RESOLUTION

At the initial stages of the war, there has been a flurry of diplomatic activity with a view to bring about a cease-fire. Yasser Arafat, the chief of the Palestinian Liberation Organisation (PLO) offered his services as a mediator but he was unable to produce results. President Fidel Castro despatched his foreign minister to Baghdad in another mediation attempt. Indonesia's Mines and Energy minister Subroto announced that Indonesia would try to play a role in ending the conflict. These individual efforts failed to end the hostilities. Equally, collective attempts by world organisations such as the UN, the Islamic Conference Organisation, and the group of non-aligned nations could not succeed in bringing about a rapprochement between the two warring nations.

The United Nations' appeal to Iran and Iraq to stop the fighting found some response from Iraq which announced an unilateral truce from October 5 to 8, 1980.[52] But Iran rejected the appeal for an end to the hostilities and spurned Iraq's offer of a cease-fire. Iran is said to have put two conditions for a cease-fire: one, Iraqi President Saddam Hussain should tender his resignation; and two, the Iraqi army should surrender to Iran. The late President Mohammed Ali Rajai said: "Iran will never sign a peace treaty with the Iraqi President Saddam Hussain even if the war lasts 10 years. The struggle shall continue until the fall of Saddam Hussain's regime".[53] The The Iranian Foreign Minister Ali Akbar Vellayati recently said that Iran will continue the war until Baghdad pays an indemnity and President Saddam Hussain appears before an international tribunal.[54]

Iraq's offer of a cease-fire too was not unconditional. Firstly, Iraq wanted Iran to refrain from any attacks or build-up of its forces on the borders and hostile propaganda against the Iraqi truce overtures. Secondly, Iraq wanted a commitment from Iran to extend the four-day truce period and start negotiations on all disputes between the two countries. With polar differences in their approach to a truce, the hope of an immediate end to the war is a distant one.

Offers of mediation to end the war came also from the Islamic Conference Organisation. First, President Zia-ul-Haq, chief spokesman of the Conference shuttled between Tehran and Baghdad exploring possibilities of reconciliation between the two conflicting parties. The Islamic initiative came to naught when Khomeini advised that the only way the Muslim leaders can use their good offices is by joining Iran in the war against Iraq. He told Habeeb Al-Shatti, General Secretary of the Islamic Organisation in Tehran on October 20, 1980, that he was prepared to receive a delegation of the Islamic heads of States if their objective was to investigate "the crimes of aggression committed by the blasphemous regime of Saddam Hussain" against Iran.[55]

The 94 member non-aligned group of nations also despatched a seven-member fact-finding good will mission consisting of India, Pakistan, Algeria, Yugoslavia, Zambia, Cuba and the PLO, to the area of conflict. The mission's main objectives were to work on the following proposals: (a) a ceasefire, (b) an unilateral Iraqi withdrawal to either the borders outlined in the 1975 Algiers Accord between Iran and Iraq or the 1913 treaty of Constantinople, (c) Iranian agreement to negotiate with Iraq on neutral grounds, and (d) non-aligned States supervise the Iraqi withdrawal, as both Iran and Iraq belong to the non-aligned group. The conference of the Non-aligned nations, held at New Delhi in 1983 reviewd the report submitted by the Conference of Foreign Ministers of non-aligned countries and further resolved to exert all possible efforts in order to contribute to the implementation of the principles of non-alignment with regard to the conflict between Iran and Iraq.[56]

Iran is not prepared to accept an in-place cease-fire. Iraq refuses to withdraw its forces to positions of September 22, 1980 before the war started. So far, neither side is willing to let the disputed areas to be turned into a demilitarised zone under the supervision of the UN or any other international organisation. In the meanwhile, there has been some reversals for Iraq on the battle front, and President Saddam Hussain has said Iraq would step up military operations in its war with Iran.[57]

So far, there has not been any concrete initiative to end the Iran-Iraq war on the part of the superpowers. While intervening in the UN debate on Iran-Iraq conflict, the US representative urged the council to work vigorously to assist Iran and Iraq to achieve a cease-fire, to begin withdrawal and to initiate a process of negotiation in a manner acceptable to both. But he said that the United States had no specific proposal to offer as to the manner or form in which those negotiations should be undertaken.[58]

The Soviet representative also said that the USSR favoured an early political settlement of the conflict, primarily through efforts made by both sides to seek solutions to the problems between them. Iran and Iraq must settle the controversial issues between them at the conference table.[59]

Earlier, President Leonid Brezhnev called upon Iran and Iraq to settle their dispute through negotiations. "Neither Iraq nor Iran will benefit from the destruction and bloodshed, and from undermining each other's economies. The only one to benefit is a third party, one to whom the interests of the peoples of this region are alien."[60] The US is particularly satisfied with the assurances of both Iran and Iraq that there will be no "infringement of the internationally recognised freedom and safety of navigation in the Persian Gulf, which was of such importance to the international community."[61]

From the debates and subsequent approaches by the superpowers what is clear is that, they seem to prefer bilateralism in the settlement of the Iran-Iraq conflict. Political expediency is not the sin only of the lesser powers. However, it should be appreciated neither the US nor the USSR is in a happy position to initiate steps in bringing the conflicting parties to the negotiating table. There are no reasons why they should be sorry for it either, for with war or without it, the superpowers stand to lose very little; their interests in the area are never affected.

Be that as it may, the superpowers have lost their importance as conflict managers in the developing world because they have often mismanaged local conflicts to suit their global interests. Despite their other differences, the two superpowers have been behaving with remarkable similarity. They determine their national interest and present the resultant policies as the revealed truth to allies, friends and followers throughout the world. Those tactics no longer work. As event unfold gradually in different parts of the world one senses a major development—the twilight of the superpowers.[62]

In the final analysis, it must be reiterated that the Iran-Iraq war is in a way a consequence of the arms build-up by the two powers. The competitive arms build-up itself was fuelled by the superpowers; but that the war did not turn out to be a proxy one is another matter. However, the spurt of arms transfers to countries like Saudi Arabia, Kuwait, UAE and Oman in the wake of the Iran-Iraq war has only increased the prospects of generating further conflicts in the region. The arms, of course, are supplied to these countries under the plea of rendering them protection from possible external attacks or threats of internal subversions from radicals.

Infusion of more weapons would eventually increase tension and instability in the region, provoking a cycle of local arms races and conflicts. Paradoxically, these are the crucial variables providing opportunities to the arms suppliers to further their political goals and consolidate their hold as well as influence over the local actors.

REFERENCES

1 The late Mohammad Reza Shah Pahlavi, the king of Iran was forced to go into exile as a result of the revolution which brought into power the Islamic fundamentalists, headed by Ayatollah Rouhollah Khomeini.

2 *Department of State Bulletin* (Washington, D.C.), Vol. 80, no. 2034, January 1980, p. 46; also see *Kayhan International* (Tehran), 13 March 1979.

3 Robert Graham, *Iran: The Illusion of Power* (London: Croom Helm, 1978), p. 179.

4 *Tehran Journal* (Tehran), 5 January 1979; see also N. Vasin, "Iran and US Imperialism," *International Affairs* (Moscow), no. 5, May 1980, p. 72.

5 *Tehran Journal*, 5 February 1979.

6 *Kayhan International*, 10 March 1979.

7 *Ibid.*, 6 March 1979.

8 By virtue of this role as defenders of the throne —not of the realm— the officer corps became a previleged class. Their pay and fringe benefits put NATO to shame, including the provision of villas, domestic personnel, low taxes on luxury goods and holiday compounds. Senior ranks were pensioned off on full pay and frequently were drafted into the boards of state companies and institutions. See Graham, n.3, p. 183.

9 95 per cent of post World War II conflicts have taken place in the developing world. See Ruth Leger Sivard, *World Military and Social Expenditures 1980* (Virginia: World Priorities, 1983), p. 30.

10 Christoph Von Imhoff, "From the Persian Gulf to the Indian Ocean," *Aussen Politik* (Bremen-Nord), Vol.26, no.1, 1st Quarter, 1975, p. 53.

11 *Flight International* (London), Vol.112, no. 3564, 2 July 1977, p. 52.

12 Harish Chandola, "Iraq After the Debacle," *Indian Express* (Cochin), 29 April 1982.

13 *The Iraqi-Iranian Conflict, Documentary Dossier* (Baghdad: Ministry of Foreign Affairs, Republic of Iraq), January 1981, p. 299.

14 *Indian Express* (Cochin), 3 October 1980.

15 Adeed I. Dawisha, "Iraq: The Wests' Opportunity," *Foreign Policy*, no. 41, Winter 1980-81, p. 139.

16 *New York Times*, 9 June 1979.

17 The foiled attempt to rescue American hostages in Iran cost $193 million. 90 commandos flew into the Iranian desert on 24 April 1980, but the mission was called off after three of their eight helicopters broke down before reaching a refuelling stop. Eight US commandos were killed when a helicopter collided with a C-13 transport plane on the way out of the desert. See *Indian Express* (Cochin), 2 November 1981.

18 *Economic Consequences of the Revolution in Iran*: A compendium of papers submitted to the Joint Economic Committee, Congress of the United States, 96th Congress, 1st Session, November 19, 1979 (Washington: US Government Printing Office, 1980), p. 88.

19 This concept underscores the notion that on a global level Iran functions as a buffer between East and West and that neither the USSR, nor US nor any Western power has any direct vital interest in Iran. They all desire to exclude one another from gaining control over a strategically important area. The effort should now be made to prevent either superpower from gaining any influence in military, political, economic or even cultural affairs. See Yair P. Hirschfeld, "Moscow and Khomeini: Soviet Iranian Relations in Historical Perspective," *Orbis*, Vol. 24, no. 2, Summer 1980, p. 223.

20 Geoffrey Kemp, "East-West Strategy and the Middle East-Persian Gulf," in Kenneth A. Myes (ed.), *NATO, The Next Thirty Years* (Colorado: Westview Press, 1980), p. 213.

21 Shahram Chubin, "US Security Interests in the Persian Gulf in the 1980s," *Daedalus* (Boston), Fall 1980, p. 43.

22 L. Medwedko, "The Persian Gulf: A Revival of Gunboat Diplomacy," *International Affairs* (Moscow), no. 12, December 1980, p. 28.

23 Iraq was separated from the Ottoman Empire following World War I and became a British mandated territory. It became independent in 1932. Iraq believes that it succeeded to the various Turkish treaties relating to the Iraqi territory and that Iran is always upto violating them.

24 *Selections from the Iraqi-Iranian Dispute* (New Delhi: Embassy, Republic of Iraq, 1981), p. 40.

25 *The Iraqi-Iranian Conflict: Documentary Dossier*, n. 13.

26 For the text of the treaty and protocols concerning the delimitation of the river frontier between Iran and Iraq, see *The Iraqi-Iranian Conflict:Documentary Dossier*, n. 13, pp. 286-92.

27 *Ibid.*, p. 290.

28 *Tehran Radio and T.V.*, 15 September 1980.

29 *Al-Hawadith* (Beirut), 22 June 1979.

30 *Al-Rai Al-Aam* (Kuwait), 16 June 1979; see also A. Ulansky, "The Iran-Iraq Conflict," *New Times* (Moscow), no. 39, September 1980, p. 11.

31 *Selections from the Iraqi-Iranian Dispute*, n. 24, p. 7.

32 *Al-Rai Al-Aam* (Kuwait), 15 March 1980.

33 *Washington Post*, April 1980.

34 *Kayhan International*, 2 October 1979.

35 Nasira Sharma, "Its Logical to Execute Terrorists," *Indian Express* (Cochin), 19 May 1982.

36 *Indian Express* (Cochin), 30 April 1982.

37 *Ibid.*, 1 November 1980.

38 *Ibid.*, 27 September 1980; see also *Patriot* (New Delhi), 9 November 1983.

39 P.K.S. Namboodiri, "Implications for the Nonaligned," *Strategic Analysis* (IDSA, New Delhi), Vol. IX, no. 7, October 1980, p. 310.

40 Michael T. Klare, "An Army in Search of War," *Progressive* (Madison), Vol. 45, no. 2, February 1981, p. 19.

41 Subrata Banerjee, "Indian Ocean: Massive US Military Presence Threat to India," *Peace and Solidarity* (New Delhi), Vol. II, no. 11, November 1980, p. 6; see also "RDF Could be Catastrophic," *Intervia* (Geneva), no. 5, May 1981, p. 369.

42 John J. Fialka, "The Rapid Deployment Force," *Washington Star*, 7-10 April 1980. Reprinted in *Strategic Digest* (New Delhi), Vol. X, no. 8, August 1980, p. 551.

43 T.V. Parasuram, "US Assault Force Ocean Bound," *Indian Express* (Cochin), 19 July 1980; see also "Defense Secretary-Designate Weinberger Discusses SALT, Military Readiness, Persian Gulf," *USICA, Official Text* (American Center, New Delhi), 9 January 1981, p. 7.

44 "Iran Threatens to Mine Gulf, Hormuz," *Indian Express* (Cochin), 16 October 1980.

45 Subrata Banerjee, n. 41; see also T.V. Parasuram, "US Pins Peace Hopes on Soviet Restraint", *Indian Express* (Cochin), 3 October 1980 and David Rees, "Strategic Problems of Indian Ocean Defense," *Asia Pacific Community* (Tokyo), no. 11, Winter 1981, p. 73.

46 "US Cruiser in Gulf," *Indian Express* (Cochin), 13 October 1980.

47 Harish Chandola, "The Gulf War—II, Fears Old and New," *Indian Express* (Cochin), 30 April 1982; see also *The Hindu* (Madurai), 26 August 1982.

48 Yuri Gudkov, "USA: Rapid Deployment Neutrality," *New Times* no. 42, October 1980, p. 13; see also *The Hindu* (Madurai), 12 March 1981.

49 *Indian Express* (Cochin), 2 February 1982.

50 *Hindustan Times* (New Delhi), 17 October 1983; The members of the GCC are: Saudi Arabia, Qatar, Bahrain, the United Arab Emirates, Kuwait and the Oman Sultanate of Oman.

51 Chandola, n. 47.

52 *UN Monthly Chronicle* (New York), Vol. XVII, no. 10, December 1980, p. 6.

53 *French News Agency*, 30 October 1980, quoted in *Selections from the Iraqi-Iranian Dispute*, n. 24, p. 88.

54 *Indian Express* (Cochin), 1 June 1982.

55 Harish Chandola, "Syria Sees No Chance of Early Gulf Peace", *Indian Express* (Cochin), 31 October 1980, Rajai also spoke in similar fashion: "Iran may host personalities who want to be familiar with the Iraqi crimes in Iran, but we do not accept any good will mission, and will never say a single word in the way of negotiations." *Tehran Radio*, 26 September 1980.

56 *Two Decades of Non-Alignment* (New Delhi: Ministry of External Affairs, 1983), p. 597; see also Chandola, n. 55.

57 *Indian Express* (Cochin), 1 June 1982.

58 *UN Monthly Chronicle*, n. 52, p. 10.

59 *Ibid.*, p. 13

60 Quoted in R. Andreasyan, "Iran-Iraq: The Oil Aspect of the Conflict," *New Times*, No. 41, October 1980, p. 8.

61 *UN Monthly Chronicle*, n. 52, p. 10.

62 T.V. Parasuram, "The Twilight of Superpowers," *Indian Express* (Cochin), 9 September 1980.

6

Prospects of Arms Control
in the Gulf Region

The States in the Gulf region have not so far either singly or collectively suggested any proposal designed to curb, limit or regulate their arms build-up. The arms suppliers—mainly the superpowers and some West European countries—without whose support and active collaboration it is impossible to maintain the arms race momentum, have also not shown so far any desire to reduce weapons sales or to decrease military assistance. That the indifference of both the suppliers and recipients to the growing danger inherent in the arms build-up is more due to their overlapping of interests—the small states having national interests and objectives and the big powers, international interests and objectives[1]—than to any other single factor. Even the recent Iran-Iraq war has not provided the Gulf States adequate incentive to abandon their arms build-up programme.

THE NECESSITY FOR ARMS CONTROL IN THE GULF AREA

The fundamental reason for suggesting curbs on an unending proliferation of sophisticated conventional weapons is based on the consequences of the arms race on security and stability of the Gulf region in general and each State in particular. For, the presence of large scale weapons invariably renders a region unstable and insecure. It is inherent in the very nature of the modern armaments race.[2] The ongoing Iran-Iraq war typifies a conflict resulting from the arms race that was going on between the two countries for a long time. Post World War II history is replete with instances of such local wars.[3]

The necessity of curbing the arms race in the Gulf region is further reinforced by the fact that the arms race in its turn has brought about great powers' presence in the region. This in itself is a matter for grave concern. Whatever may be the nature of their presence, it smacks of neo-colonialism and would affect not only the foreign policies but also the domestic affairs of the countries in the region.[4] Above all, foreign presence would tend to stimulate rather than decelerate a regional arms race.

Besides, attempts by each state of the Gulf region to increase its stockpile of arms do not help in creating favourable conditions for building up enduring mutual confidence. It paves the way for mutual distrust and suspicion among the States. For example, the Gulf States were worried about the way in which the deposed Shah of Iran was strengthening his military forces. They grew suspicious of his intentions.

It is to be further noted that local tension and conflicts, resulting from an uncontrolled regional arms race, can in due course escalate into a global one more so in the context of preferential treatment in the matter of arms supplies given to countries like Saudi Arabia in the Gulf region by one of the superpowers. The discriminatory nature of arms supplies clearly reflects the suppliers' predilection to support and balance these powers for their own ends rather than to help the developing nations of the area. In sum, the need for curbing the arms race arises mainly from the dangerous implications of regional insecurity, instability and the ever increasing problem of restricting foreign interventionism, inherent in the weapon-building programme of the Gulf States.

PROBLEMS OF ARMS CONTROL IN THE GULF AREA

Before attempting to propose some arms control measures in the Gulf region, it would be pertinent to take cognizance of the strategic realities or problems which would pose insurmountable difficulties in the path of arms control.

1. The Gulf region is of strategic interest to the great powers who have, since World War II, kept a close watch over this area. The world-wide importance of oil has further deepened the involvement of most of the industrialised powers in the area since 1973 with the result that a strategic retreat of these powers from the Gulf region in the near future appears to be very unlikely. They maintain their presence by keeping the arms race steadily going with their active support. Hence, any arms control attempt in the region by local powers is likely to be influenced by the interests of the superpowers.

2. Weapons are being supplied by the US to Saudi Arabia on an increasing scale. With the loss of Iran the US has assigned a significant role in the maintenance of security of the Gulf to Saudi Arabia. It is evident that the military influence of the US would be more on Saudi Arabia than on any other littoral States of the Gulf. As such, it is quite unlikely that Saudi Arabia would function as a constant factor in any regional arms control negotiation.

3. Most of the States in the region have surplus oil revenues, which they cannot possibly absorb into their domestic economy for the present. Hence, they can easily set apart enough money for weapon purchases.

4. Some of the regimes in the area fear radical takeover by revolutionaries as happened in Iran in 1979. To avert such a crisis, they are prepared to depend on foreign powers in times of crisis.

5. The Gulf region is an arms sellers market. Heavily depending on the Gulf oil the industrialised nations of the West are willing to supply the Gulf countries the latest generation of weapons in exchange for oil, the vital fluid that sustains their industrial economy. The 'weapons-for-oil' policy appears to play a decisive role in the Arab-European relations which would possibly influence and almost determine the trend of any regional arms control agreement.

6. The arms race in the Gulf region is also inextricably intertwined with the Arab-Israeli conflict and hence the possibilities of regional arms control in this area cannot be contrived in isolation without giving serious consideration to the resolution of this conflict.

7. Another factor that would possibly influence the Arabs is Khomeini's clarion call to export the Iranian revolution into other Arab countries. The ongoing Iran-Iraq war is the immediate result of such a call. As against Khomeini's Shia fundamentalism and hegemony, his Arab neighbours could be expected to arm themselves vigorously.

TWO METHODS OR APPROACHES

There are two classical approaches to the problem of arms race; *a*) the traditional approach of disarmament which was suggested as a panacea for all the arms build-up before World War II, and *b*) arms control approach that has come in vogue after World War II. Whether or not any one of these two approaches could be applicable to the problem of arms race in the Gulf region is to be examined in some detail.

Disarmament Approach: Arms Regulation, Reduction, Limitation and Elimination

Disarmament talks have been an important feature of international relations for about a century now.[5] Disarmament, in the traditional sense, has now been practically abandoned by the great powers who prefer the arms control approach. Even though disarmament approach as such may prove to be of little use to the great powers, it may not be wholly useless for the developing nations, engaged in competitive conventional arms build-up. Hence it justifies the relevance of seeking types and precedents to base the structuring of a model of regional arms limitation in the Gulf.

The word disarmament has been used to signify four distinct conception:[6] *a*) the penal destruction or reduction of the armament of a country defeated in war; *b*) bilateral disarmament agreements applying to specific geographic areas; *c*) the complete abolition of all armaments; and *d*) the reduction and limitation of national armament by general inter-national agreement.

Disarmament in the first sense has been enforced as a penalty following loss of war.[7] Ancient history of the West as well as the East is full of such episodes of compulsory disarmament imposed by victors over the vanquished States. The most recent cases of involuntary disarmament were those of Japan and Germany which came under the occupation of allied forces after the Second World War.

The application of compulsory disarmament as such is totally irrelevant to the Gulf situation where there are neither victors nor vanquished. The era of compulsory disarmament is over.

The Rush-Bagot agreement of 1817 between the United States and Canada exemplifies disarmament in the second sense.[8] By this agreement the US-Canadian border continues to remain disarmed even today.

The Rush-Bagot model would be easy enough to consider as a prototype where only two rivals are involved in an arms race. But in a region like the Persian Gulf where the territorial boundaries of many States are under dispute and over which many a battle have been fought and where arms race tends to be a multilateral one, the Rush-Bagot model cannot presumably be applicable to the situation.

Thirdly, complete abolition of all armaments appears utopian to some;[9] but there are goverments and people advocating complete voluntary abolition of all arms. For example there is a fundamental difference in disarmament approaches between the Soviet Union and the United States. "The Soviet programme envisages complete abolition of all armed forces and all types of armaments. Thus, when universal and complete disarmament is achieved all states will be without soldiers or armaments which means that the menace of war will be removed once and for all."[10] On the other hand, the United States wants "to institute control over existing armaments instead of concluding an agreement on universal and complete disarmament."[11]

Article 2, paragraph 4 of the Charter of the United Nations reflects the view in support of comprehensive ban on the use of force in international relations. Hence also, the interpreters of international law seem to be in favour of abolition of weapons which are the instruments of force and coercion. It is not "just the use of force but even the threat of it in relation to other states is contrary to international law."[12]

However, it can be argued that complete elimination of weapons and as a matter of fact, force can only follow a basic structural change of the international order. In the context of such a preferred international system, where conditions of conflicts and violence are reduced to zero point, perhaps total and complete disarmament at all levels, global as well as regional, could be thought of as a feasible proposition.[13]

It could be argued that there is no reason why the smaller powers like those of the Gulf region should give up all weapons when the great powers are not prepared to impose on themselves such an abnegation which would help to advance the cause of universal peace and harmony in international relations. But there are, of course, reasons as has been already explained, why the Gulf States should stop or at least curb the regional arms race even if the big powers are totally unwilling to abandon or to curb the global arms race.

Fourthly, reduction or limitation of arms was attempted since the Hague Conferences of 1899 and 1907. Qualitative as well as quantitative reduction or limitation of armaments became the main objective of most nations which were represented at the World Disarmament Conference of 1932.[14] The nearest approximation to any measure of conventional disarmament was the Washington treaty of 1922 by which US, Britain and Japan agreed to reduce their capital ships by 40 per cent. However, this was only a temporary agreement which stipulated that replacements to begin in 1931 and should establish by 1942 a 5 : 5 : 3 : 1.67 : 1.67 ratio for the capital ships of the British Empire, the United States, Japan, France, and Italy.[15]

Disarmament in the sense of limitation, reduction and regulation of arms trade have been tried towards the end of the 19th century. The Brussels Act of 1890 was "the only international measure regulating the arms trade which ever came into force."[16] Further, there was intense international negotiation at the end of the First World War within the framework of the League of Nations; the high water-mark of interest was the Geneva Conference of 1925, which dealt exclusively with the arms trade.[17] However, the 1925 Geneva convention on regulation of the arms trade never came into force and thereafter there has never been any prospect of an agreement particularly after the failure of the Disarmament Conference in 1933.[18]

Arms trade is one of the major aspects of the arms race problem in the developing region.[19] If it has to be solved, the arms traders should also equally cooperate in regulating their military sales and also reduce their military assistance. It is the arms acquisition policies of the developing nations which have to finally determine whether they should accept or reject armaments from outside sources. If the arms acquisition policies of the developing nations are mainly responsible for the arms spiral in particular regions, efforts must be made to reverse those policies partially or totally. If a total or partial reversal of arms acquisition policies of developing States can be effected, it could be called a regional arms control measure. The term disarmament is not preferred here for, it implies the ultimate elimination of all weapons; *a fortiori*, it does not also mean arms control conceived in the nuclear context. Hence, regional arms control in this context may be defined as a *deliberate reversal of the arms acquisition policies of developing nations, designed to restrict and/or reduce the level of conventional armaments in order to prevent regional wars or to diminish the presence of weapons in large scale and the possible outbreak of regional conflicts.*

Regional arms control is not intended to be a partial measure towards total and complete disarmament of a particular region. It is also not a technique or device to legitimise various types of conventional weapons at mutually agreed levels. It does not leave scope for regional powers to step up stockpiling conventional weapons either qualitatively or quantitatively. In sum, regional arms control focusses attention on drastic restriction of arms acquisition on the one hand, and adopts measures to reduce the existing levels of sophisticated conventional armaments in specific regions on the other.

Arms Control Approach

Since World War II a number of arms control agreements such as the Antarctic Treaty (1959), Hot Line Agreement (1963, 1971), Limited Test Ban Treaty (1963), Outer Space Treaty (1967), Treaty for the Prohibition of Nuclear Weapons in Latin America (1967), Non-Proliferation Treaty (1968), Seabed Arms Control Treaty (1971), Nuclear Accidents Agreement (1971), B.W. Convention (1972), SALT I Agreement (1972) and SALT II Agreement (1979) have been concluded between the superpowers.[20] The primary aim of these agreements has been the prevention of a cataclysmic thermo-nuclear war between the United States and the Soviet Union. The objectives of the contracting parties to these agreements are not comprehensive and complete elimination of thermo-nuclear weapons from their war arsenals but they are mainly concerned with the legitimisation of certain levels of weapons on either side with a view to establish a central strategic balance. If international security and peace are desirable objectives, the same could be achieved by increasing the military stability,[21] which would ensure a balance of power among nations. This implies that arms control approach seeks to create an arms relationship between rival nations or military cooperation with potential enemies,[22] wherein the use of arms is discouraged because of equality of armaments.[23] Therefore, arms control approach would take into account all "forms of military co-operation between potential enemies in the interest of reducing the likelihood of war, its scope and violence if it occurs and the political and economic costs of being prepared for it."[24] They are also intended to legitimise or institutionalise the arms race particularly the qualitative and technological one; to preserve the *status quo* of the international system by strictly trying to limit the membership of the nuclear club; and to permit a certain amount of violence and limited war at the periphery of the central powers.[25] Hence arms control approach or strategy[25] "offers to curb the race without abolishing the arms, and promise to build security and peace by reliance on arms rather than by their annihilation."[26]

Judging from the point of view of its aims and objectives, arms control approach as such applied in the nuclear context does not appear to have any relevance for the Gulf region. In other words, the assumptions involved in the nuclear arms control doctrine, such as mutual deterrence, strategic stability, legitimisation of certain required levels of weapons systems, mutual assured destruction (MAD) capability, first strike capability, second strike capability, etc., are incompatible with the situation in the Gulf region. That this would be so follows logically from the very concept of regional arms race between two developing nations which is basically a conventional arms race and hence so different from that of the global nuclear arms race between the United States and the Soviet Union. This arms control approach is designed to restrain the superpower arms policy rather than the arms race itself and hence is less likely to be a model which can be applied to the Gulf region. The problems related to the controlling of the arms race in the Gulf area are not identical with those of global arms control. The methods or approaches to achieve specific measures of arms control in the Gulf area would naturally differ from the nuclear arms control measures.

The participants of the arms race in the Gulf area cannot, for example, have as their main aim of arms control the prevention of a thermo-nuclear war. It is evident that the Gulf States, for the present, are engaged in a conventional arms race. What they have to prevent consequently is a conventional war at the regional level. The ongoing Iran-Iraq war inflicted serious damages to the conflicting States, but it did not reduce to ashes the entire region; much less did it sent up flames to the whole world.

It is quite unlikely that the current competitive arms build-up can ensure national security and stability of the Gulf States, for no State in the region has adequate military power, credible enough to deter a potential aggressor in a crisis situation of a regional dimension. By regional standards, Iran's arms build-up before the 1979 political crisis looked very impressive vis-a-vis her neighbours. But even such an arms build-up did not provide national security as was amply demonstrated in the recent war with Iraq. It would be very much a matter for surmise whether or not any semblance of mutual deterrence in the foreseeable future could ever be built up by the local powers who for their arms requirements have to depend entirely on external sources. It should be beyond doubt that arms supply is an unpredictable variable. Once arms suppliers, for one reason or other, decide to discontinue the supplies, the tenuous deterrence presumed to have been built up by the help of imported arms at the local level inevitably collapses by itself.

The objective, further, of legitimisation of certain levels of strategic weapons as is envisaged in, say SALT, need not be true of the arms build-up in the Gulf region. Yet legitimisation of certain levels of conventional weapons cannot be ruled out of a possibility provided regional powers are self-sufficient in their arms production and are insulated against big power interventionism.[27] In order to have an agreement on levels of conventional weapons between two regional rivals, there should be some guarantee that all illegal and clandestine supply of weapons by third parties will be effectively plugged.

How could, for example, Iran and Iraq or Iraq and Saudi Arabia mutually agree to legitimise their levels of conventional arms when all of them are incapable of producing their own weapons systems and therefore have to constantly depend on arms suppliers? The arms suppliers would be ready to transfer only those weapons of their choice and not those demanded by clients and moreover their supplies would be invariably tied up with preconditions.

It has been argued that "conflict control objectives may in some circumstances require an increase in quantities of certain types of arms transferred."[28] Further, the big powers, as conflict managers are accustomed to increase the supply of weapons to rival nations to maintain what is called the "regional balance of power". This reasoning is a corollary to the arms control doctrine in the superpower context which can also mean an incremental augmentation of weapons in the process of an arms control agreement. According to Mack "arms control means the controlled qualitative escalation of the arms race within agreed limits."[29]

Any idea that the big powers would be able to maintain a balance of power among the various Gulf States is not a feasible proposition. Admittedly, the will or desire on the part of the big powers to balance the forces of two or more

States is not enough; they should be acceptable to all the Gulf States. The important question is whether they would respond to it voluntarily or under coercion. If they choose to accept the proposition, then it is easier to work out the technicalities of the balance of forces either on the lines suggested at the Washington Naval Agreement of 1922 or the World Disarmament Conference of 1932. Even the ratio in the reduction of manpower and other categories of conventional armaments contained in the Soviet and Western proposals upto 1957 could also be considered in this context.

In the absence of universally acceptable criteria for actual control and verification systems, any compulsory enforcement of the balance of forces principle would be totally unacceptable to the Gulf States. As against voluntary disarmament, no nation would accept disarmament to be imposed on them, unless of course it is a part of the peace settlement as in the case of Germany and the Treaty of Versailles after the First World War.

A regional balance of power which is workable in a bilateral relationship need not necessarily succeed in a multilateral situation as in the case of the Gulf States. How could a regional balance in the Gulf region be established when arms are flowing without any restraint from diverse sources into Saudi Arabia, Iraq, Kuwait and the rest of the Gulf States where the arms supply is motivated by the economic and national interests of each arms supplier in addition to diverse interests and conflicting policies of recipient States? Even if it is assumed that the major supply of weapons to Saudi Arabia, Kuwait or Iraq for example, originate from a single source, say the United States, could there be any guarantee that the US would always be prepared to restrict the supply of arms to these clients strictly based on a mathematical calculation of the regional balance of power among them? The concept of military balance which is used so often in world politics may not be relevant to the Gulf region.[30]

As Thayer observes: "While balancing may keep antagonists temporarily at bay, it also creates at least three unhealthy effects: it tends to increase the level of the balance, thus making any conflict that much more violent; it tends to make a war that much more difficult to stop, since both sides are militarily each other's equal; and above all, it tends—in most cases by the mere presence of arms—to provoke war itself, the one act such a policy is designed to prevent.[31]

Evidences have been accumulating to strengthen the contention that the arms suppliers are more inclined to supply arms to the Gulf States to exploit their natural resources than to the chimerical notion of balancing their forces. Hence, the so-called built-in mechanism of arms control[32] in the very arms transfers to developing countries is only a device to justify or explain away huge trafficking in arms by the big powers.

In one scenario, the arms suppliers agree among themselves to transfer specific types of weapons to their respective clients in the Gulf region with a view that a regional balance may be maintained by the recipients. But this is hardly an attractive business venture for the weapons suppliers who themselves are engaged in intense arms competition and frequently vie for influence and market in the less developed world; and the Gulf region is now the best market.[33] Among major issues facing arms control experts is how to check international competition between the main suppliers of arms.[34] Because of regional imbalances, tensions and conflict situations, regional powers are made to rush to the 'Merchans of Death' and mortgage all their available resources to secure more arms. Despite global arms control agreements, the superpowers would be willing to supply arms to regional powers and permit conflicts to occur at the periphery. For, the big powers are not so concerned about the dangers of conventional wars at the local level.

When the superpowers speak of international security and peace, they speak in terms of security for themselves and perhaps for their allies. It does not necessarily include security for smaller nations in the developing regions of the world. It becomes all the more evident when it is known that weapons used in all the local wars since World War II have originated from the factories of the industrial powers.[35] Besides, foreign participation in such conflicts has become a general practice. For, according to Kende, in certain regions as in the Middle East and Black Africa, there has not been a single internal war without foreign participation.[36] Besides, the big powers by their arms supply policies act as catalysts in the sporadic eruption of local wars which they would devise as a means of diffusing the pressure at the centre. Instances of such wars are those fought in Korea, Vietnam and West Asia.

Searching for precedents or prototypes to fashion out a regional arms control measure in the Gulf region would be of no avail. All the same there have been a number of proposals and counter-proposals by way of draft resolutions in the UN brought forward by several countries without there being any concrete agreement to limit or regulate the regional arms race. There have also been exhortative statements made by representatives of various countries in the Eighteen-nation Disarmament Committee for regional agreements but they all did not proceed beyond the realm of proposals and discussions.[37]

CONDITIONS FOR ARMS CONTROL IN THE GULF AREA

a) Co-operation of arms suppliers

One of the essential conditions of reaching a favourable atmosphere for negotiating arms control agreements will depend on the cooperation of the arms exporting nations in adopting a restrictive policy in the promotion of weapons sales and military assistance to the region. Only with their cooperation could the Gulf States negotiate arms control agreement among themselves. There are several possibilities open to arms supplying nations:

First, the arms exporting nations, individually can stop the supply of weapons to the Gulf region.

Second, it could be that the arms exporting nations collectively take a decision to stop all arms exports to the Gulf region.

Third, it could be that an individual arms exporter curtails the supply of certain types of war material which in turn would lessen the intensity of the arms race in the Gulf region.

Fourth, it could be that all the weapon suppliers collectively take decision not to export certain types of strategic weapons falling into the war arsenals of the Gulf States.

All these possibilities are fraught with problems. If an arms supplier voluntarily stops the supply nothing forbids the recipient country from approaching other weapons suppliers. It is also important to note that such unilateral action by one weapons supplier need not necessarily inhibit other suppliers from obliging a recipient country. As many sources of weapons are readily available to the Gulf States, an unilateral decision by one country to stop supply cannot substantially affect the nature of the regional arms race.

The second possibility of a collective decision by all weapons suppliers to stop delivering all types of weapons to the Gulf region does not appear to be pragmatic. As already noted, the motives and intentions of different weapons suppliers are not even incidentally identical. And therefore, each one would try to promote its own interests, in terms of the fulfilment of some military, commercial or political objective in the Gulf region.

The third possibility of an individual arms supplier restricting the supply of certain types of weapons to the arms race participants in the Gulf region may be presumed to have an unsteady effect on the course of the arms race in progress. It may help to reduce the intensity of the competition. Here again, it is altogether immaterial if such supplies as required by the competitors are not available from one source. If the affected parties have the political will and purchasing capability (which it is presumed that almost all the Gulf States are beginning to acquire) they can always have recourse to alternative sources of arms supply.

The fourth possibility of all the arms exporters collectively deciding to prohibit only certain types of weapons falling into the war arsenals of the Gulf States may be viewed as an important step towards regional arms control. But it could be considered only as a first step towards the objective of regional arms control. It should be followed by a collective agreement to stop both quantitative and qualitative increase in all types of weapons—an inconvenient proposition which every arms exporter would be eager to evade for their own interests.

b) *Co-operation Among Gulf States*

The success of any arms control negotiation would also greatly depend on the restraints the Gulf States themselves are prepared to have. Essentially there appears to be two basic prerequisites for arms control measures: conflict resolution and non-alignment.

i) *Conflict Resolution*

If the basic objective of regional arms control is to limit or to reduce the weapons acquired by regional powers, thereby creating a favourable climate of peace and security for all the States in a region, it can hardly be achieved unless grounds are prepared to fashion their politico-socio-economic relationship. The arms race as such portrays deeper symptoms of interstate conflicts. Conflicts, whether actual or potential would stimulate pursuit of weapons production or procurement. To induce regional conditions, conducive to the resolution of actual or latent conflicts by mutual cooperation and understanding, non-interference of any extra-regional power is a *sine qua non*. It does not necessarily follow that regional arms races will cease simultaneous with the resolution of all political conflicts between competing nations in the developing world. It would be more correct to say that regional arms races, including that of the Gulf region would cease if the regional powers agree among themselves to insulate the big powers from exploiting conflict situations in the developing regions.

The purposes of a policy of regional insulation of big powers would be three-fold: first, it prevents the big powers from becoming militarily allied with particular countries in the region, thereby increasing the danger of war among the big powers themselves; second, it will reduce the destructiveness of war within the region as it would restrict the flow of arms into the region. The destructions caused in the Iran-Iraq war would have been greater, had not the superpowers agreed to maintain a strict neutrality. The superpowers also discouraged transferring weapons to the local belligerents; and third, it would avoid the economic burdens of armaments.[38]

ii) Non-alignment

The second condition which might possibly help to find regional arms control agreements in the Gulf region is a vigorous political attempt by every individual state in the region to adhere to the cardinal principle of non-alignment. Iran's unilateral decision to wind up all foreign military bases and expel all foreign military personnel and the declaration to follow a non-aligned policy in the wake of the late Shah's ouster in early 1979, held out bright prospects for reducing armaments in the region. However, other circumstances induced the Khomeini regime to enter into a war with neighbouring Iraq, thereby spoiling the chances of arms reduction. The war has, on the other hand, encouraged countries like Saudi Arabia, Kuwait, Bahrain, Qatar, United Arab Emirates and the Sultanate of Oman to set up a joint military defence force. Its purpose was stated to be to defend the region from external threat, establish a joint air defence system, and coordinate arms purchases.[39] This would mean that the prospects of arms limitation in the region have diminished to some extent. For the moment, the Iran-Iraq war remains a major hurdle for any arms limitation proposal. The redeeming feature is that both Iran and Iraq are non-aligned nations and they cannot now easily be drawn into any alliance with the big powers.

Though countries like Saudi Arabia, Bahrain and Oman are independent sovereign States, their policies indicate a pro-western tilt, which would make them dependent on big powers. This very dependence on external powers impose difficulties for any arms control in the region. To make the point clearer: Assume that ABCDEF are the component states of a specific region in which A and B are aligned or are under the influence of external powers and CDEF are non-aligned. In such a regional system A and B could be said as unstable variables, responsible for an arms race at the regional level simply by virtue of being allies of extra regional powers. They are beneficiaries of the alliance system; they are given military assistance and economic aid from time to time, according to the increasing demands of the allies; military advisers and instructors are sent to the arms recipients to train and influence the force structure and defence policies.

The defence expenditure of CDEF—the non-aligned in the

region—swells higher in accordance with the free flow of weapons to A and B from their allies. Even if CDEF are prepared to agree upon some arms control measures at the regional level, all attempts would be thwarted because A and B are aligned to extra-regional powers and they are more often than not under their manipulation. A successful attempt at arms control could be made only when A and B are weaned away from the alliance or influence of the external powers. If A and B, by a deliberate design decide to be non-aligned and thus cooperate in the efforts of regional arms control, a probable scenario could be constructed in the following manner:

i) A and B would willingly send out all foreign military personnel sent in charge of training and instructing indigenous forces.

ii) A and B would reject all offers of further weapons supplies under the military assistance or military sales programme.

iii) A and B would also reject all economic aid tied to weapons transfers under the military assistance programme.

iv) A and B would not allow their defence policies to be tailored as an adjunct to the global defence policy of an external power.

v) A and B would eliminate all foreign bases and vestiges of neo-colonialism.

Once A and B have taken a bold step in breaking away from an alliance system and adopt a strictly non-aligned policy, the possibilities of regional cooperation among all the component states of the region appear to be bright.

First of all they could together devise a regional security system which should not be allowed to be propped up by an outside power.

Secondly, they could agree among themselves not to allow any extra-regional power to interfere with or influence their domestic affairs either politically, militarily, or commercially.

Thirdly, they could agree among themselves to effectively boycott the arms sellers in the region.

Fourthly, they could practically arrive at measures designed to limit, reduce and even finally eliminate highly destructive weapons from the region with the confidence that no extra-regional power ever would be able to influence the independent decisions of each State in the region.

Finally, they could collectively agree to divert their economic resources thus released, to joint ventures in various fields of trade and commerce and support one another in their socio-economic development.

Arms Control Proposal for the Gulf

The root-cause of the arms race in the Gulf region has been the excessive involvement of the arms supplying nations and their arms supply policies towards this region. The regional powers of the Gulf area should realise that without self-sufficiency in arms through their indigenous production, they cannot afford to sustain a policy of arms build-up, if not arms race, by almost exclusively relying on arms supplies from outside. Arms supply virtually invites big power interventionism which in turn only serves to aggravate the regional arms race, jeopardising regional security and stability. The menace of big power interventionism is to be eliminated from the Gulf region which alone can ensure the stability, security and peaceful economic development of the region.

In the light of the strategic problems just discussed above, the six principles as outlined by the Islamic foreign ministers conference held as early as in July 1975 should be considered as important. These principles reflected the thinking of the Gulf States for the initiation of a practical step towards regional arms control in the region. The six principles drawn up by the Islamic Ministers Conference are:[40]

1) Denial of the Gulf to foreign fleet;
2) Peaceful cooperation to guarantee free navigation;
3) Peaceful resolution of regional disputes;
4) Guarantees for the territorial integrity of Gulf States;
5) Denial of military bases for outside powers; and
6) General agreement on territorial waters between the littoral States.

A programme of regional arms control in the Gulf would possibly progress provided the following proposals are given serious consideration.

1. Efforts towards forming a Gulf Arms Control Conference should be made under the auspices of the United Nations at which a non-aggression pact could be negotiated and agreed upon to guarantee the territorial integrity and political independence of all the States of the region. A minimum force level for internal security could be maintained by each State according to common agreement.

2. The immediate task of dismantling military base of foreign powers in the region should be taken up under the supervision of the UN.

3. The military personnel made available to various States of the region, consequent to the military assistance programme or military sales programme, should be asked to return within a stipulated period.

4. A high level committee, representing all the States of the Gulf region should be constituted with a view to settle bilateral and multilateral disputes related to interstate boundaries and territorial waters between the littoral States. Those disputes which cannot be solved by this regional committee should be referred to the International Court of Justice for arbitration and its verdict shall be accepted as final.

5. The Gulf region should be declared a demilitarised zone and the movement of foreign fleet should be totally prohibited in the area by a UN resolution.

6. The heads of States of the Gulf region, in a joint action should boycott the arms sellers in the area and impose a total freeze of arms acquisition by all the States of the region.

Will such regional measures succeed without the active cooperation of the big powers? Some are of the view that such measures may not succeed without the support of the superpowers. According to Smithies, the big powers are in a position to ensure the working of a regional arrangement. No such arrangement will be possible unless the major powers are willing to accede to it; and if they are, they can provide the arrangement with its ultimate sanction.[41] As against this view, it may be observed that the overthrow of the late Shah of Iran in 1979, despite US backing and the consequent expulsion of all foreign military personnel and freezing of weapon purchases were all accomplished by a determined people, imbued with the spirit of independence and nationalism. Similar things can happen in other countries of the Gulf region. The crucial problem is to what extent the people of these countries are prepared to extricate themselves from the tentacles of neo-colonialism.

Any regional arms control arrangement therefore is a workable proposition even without superpower cooperation. No regional powers need solicit an ultimate sanction from external big powers, provided mutual understanding and cooperation exist among themselves. A good example of the regional co-operation to limit the flow of weapons from outside sources and to ensure regional peace and security in the unprecedented declaration of Ayacucho, signed by eight Latin American countries,[42] on December 9, 1974.

They declared their intention "to create the conditions which will make possible the effective limitations of armaments and an end to their acquisition for offensive purposes so that all possible resources may be devoted to the economic and social development of every country in Latin America."[43] A similar move by the Gulf States would most likely draw international recognition and respect from all quarters. The precise question is whether or not all the States in the Gulf region are willing to exercise their sovereign rights and give shape to a self-reliant domestic and foreign policy which, on the one hand, would be conducive to consolidate their own regional peace and security, and, on the other hand, lessen tension and insecurity, generally visible in international relations today.

REFERENCES

1 Gunnar Skagestad, "Small States in International Politics: A Polar—Political Perspective," *Nordic Journal of International Politics*, Vol. I, 1974, p. 187.
2 A.N. Kaliadin, "Problems of Disarmament Research," *Journal of Peace Research*, Vol. I, 1972, p. 238.

3 George Thayer, *The War Business* (London: Weidenfeld and Nicolson, 1969), p. 351.

4 Geoffrey Kemp, *Classification of Weapons Systems and Force Designs in Less Developed Country Environments: Implications for Arms Transfer Policies* (Cambridge, M.I.T.C./70-3, February 1970), p. 207.

5 Philip Noel-Baker, *The Arms Race* (London: Atlantic Book Publishing Co., 1958), p. 31; see also Nicholas A. Sims, *Approaches to Disarmament* (Panjim: Printwell Press, 1975) p.14.

6 *The New Encyclopaedia Britanica*, Vol. I, 1974, p. 529.

7 Frederick H. Hartmann, *The Relations of Nations* (New York: Macmillan, 1967), p. 266.

8 For a historical and analytical account of the Rush-Bagot Agreement, see James Eayrs, "Arms Control on the Great Lakes", *Disarmament and Arms Control* (Oxford), Vol. 2, 1964, pp. 373-402.

9 Complete universal disarmament as a road to world order is not only utopian but would fail to reach the desired destination, see Raymond L. Wise, *Order Please* (Brooklyn: Central Book Company, 1970), p. 255.

10 O. Grinyov, "Soviet Efforts for Disarmament," *International Affairs* (Moscow), n. 12, December 1967, p. 65.

11 *Ibid.* For an account of an active disarmament policy, pursued by the Soviet Union at the United Nations along with the support of other socialist countries, see V. Izaraelyan, "The United Nations and the Curbing of the Arms Race," *International Affairs* (Moscow), n. 3, March 1976, pp. 54-62.

12 B. Graefrath, "Disarmament and International Law," *Scientific World*, Vol. XVI, n. 1, 1972, p. 8; see also Andrew Martin, *Legal Aspects of Disarmament* (London: Stevens, 1963).

13 "A change of the world structure would come closest to a built-in control, provided the change were towards a more just, equal and peaceful world," see Jan Oberg, "Arms Trade with the Third World as an Aspect of Imperialism," *Journal of Peace Research*, Vol. XII, n. 3, 1975, p. 230.

14 E.H. Carr, *International Relations between the Two Wars, 1919-1939*, (London: Macmillan Ltd., 1967), pp. 183-90.

15 For a brief but lucid exposition of the success and failures of disarmament, see Hans J. Morgenthau, *Politics Among Nations* (Calcutta: The Indian Press Pvt. Ltd., 1973), pp. 383-406.

16 SIPRI, *Arms Trade with the Third World* (Middlesex: Penguin, 1975), p. 299.

17 *Ibid.*

18 *Ibid.*

19 For a very good study on international trade in armaments and their related problems, see Thayer, n. 3.

20 For brief details of these treaties, see *Arms Control Agreements*

1959-1972 (Washington, D.C.: Arms Control and Disarmament Agency Publication, 1963-72), pp 1-15.

21 Hans J. Morgenthau, n. 15, p. 404; see also, "President Carter Urges Increased Defense Spending," (*USICA, Official Text* (American Centre, New Delhi), December 13, 1979.

22 Kenneth E. Boulding, "Economic Implications of Arms Control," in Donald G. Brennan, ed., *Arms Control, Disarmament, and National Security* (New York: George Braziller, Inc., 1961), p. 153.

23 Robert M. Lawrence, *Arms Control and Disarmament: Practice and Promise* (Minneapolis: Burgess Publishing Company, 1972), p. viii.

24 Thomas C. Schelling and Morton A. Halperin, *Strategy and Arms Control* (New York: Twentieth Century Fund, 1961), p. 2; see also Robert R. Bowie, "Basic Requirements of Arms Control," in Brennan, n. 22, p. 43.

25 Jeremy J. Stone, *Containing the Arms Race* (Cambridge: MIT Press, 1966), pp. 13-20.

26 Amitai Etzioni, *The Hard Way to Peace* (New York: Crowell-Collier, 1962, p. 114; see also William C. Foster, "Technological Peace," *Impact of Science on Society*, Vol. XXII, n. 3, 1972. Reprinted in *Strategic Digest* (IDSA, New Delhi), Vol. II, n. 8, August 1972, p. 30. US Ambassador to the Committee on Disarmament in Geneva said that nuclear deterrence "must remain a key element in maintaining stability and peace." See "US Statement on Arms Control," *USICA, Official Text* (American Centre, New Delhi), 8 April 1981.

27 William Gutteridge, *Military Institution and Power in the New States* (London: Pall Mall Press, 1964), p. 70.

28 Amelia C. Leiss, *Arms Transfer to Less Developed Countries* (Cambridge: MIT C/70-1, February 1970), p. 8.

29 Andrew Mack, "The Undercover Arms Race," *New Scientist*, Vol. 60, n. 874, November 19, 1973, p. 638; it is argued that arms control is purported to be a middle ground between an unrestrained competition of armaments and complete disarmament. See Richard J. Barnet, *Who wants Disarmament* (Boston: Beacon Press, 1960), p. 99.

30 *New Perspectives on the Persian Gulf:* Hearings, Sub-committee on the Near East and South Asia, Committee on Foreign Affairs, House of Representatives, 93rd Congress, First Session, June 6, July 17, 23, 24 and November 28, 1973 (Washington, D.C.: US Government Printing Office, 1973), p. 73.

31 Thayer, n. 3, p. 369.

32 The Concept of built-in-mechanism of arms control reflects the view that military build-up may help to reduce the prospects for conflict among local countries. See Geoffrey Kemp, "The New Strategic Map," *Survival*, Vol. XIX, n. 2, March/April, 1973, p. 53.

33 Leiss, n. 28, p. 18.

34 *Asian Defence Journal*, n. 3, June 1976, p. 69.
35 Geoffrey Kemp, "Arms Traffic and Third World Conflicts," *International Conciliation*, n. 577, March 1970, p. 5.
36 IstvanK ende, *Bulletin of Peace Proposals* (Oslo), n. 3, 1973, p. 205.
37 *Documents on Disarmament, 1970*, pp. 3, 32 and 406-8, Statement by United States Representative (Leonard) to the Conference of the Committee on Disarmament: Restraints on Conventional Armaments, 26 August 1971. CCD/PV. 533, pp. 5-16; see also CCD/PV. 491, p. 27 and CCD/PV. 501, p. 17.
38 Arthur Smithies, "Regional Arms Limitation," in David H. Frisch, ed., *Arms Reduction Program and Issues* (New York: The Twentieth Century Fund, Inc., 1961), pp. 76-77.
39 Harish Chandola, "Six Nations Enter into Gulf Security Pact," *Indian Express* (Cochin), 29 January 1982.
40 *Strategic Survey 1975*, 1976, p. 87.
41 Smithies, n. 38, p. 78.
42 The Signatories to the declaration of Ayacucho are: Argentina, Bolivia, Chile, Colombia, Ecuador, Panama, Peru and Venezuela.
43 Quoted in *Arms Control Today* (Washington, D.C.), Vol. 5, n. 9, September 1975, p. 2; for the full text of the Declaration of Ayacucho, see "Eight Latin American Governments Sign Declaration Aimed at Limiting Armaments," *UN Monthly Chronicle*, March 1975, pp. 54-57.

7

Conclusions

I

Since World War II, a plethora of modern weapon technologies provided a rocket-boost to the gigantic arms industries of the developed nations of the world. Governments in those countries encourage and promote arms sales and even provide generous credits and other financial incentives to further the arms trade. As Ruth Sivard has observed, the most buoyant sector of the world economy is the arms business today. Annual sales of military equipment, for both nuclear and conventional war now amount to over $120 billion a year.[1] As a result, not only the industrialised nations armed to the teeth, but the developing nations which already account for a quarter of the world's expenditure on military equipment, are also in the process of intensive militarisation.

Besides, the arms supply policies of the donor nations have created a climate of competitive arms procurement in the developing world, leading to regional arms races. The quantitative and qualitative expansion of the international trade in conventional arms is one of the most significant indicators of an evident international trend towards increased global militarisation.[2]

II

In trying to generate regional arms races and maintain their momentum, the arms suppliers have various motives. They are recognised as political, hegemonic or economic-industrial. These motives may not be mutually exclusive and indeed emphasis may be laid on one or the other at different points of time.

Political-hegemonic motivations became evident when the arms suppliers attempt to influence and mould the domestic and foreign policies of recipient states to suit their interests. Developing nations might be provided with weapons to protect them from potential external or internal threats to security. Sophisticated arms may be infused into particular regions with a view to stabilise artificial intra-regional balances or to maintain a perferred local elite in power or to exclude adverse foreign influences. In order to ensure preferred political behaviour by the recipients, the donor country may utilise the initiation, reduction or resumption or stoppages of arms supplies and provision of technical personnel, training, spares and ancillaries, etc., as political leverages. In other words, arms supplies could be utilised as an instrument of coercive and persuasive diplomacy.

Political considerations and superpower rivalries are, no doubt, major factors in arms transfers, but equally important are the economic-industrial or commercial motives of the supplier nations. It often happens that the armed forces in arms manufacturing countries may be unable to adsorb the entire arms production. In any case, discarded obsolescent weapons are exported to developing nations when new generations of weapons are produced. Arms exports would permit longer production runs, reduce unit costs, ensure larger employment of the work-force, and satisfy domestic pressures. After the oil crisis of 1970s the arms exports enabled, to a great extent, the recycling of the oil wealth and thereby, a balancing of trade deficits.

III

The motivations of the arms importing countries, are varied

and more complex. Firstly, military power is said to be an attribute of national sovereignty. With the dawn of decolonisation, the liberated nations found themselves militarily weak. Lingering historical animosities and unresolved disputes have influenced the security perceptions of national elites and strengthened the demand for arms. The increasing power of military elites in many of the new nations added fuel to the fire.

Secondly, arms purchases are necessitated by the lack of indigenous defence production facilities. Even if some of the developing nations have partially succeeded in producing ships, aircraft, missiles and armoured fighting vehicles, their production is limited to older generation weaponry. However, if the latest and sophisticated weapons are considered necessary for meeting perceived security threats, recourse to major arms producers cannot be avoided.

Thirdly, the influence of the military elites in the decision-making process relating to weapons acquisition cannot be minimised. Some developing nations have came under military rule; while in some others, the ruling elites remain in power with the support of the military forces. The influence of the military establishments often leads to exaggerated assessments of arms requirements. Sometimes, these purchases are associated with questionable practices. Further, arms procurement serves to enhance the power of the military which is often used to suppress popular aspirations. Arms, in such cases become instruments in the hands of repressive regimes to hold on to power. The trend towards the rise of military dictatorships is thereby strengthened and so is the correlation between such regimes and the arms supplying nations. Even in democratic countries, the armed forces always make demands for acquiring new weapon systems to which generally the civilian authorities acquiesce lest they be accused of neglecting defence.

Fourthly, the possession of sophisticated weapons is said to confer prestige at home and abroad. Hence, some of the developing countries spend vital resources on weapon purchases. Even if the transferred weapon systems cannot be operated by local personnel, prestige considerations have generated an increased demand for such arms imports.

Lastly, arms procurement policies often reflect a basic desire to overinsure against real or imagined threats. Fundamentally, the security threat which a country visualises is the result of its elite perceptions. A tendency to exaggerate such threat perceptions is common because military planning is based on the hypothesis that, while hoping for the best, it is prudent to develop military capabilities to deal with the worst situations. Since military preparations against potential threats by one country tend to affect the threat perceptions of the neighbouring countries, a chain reaction starts, accelerating the arms race further. The result is the creation of a climate, conducive to international arms trade.

IV

An intensive regional arms race is possible only through a military alliance, explicit or implicit, with either of the super-powers because only these are in a position to supply arms consistently for a longer duration of time. The intensity, duration and capability of such an arms race are conditioned more by the motives and intentions of the donor country than by the will and vigour of the recipient country. It cannot, however, be argued that regional arms races are an integral part of a global arms build-up phenomenon in which the super-powers play the leading role, followed by the other industrially advanced nations who have also sizeable arms industries.

The donor country is not always capable of controlling, even influencing the actions of the recipient nations. The donor country may cripple the latter's war making power, by shutting off supply of spares or by refusing to replenish losses. But such acts of refusal generate political reactions which destabilise both the recipient regime as well as the relationship between the recipient and the donor.

The analysis of the role of the big powers in the military build-up of the developing nations has demonstrated that regional arms races are the by-products of great power involvement in the politics of developing nations. Apart from their pernicious effects on the regional security, they tend to destabilise a whole region for a long period. It is immaterial whether a region is strategically less important or not. Its immediate consequence has been to induct big power rivalry into a region. The intention is to exploit the economic backwardness and political instability by diverting domestic resources and energy to proxy arms races to serve big power interests.

None can deny that one of the deleterious consequences of arms transfers to the developing countries, is the distortion of economic priorities and the arrest of economic growth.

Regional tensions are also greatly intensified. Induction of more arms do not necessarily increase the security of a developing nation. On the contrary, there is a greater risk of national autonomy being eroded. For, along with the arms enter the military advisers and foreign technicians for operating the new weapon systems. Military advisers can act as levers of subversion in the host country.

Besides, it becomes necessary at times for the local personnel to go abroad to the arms supplier countries for acquiring the necessary training and skill to operate the imported weapons. In that process, they get indoctrinated in militant traditions and are encouraged to retain military links. Military advisers reinforce these links further by encouraging imports of high technology weapons, and thus perpetuate the recipients' dependence. Viewed in this perspective, international tranfer of arms may be seen as an instrument for achieving neo-colonialist objectives by accentuating dependency patterns.

It has been said that the military and police programme of the US have political and ideological objectives. These programmes seek "to win friends and influence people who are destined to be in power in their respective countries. The ideological direction of these programmes has been to inculcate these participants with negative enemy images of communism, neutralism, leftist revolution, forces of disruption, revolutionary ideas, political dissidents, insurgents, extremists, radicals, ultra-nationalists, and political instability in general."[3] According to Andre Frank, by and large, the western and particularly US military training and assistance programmes have been eminently successful in introducing an armed fifth column to defend 'Western Values" within the societies of the Third World.[4]

V

The multilateral arms race in the Persian Gulf region has certain special characteristics. It is not so conspicuous as the arms race between the superpowers. In the case of Gulf countries, their annual military budgets, the GNP percentage of military expenditure and other barometers indicating the arms race do not reflect parallel arms race. It is a more subtle form of arms race. All the same, it can be seen and its effects can be felt. The ever increasing stockpile of highly sophisticated weapons and equipment in each one of the Gulf countries is evidence of the typical regional arms race.

In the multilateral arms race, Iran stood in the front line. Iran's participation in the alliance system of the United States in the fifties enabled it to have large quantities of US weapons and military assistance. To offset Iran's military build-up, Iraq took initiative to acquire arms from the Soviet Union. When petro-dollars began to flow into the Gulf as a result of the 1973 oil-price-hike. Saudi Arabia, Kuwait, the UAE, Bahrain, Qatar and Oman started vying with one another to purchase the most sophisticated weapons, thereby giving a sudden spurt to the militarisation of the region. The ambition of the late Shah of Iran to dominate the Gulf coupled with the US strategy of making him a surrogate to safeguard western interests in the area added momentum to the arms race, giving Iran a preponderant position. The strategy of building up the Iranian forces that would match the combined forces of all the other countries of the region vanished as a result of the Iranian revolution in late 1978. The Khomeini regime put an abrupt end to the Western arms market in Iran. Since then, Iran lost the race and this was convincingly proved in its recent war with Iraq.

However, it is a proxy arms race because the major sources of the arms supplies are the big powers particularly the United States, Britain, France and the Soviet Union. Once these supplies are stopped or withheld, the arms race would automatically come to an end. This reveals the artificial character of the regional arms race which is entirely dependent on foreign interventionist powers. Whereas the superpowers have complete control over the global arms race which is entirely of their own making, the regional arms race is propped up and manipulated from outside. Needless to say a global arms race is characterised by its nuclear component and by its enormous cost. But the regional arms race is still conventional and less expensive. Symptoms like tension, distrust, suspicion, fear and regional destabilisation are common for both the global and regional arms races.

It is evident that the regional or local powers are incapable of sustaining a continuous and costly military build-up. However, their mutual hostility drives them into the open arms of the weapon producers on whom they depend very much.

VI

The hypothesis that imported arms would often maintain regional balance of forces and would prevent local wars has been disproved by the ongoing Iran-Iraq war. What is deplorable is that the competitive arms build-up by these countries over a decade has drained huge funds for defence which could have been better utilised for socio-economic developments. The war threatens to impoverish these nations and deprive them of their productive resources.

The arms suppliers have nothing to lose because of the war. As a matter of fact, local wars in the developing world are often encouraged by the big powers. The possibility of local or regional war turning into a major nuclear war is very remote. This is because the big powers have defined in advance the escalation threshold of such third world wars. The main thrust of the regional arms race is to maintain the conventional character of regional conflicts since the objectives of regional arms race are normally confined to local issues. Even with superpower intervention, the basic conventional character of a regional war between developing nations does not change. There is a precise reason for this. As the great powers are the main weapon suppliers, they can, to a very great extent, influence the course of regional wars and maintain such wars at the conventional level. However, a local war may be of a low intensity or high intensity depending on the type of sophisticated arms introduced into the war. This will entirely depend on the arms suppliers. As a corrollary, one could assume that a regional arms race permitted and manipulated by the superpowers, would be of a low intensity or high intensity depending on their arms supply policies, and their economic, political and strategic interests.

VII

No doubt, there are many domestic and regional problems in the Persian Gulf, potentially threatening regional security and stability. Many disputes among the States of the region have been successfully settled by the regional powers themselves without any intervention by outside powers. However, it is not impossible for external powers to gain access and influence in this area by reactivising frozen issues. This has been the style of functioning of the big powers in the past. Can the United States with its overwhelming presence act differently now?

Regional security and stability of the Gulf region are best ensured provided all the regional powers are actively involved in the pursuit of such aims without the intervention of outside powers. An orderly development of the Gulf region is to be the primary concern of the littoral States of the Gulf and it is to be left to them to plan and execute their development programmes without outside interference. Any attempt on the part of outside powers to influence the policies of development of the littoral States by introducing foreign developmental models would only serve to aggravate the problems of these developing nations.

The presence of one external power within a regional system—however disparate the nature of that system—tends to create destabilising conditions by inviting other powers into the region. It may evoke fear or suspicion among the regional powers about the interventionist policies of foreign powers. Would it be possible now for the Gulf Sheikdoms to devote themselves to the task of nation-building against the background of the intimidating presence of the United States?

Unfortunately, the developing nations of the Gulf region are the victims of their own making, though one is inclined to blame the interventionist policies of the big powers. Perhaps, these nations could have turned their attention to the serious problems of development, had they not been influenced by these policies. Keeping themselves strictly equidistant from the superpowers and following a non-aligned stance in world politics would appear most beneficial to them in the task of nation-building and progress rather than cultivating one or the other of the big powers to boost their war arsenals with the latest weapons. The Iran-Iraq war should remind all the Gulf States that no local war can be won with imported arms without their being fully assimilated into the indigenous military infrastructure. Nor can such wars solve contentious political issues ensuring peace, security and stability of the region.

VIII

The necessity for arms control in the Gulf region is evident. It may be argued that most developing nations would be reluctant to adopt bold arms control measures without first evolving some mechanism for regional conflict control, underscoring a coherent and integrated security policy for all States within a regional system. This argument is fallacious, except that it serves to justify and encourage the arms transfer policies of big powers. Firstly, it is hardly possible to contrive a stereotype, agreeable mechanism for regional conflict control which would satisfy all. Secondly, the establishment of a mechanism for regional conflict control as a pre-condition or *sine qua non* tends to restrict the freedom of individual States to initiate at will unilateral arms control measures.

Since the root-cause of all major conflicts in the developing regions of the world has always been the involvement of the big powers and their arms supply policies, it is important to pre-empt local conflicts through the introduction of some form of arms control measures. It might be asked what sort of arms control measures can be envisaged in the context of regional and local rivalries.

One measure that could be thought of is self-reliance in the matter of arms production rather than a dependent policy of procuring arms from outside. This would enable them to evolve their own arms policies. A second arms control measure could probably be to agree bilaterally or otherwise not to enter into an arms race either by direct arms supply deal with others or by joining any military alliance. A final 'radical' measure would be for the developing nations to discuss the common problems related to regional arms build-up and draw up mutually beneficial agreements which would include enforcing an effective boycott of big power arms sale in specific regions. For, the basic pre-requisite for the realisation of regional peace, security, stability and steady economic growth is the total abolition of the "arms sellers markets" from the developing regions of the world.

REFERENCES

1 Ruth Leger Sivard, *World Military and Social Expenditures*, 1979 (Virginia: World Priorities, 1979), p. 5.
2 *The United Nations Disarmament Yearbook* (New York), Vol. 4, 1979, p. 275.
3 M.D. Wolpin, *Military Dependency Vs Development in the Third World* (New York: State University of New York, Department of Political Science (Mimeo), p. 8.
4 Andre Gunder Frank, "Arms Economy and Warfare in the Third World," *Third World Quarterly* (London), Vol. II, n. 2, April 1980, p. 229.

Selected Bibliography

Primary Sources

"Agreement of Cooperation between the Government of United States of America and the Imperial Government of Iran, 5 March 1959," United Nations, *Treaty Series*, Vol. 327, pp. 277-83.

Hussain, Saddam (President of the Republic of Iraq), *Inauqurating the Foreign Ministers Conference of the Islamic Countries* (Baghdad), 1st-6th June 1981.

Iraq, Embassy in India, *Selections from the Iraqi-Iranian Dispute* (New Delhi, 1981).

——, Ministry of Foreign Affairs, *The Iraqi-Iranian Conflict: Documentary Dossier* (Baghdad, January 1981).

Kuwait, Printing and Publishing Department, *The Kuwait-Iraqi Crisis*, August 1961.

United Nations, *Report of the Secretary General, Economic and Social Subsequences of the Arms Race and of Military Expenditures* (New York, 1972).

US Cong., Committee on Congress, Subcommittee on the Near East and South Asia, 1st sess., Hearings, *New Perspectives on the Persian Gulf* (Washington: GPO, 1973).

US, 96th Cong., 1st sess., Joint Economic Committee, *Economic Consequences of the Revolution in Iran: A Compendium of Papers Submitted to the Joint Economic Committee, November 19, 1979* (Washington: GPO, 1980).

US, Department of State, "Foreign Policy Challenges in the 1980," *Current Policy No. 161*, April 12, 1980.

——, "Middle East: Progress in the Peace Negotiations," *Current Policy No. 129*, January 17, 1980.

——, "The U.S. Course in a Changing World," *Current Policy No. 159*, April 10, 1980.

US House, 92nd Cong., 2nd sess., Committee on Foreign Affairs, Subcommittee on Europe and the Middle East, Hearings, *Review of Recent Developments in the Middle East, 1979* (Washington: GPO, 1979).

US House, 95th Cong., 2nd sess., Committee on International Relations, *Peace in the Middle East: A Delicate Balance, Report of a Study Mission to the Mideast and Ireland, January 2 to January 20, 1978* (Washington: GPO, 1978).

US House, 92nd Cong., 2nd sess., Subcommittee on Foreign Affairs, Hearings, *U.S. Interests in and Policy towards the Persian Gulf* (Washington: GPO, 1972).

US Senate, 96th Cong., 1st sess., Committee on Foreign Relations, *Prospect for Multilateral Arms Export Restraint* (Washington: GPO, 1979).

——, 96th Cong., 2nd sess., Committee on Foreign Relations, Report, *US Conventional Arms Transfer Policy* (Washington: GPO, 1980).

SECONDARY SOURCES

Abdullah, Muhammad Morsy, *The United Arab Emirates: A Modern History*, London: Croom Helm Ltd., 1978.

Adie, W.A.C., *Oil Politics and Seapower, the Indian Ocean Vortex*, New York: Crane, Russak, 1975.

Ahmad, Maqbul, *Indo-Arab Relations*, New Delhi: Indian Council for Cultural Relations, 1969.

Amirie, Abbas, ed., *The Persian Gulf and Indian Ocean in International Politics*, Tehran: Institute for International Political and Economic Studies, 1975.

Barnaby, Frank and Huisken, Ronald, ed., *Arms Uncontrolled*, Cambridge: Harvard University Press, 1975.

Be'eri, Eliezer, *Army Officers in Arab Politics and Society*, New York: Frederick A. Praeger, 1970.

Beling, Willard A., ed., *King Faisal and the Modernization of Saudi Arabia*, London: Croom Helm, 1980.

Bloomfield, Lincoln P., and Leiss Amelia C., *Controlling Small Wars: A Strategy for the 1970s*, New York: Alfred A Knopf, 1967.

Bramson, Leon, and Goethals, George, W., ed., *War*, New York: Basic Books, 1964.

Brezhnev, L.I., *On Problems of Peace and Security*, Bombay: Allied Publishers, 1973.

Burrell, R.M., and Cottrell, Alvin J., *Iran, the Arabian Peninsula and the Indian Ocean*, New York: National Information Centre, 1972.

Burton, John W., *Peace Theory: Preconditions of Disarmament*, New York: Alfred A. Knopf, 1962.

Campbell, John C., *Defence of the Middle East: Problems of American Policy*, New York: Harper and Brothers, 1960.

Carr, E.H., *International Relations Between the Two Wars, 1919-1939*, London: Macmillan 1967.

Coffin, Frank M., *Witness for Aid*, Boston: Houghton Mifflin, 1964.

Crabb, Cecil V., *American Foreign Policy in the Nuclear Age*, New York: Row, Peterson and Co., 1960.

Duignan, Peter and Rabushka, Alvin, eds., *The United States in the 1980s*, New Delhi: Kalyani Publishers, 1980.

Falk, Richard A., Medlowitz, Saul H., eds., *Strategy of World Order, Vol. IV*, New York: World Law Fund, 1967.

Fisher, Sydney Nettleton, *The Middle East*, New York: Alfred A. Knopf, 1968.

Frank, Jerome D., *Sanity and Survival*, New York: Alfred A. Knopf and Random House, 1967.

Frank, Van der Linden, *Nixon's Quest for Peace*, Washington: D.C.: Robert B. Luce, 1972.

Frisch, David H., ed., *Arms Reduction Program and Issues*, New York: Twentieth Century Fund, 1961.

Fulbright, William J., *Prospects of the West*, Cambridge, Mass: Harvard University Press, 1963.

Gross, Feliks, *World Politics and Tension Areas*, New York: New York University Press, 1966.

Gutteridge, William, *Military Institutions and Power in the New States*, London: Pall Mall Press, 1964.

Hammond, Paul Y., and Alexander, Sidney S., eds., *Political Dynamics in the Middle East*, New York: American Elsevier, 1972.

Hartmann, Frederick H., *The Relations of Nations*, New York: Macmillan, 1967.

Selected Bibliography   209

Hawley, Donald, *The Trucial States*, London: George Allen and Unwin, 1970.

Hitti, Philip K., *History of the Arabs*, London: Macmillan, 1970.

Holbread, Carsten, ed., *Super Powers and World Order*, Canberra: Australian National University Press, 1971.

Holsti, K.J., *International Politics*, New Jersey: Prentice-Hall 1967.

Hovey, Harold A., *United States Military Assistance: A Study of Policies and Practices*, New York: Praeger, 1965.

Huntington, Samuel P., *Political Order in Changing Societies*, New Haven: Yale University Press, 1968.

Hurewitz, J.C., *Middle East Politics: The Military Dimension*, New York: Frederick A. Praeger, 1969.

Ismael, Tareq Y., *Governments and Politics of the Contemporary Middle East*, Illinois: Dorsey Press, 1970.

Kelidar, Abbas, *The Integration of Modern Iraq*, London: Croom Helm, 1979.

Kelly, J.B., *Britain and the Persian Gulf, 1795-1880*, London: Oxford University Press, 1968.

Kennedy, Gavin, *The Military in the Third World*, London: Gerald Duckworth, 1974.

Kerr, Malcolm H., *The Arab Cold War*, London: Oxford University Press, 1971.

Khalifa, Ali Mohammed, *The United Arab Emirates: Unity in Fragmentation*, Colorado: Westview Press, 1979.

Knorr, Klaus, *The Power of Nations*, New York: Basic Books, 1975.

Kothari, Rajni, *Footsteps into the Future*, New Delhi: Orient Longman, 1974.

Laqueur, Walter Z., ed., *The Middle East in Transition*, London: Routledge and Kodgan Paul, 1958.

Lawrence, Robert M., *Arms Control and Disarmament: Practice and Promise*, Minneapolis: Burgess Publishing, 1972.

Leiss, Amelia C., *Arms Transfers to Less Developed Countries*, Cambridge: M.I.T. C/70-1, February 1970.

Lerche, Charles O., and Said, Abdul A., *Concepts of International Politics*, Englewood Cliffs: Prentice-Hall, 1964.

Luard, Evan, *Conflict and Peace in the Modern International System*, London: University of London Press, 1970.

Malone, Joseph J., *The Arab Lands of Western Asia*, New Jersey: Prentice-Hall, 1973.

Mansfield, Peter, *The Middle East: A Political and Economic Survey*, London: Oxford University Press, 1973.

Marlowe, John, *Arab Nationalism and British Imperialism*, London: The Cresset Press, 1961.

Millar, T.B., *Soviet Policies in the Indian Ocean Area*, Canberra: Australian National University Press, 1970.

Morgenthau, Hans J., *Politics Among Nations*, Calcutta: Indian Press, 1973.

Myes, Kenneth A., ed., NATO, *The Next Thirty Years*, Colorado: Westview Press, 1980.

Narayan, B.K., *Lessons and Consequences of the October War*, New Delhi: Vikas, 1977.

Noel-Baker, Philip, *The Arms Race: A Programme for World Disarmament*, London: Oceana, 1958.

Northedge, F.S., ed., *The Use of Force in International Relations*, London: Faber and Faber, 1974.

Peterson, J.E., *Oman in the Twentieth Century*, London: Croom Helm, 1978.

Pruitt, Dean G., and Snyder, Richard C., eds., *Theory and Research on the Cause of War*, Englewood Cliffs: Prentice-Hall, 1969.

Pursell, Carrol W., *The Military Industrial Complex*, New York: Harper and Row, 1972.

Ramazani, Rouhollah K., *The Persian Gulf: Iran's Role*, Charlottesville: University Press of Virginia, 1972.

Refson, Jacob S., *US Military Training and Advice: Implications for Arms Transfer Policies*, Cambridge: MIT, C/170-4, February 1970.

Richardson, Lewis F., *Arms and Insecurity*, Pittsburg: The Boxwood Press, 1960.

Rubin, Barry, *Paved with Good Intentions*, New York: Oxford University Press, 1980.

Sarkesian, Sam C., ed., *The Military-Industrial Complex: A Reassessment*, Vol. II, Beverly Hills: Sage Publications, 1972.

Schelling, Thomas C., and Halperin, Morton A., *Strategy and Arms Control*, New York: Twentieth Century Fund, 1961.

Sid-Ahamed, Mohammed, *After the Guns Fall Silent*, London: Croom Helm, 1976.

Singer, Marshall R., *Weak States in a World of Powers*, New York: The Free Press, 1972.

Sivard, Ruth Leger, *World Military and Social Expenditures, 1980*, Virginia: World Priorities, 1980.

Stoessinger, J.C., *The Might of Nations*, New York: Random House, 1965.

Stone, Jeremy J., *Containing the Arms Race*, Cambridge: M.I.T., 1966.

Stone, Julius, *Legal Controls of International Conflicts*, London: Stevens, 1959.

Sveics, V.V., *Small Nation Survival*, New York: Exposition Press, 1970.

Sykes, Percy, *A History of Persia*, London: Macmillan, 1963.

Tahtinen, Dale R., *Arms in the Persian Gulf*, Washington, D.C.: American Enterprise Institute of Public Policy Research, 1978.

Thayer, George, *The War Business: The International Trade in Armaments*, New York: Simon and Schuster, 1969.

Theberge, James D., *The Soviet Presence in Latin America*, New York: Crane, Russak, 1974.

Tzabar, Shimon, *The White Flag Principle*, London: Allen Lane, 1972.

Van Doorn, Jacques, *Armed Forces and Society*, The Hague: Mouton, 1968.

Wainhouse, David W., et. al., *Arms Control Agreements: Design for Verification and Organization*, Baltimore: John Hopkins Press, 1968.

Wells, Donald A., *The War Myth*, New York: Western Publishing, 1967.

Wilson, Arnold T., *The Persian Gulf: A Historical Sketch from the Earliest Times to the Beginning of the Twentieth Century*, London: George Allen and Unwin, 1928.

Windsor, Philip, *Oil*, London: Maurice Temple Smith, 1975.

Wise, Raymond L., *Order Please*, Brooklyn: Central Book Co., 1970.

Wright, Quincy, *A Study of War*, Chicago: University of Chicago Press, 1965.

Yarmolinsky, Adam, *The Military Establishment: Its Impact on American Society*, New York: Harper and Row, 1971.

Young, Oran R., *The Politics of Force*, Princeton: Princeton University Press, 1968.

ARTICLES

Abbot, George C., "Size, Viability, Nationalism and Politico-Economic Development," *International Journal* (Toronto), vol. 25, 1969-70, p. 54.

Abrams, Paul, "Saudis Want US Missiles," *Jewish Observer and Middle East Review* (London), vol. 25, no. 26, 25 June 1976, p. 8.

Afaf, Mohammad, "The Drives Behind Defence Spending," *Islamic Defence Review* (London), vol. 6, no. 1, 1981, p. 38.

Akins, James E., "The Oil Crisis: This Time the Wolf is Here," *Foreign Affairs* (New York), vol. 51, no. 3, April 1973, pp. 462-90.

Albrecht, U., Ernst, D., Lock P. and Wulf, H., "Militarization, Arms Transfer and Arms Production in Peripheral Countries," *Journal of Peace Research* (Oslo), vol. 12, no. 3, 1975, p. 197.

Alhegelan, Faisal, "The Economic Policy of Saudi Arabia," *Vital Speeches of the Day* (New York), vol. 47, no. 5, 15 December 1980, p. 158.

Andreasyan, R., "Iran-Iraq: The Oil Aspect of the Conflict," *New Times* (Moscow), no. 41, October 1980, p. 8.

Aubert, Vilhelm, "Competition and Dissensions: Two Types of Conflict and Conflict Resolution," *Journal of Conflict Resolution* (London), vol. 7, no. 1, 1963, p. 26.

Avery, Peter, "The Many Faces of Iran's Foreign Policy," *New Middle East* (London), no. 47, August 1972, p. 19.

Bailey, Robert, "Superpower War Games Muddy Gulf Waters," *Middle East Economic Digest* (London), 28 March 1980, p. 8.

Beckett, Brian B., "Giants in the Gulf," *Middle East International* (London), no. 69, March 1977, p. 27.

Bedore, James M., "Saudi Arabia: Greatness Thrust Upon Them," *Middle East International* (London), no. 79, January 1978, pp. 14-15.

Beedham, Brian, "Look Beyond the Oil," *The Economist* (London), 17-23 May 1975, p. 11.

Ben-Dor, Gabriel, "Civilization of Military Regimes in the Arab World," *Armed Forces and Society*, vol. 1 no. 3, Spring 1975, p. 317.

Binder, Leonard, "The Middle East Crisis: A Trial Balance," *Bulletin of the Atomic Scientists* (Chicago), vol. 23, no. 7, September 1967, p. 7.

Borchgrave, Arnaud, "Colossus of the Oil Lanes," *Newsweek* (New York), 21 May 1973, p. 41.

Bowles, Chester, "America and Russia in India," *Foreign Affairs* (New York), vol. 49, no. 4, July 1971, p. 636.

Burhop, E.H.S., "ABC Weapons, Disarmament and the Responsibility of the Scientist," *Scientific World* (London), vol. 16, no. 1, 1972, pp. 5-6.

Burrell, R.M., "Rebellion in Dhofar," *New Middle East* (London), March 1972, pp. 55-58.

Burrell, R.M., "Iran in Search of Greater Responsibilities," *New Middle East* (London), no. 49, October 1972, p. 28.

Burton, John W., "Regional Disarmament: South-East Asia," *Disarmament and Arms Control* (Oxford), vol. 1, 1963, p. 168.

Carrey, Jane Perry Clark, "Iran and Control of Its Oil Resources," *Political Science Quarterly* (New York), vol, 89, no. 1, March 1974, p. 157.

Charlfont, Lord, "Russia and the Indian Ocean: New Attitudes to Sea Power," *New Middle East* (London), no. 44, May 1972, pp. 4-6.

Chubin, Shahram, "US Security Interests in the Persian Gulf in the 1980," *Daedalus* (Boston), Fall 1980, p. 43.

Connery, Robert H. and David, Paul T., "The Mutual Defence Assistance Programme," *American Political Science Review* (Washington, D.C.), vol. 45, no. 2, June 1951.

Cooley, John K., "Iran, the Palestinians, and the Gulf," *Foreign Affairs* (New York), vol. 57, no. 5, Summer 1979, p. 1019.

Cottrell, Alvin J., "Iran, the Arabs and the Persian Gulf," *Orbis* (Philadelphia), vol. 17, no. 3, Fall 1973, pp. 978-88.

Dawisha, A-deed I., "Iran: The West's Opportunity,"

Foreign Policy (New York), no. 41, Winter 1980-81, p. 139.

Dinerstein, Herbert, "Moscow and the Third World: Power Politics or Revolution," *Problems of Communism* (Washington, D.C.), January-February 1968, p. 52.

Editorial, "Middle East Trends: The Dangers of Recolonisation," *New Middle East* (London), no. 16, January 1970.

Eilts, Hermann F., "Security Considerations in the Persian Gulf," *International Security* (Cambridge), vol. 5, no. 2, Fall 1980, p. 89.

Enders, Thomas O., "OPEC and the Industrial Countries: The Next Ten Years," *Foreign Affairs* (New York), vol. 53, no. 4, July 1975, pp. 625-37.

Enlone, Cynthia H., "The Military Uses of Ethnicity," *Journal of International Studies* (London), vol. 4, no. 3, Winter 1975-76, pp. 220-35.

Farris, F., "Arabs Get Kissinger Warning," *International Herald Tribune* (Paris), 7 February 1974.

Feoktistov, A., "Saudi Arabia and the Arab World," *International Affairs* (Moscow), no. 7, July 1977, p. 101.

Field, Michael, "Struggle for Stability," *Middle East International* (London), no. 6, September 1971, pp. 42-43.

Foster, William C., "Technological Peace," *Impact of Science on Society*, vol. 22, no. 3, 1972. Reprinted in *Strategic Digest* (IDSA, New Delhi), vol. 2, no. 8, August 1972, p. 30.

Frank, Andre Gunder, "Arms Economy and Warfare in the Third World," *Third World Quarterly* (London), vol. 2, no. 2, April 1980, p. 229.

Freedman, Lawrence, "Britain and the Arms Trade," *International Affairs* (London), vol. 54, no. 1, July 1978, p. 378.

Glubb, Faris, "Backdoor to Arabia," *Middle East International* (London), no. 45, March 1975, p. 12.

Gotthel, M. Fred, "An Economic Assessment of the Military Burden in the Middle East, 1960-1980," *Journal of Conflict Resolution* (London), vol. 18, no. 3, September 1974, p. 504.

Graetfrath, B., "Disarmament and International Law," *Scientific World* (London), vol. 16, no. 1, 1972, p. 8.

Graham, Robert, "Iraq and Iran: Gulf Power Struggle

Sharpens," *New Middle East* (London), no. 45, June 1972, pp. 14-16.

Gray, Colin S., "The Arms Race Phenomenon," *World Politics* (Princeton), vol. 24, no. 1, October 1971, p. 40.

Griffiths, David R., "Congress Probes Yemeni Arms Policy," *Aviation Week and Space Technology* (New York), vol. 112, no. 21, 26 May 1980, p. 79.

Grinyov, O., "Soviet Efforts for Disarmament," *International Affairs* (Moscow), no. 12, December 1967, p. 63.

Gudkov, Yuri, "USA: Rapid Development Neutrality," *New Times* (Moscow), no. 42, October 1980.

Gupta, Bhabani Sen, "Soviet Foreign Policy Strategic Thinking for the Seventies," *India Quarterly* (New Delhi), no. 4, October-December 1975, p. 331.

Hirschfeld, Yair P., "Moscow and Khomeini: Soviet-Iranian Relations in Historical Perspective," *Orbis* (Philadelphia), vol. 24, no. 2, Summer 1980, p. 223.

Hoagland, John H., "Arms in the Developing World," *Orbis* (Philadelphia), vol. 12, no. 1, Spring 1968, pp. 167ff.

Holden, David, "Peace or Southern Arabia's Hundred Year War," *New Middle East* (London), no. 50, November 1972, p. 32.

Hottinger, Arnold, "King Feisal, Oil and Arab Politics," *Swiss Review of World Affairs* (Zurich), vol. 23, no. 7, October 1973, p. 9.

Hurewitz, J.C., "From Pax Britannica to Withdrawal," *Headline Series* (New York), no 220, April 1974, p. 25.

Hurni, Ferdinand, "The Complex Middle East," *Swiss Review of World Affairs* (Zurich), vol. 31, no. 3, June 1981, p. 6.

Husain, M.A., "Third World and Disarmament; Shadow and Substance," *Third World Quarterly* (London), vol. 2, no. 1, January 1980, p. 96.

Joseph, Ralph, "Iraq: The Baath Settles in," *The Middle East* (London), no. 22, August 1976, p. 12.

Kaiser, Robert G., "US-Soviet Relations: Goodbye to Detente," *Foreign Affairs* (New York), vol. 59, no. 3, 1981.

Kaliadin, A.N., "Problems of Disarmament Research," *Journal of Peace Research* (Oslo), vol. 1, 1972, p. 238.

Kaysen, Carl, "American Military Policy," *Survival* (London), vol. 11, no. 2, February 1969, p. 51.

Kende, Istvan, *Bulletin of Peace Proposals* (Oslo), no. 3, 1973, p. 205.

Kennedy, Edward K., "The Persian Gulf: Arms Race or Arms Control?" *Foreign Affairs* (New York), vol. 54, no. 1, October 1975, p. 19.

Kemp, Geoffrey, "Arms Traffic and Third World Conflicts," *International Conciliation* (New York), no. 577, March 1970, p. 5.

Kislow, A., "The Arms Race in the Middle East," *International Affairs* (Moscow), no. 7, July 1978, p. 91.

Klare, Michael T., "The Political Economy of Arms Sales," *Bulletin of the Atomic Scientists* (Chicago), vol. 22, no. 9, November 1976, p. 11.

Knorr, Klaus, "The Limits of Economic and Military Power," *Daedalus* (Cambridge: Mass), vol. 104, no. 4, 1975, p. 231.

Kolodziej, Edward A., "France and the Arms Trade," *International Affairs* (London), vol. 56, no. 1, January 1980, p. 61.

Korb, Laurence J., "The FY 1980-1984 Defence Program: Issues and Trends," *AEI Foreign Policy and Defense Review* (Washington, D.C.), vol. 1, no. 4, 1979, p. 53.

Kortunove, V., "Arms Race Policy Historically Doomed," *International Affairs* (Moscow), no. 10, October 1976, p. 4.

Kramer, Helmut, and Bauer, Helfried, "Imperialism, Intervention Capacity and Foreign Policy Making," *Journal of Peace Research* (Oslo), 1972, p. 285.

Kudryavtsev, K., "Oman: Looking for a New Prop," *New Times* (Moscow), no. 11, March 1979, p. 12.

Lateef, Abdul, "Riyadh and Washington: A Mutual Reliance," *Middle East International* (London), no. 85, July 1978, pp. 16-18.

Lewis, Bernard, "Russia in the Middle East," *Round Table* (London), July 1970. Reprinted in *Survival* (London), October 1970, pp. 332-36.

Li Richard, P.Y. and Thomas, William, "The Coup Contagion Hypothesis," *Journal of Conflict Resolution* (London), vol. 19, no. 1, March 1975, p. 87.

Linder, Willy, "The Price of Oil: A Political Time Bomb," *Swiss Review of World Affairs* (Zurich), vol. 24, no. 11, February 1975, pp. 4-6.

Long, David E., "United States Policy Towards the Persian Gulf," *Current History* (Philadelphia), vol. 68, no. 402, February 1975, p. 170.

Luce, William (Sir), "Britain's Withdrawal," *The Royal United Service Institution Journal*, March 1969. Reprinted in *Survival* (London), vol. 11, no. 6, June 1969, p. 190.

Mack, Andrew, "The Undercover Arms Race," *New Scientist* (London), vol. 60, no. 874, 29 November 1973, p. 638.

Mansur, Abdul Kasim, "The American Threat to Saudi Arabia," *Survival* (London), vol. 23, no. 1, January-February 1981, p. 37.

Maull, Hanns W., "Oil and Influence: The Oil Weapon Examined," *Adelphi Papers*, no. 117 (ISS, London), Summer 1975, p. 25.

McDermott, Antony, "Japan and the Arabs," *Middle East International* (London), no. 63, September 1976, p. 13.

Medwedko, L. "The Persian Gulf: A Revival of Gunboat Diplomacy," *International Affairs* (Moscow), no. 12, December 1980, p. 28.

Meister, Jurg, "Iran's Naval Build-up," *Swiss Review of World Affairs* (Zurich), vol. 23, no. 4, July 1973, pp. 14-16.

Myrdal, Alva, "The Game of Disarmament," *Impact of Science on Society*, vol. 22, no. 3, 1972.

Nes, David G., "The US Energy Crisis and the Middle East," *Military Review* (Leavenworth, K.S.), vol. 53, no. 3, March 1973, pp. 3-7.

Newsom, David D., "America Engulfed," *Foreign Policy* (Washington, D.C.), no. 43, Summer 1981, p. 25.

O'Ballance, Edgar, "The Kurdish Factor in the Gulf," *The Army Quarterly and Defence Journal* (London), vol. 104, no. 5, October 1974, p. 570.

Oberg, Jan, "Arms Trade with the Third World as an Aspect of Imperialism," *Journal of Peace Research* (Oslo), vol. 12, no. 3, 1975, p. 230.

Orudjev, S., "Soviet Oil," *New Times* (Moscow), no. 50, December 1968, pp. 5-7.

Owen, R.P., "The British Withdrawal from the Persian Gulf," *World Today* (London), vol. 28, no. 2, February 1972, pp. 76-77.

Penzin, D., "Oil and Independence", *International Affairs* (Moscow), no. 10, October 1972, pp. 34-40.

Petrov, R., "The Soviet Union and Arab Countries," *International Affairs* (Moscow), no. 11, November 1972, pp. 22-29.

Polk, William R., "The Middle East: Analysing Social Change," *Bulletin of the Atomic Scientists* (Chicago), January 1967, p. 17.

Ramazani, Rouhollah K., "Iran's Search for Regional Co-operation," *Middle East Journal* (Washington, D.C.), vol. 30, no. 2, Spring 1976, p. 181.

Rees, David, "Strategic Problems of Indian Ocean Defence," *Asia Pacific Community* (Tokyo), no. 11, Winter 1981, p. 73.

Rubin, Barry, "Sub-Empires in the Persian Gulf," *The Progressive* (Madison), vol. 39, no. 1, January 1975, p. 30.

Rubinstein, Alvin Z., "Soviet-American Rivalry in the Middle East," *Middle East Review* (New York), vol. 9, no, 3, Spring 1977, p. 34.

Safran, Nadav, "Engagement in the Middle East," *Foreign Affairs* (New York), vol. 53, no. 1, October 1974, p. 56.

Saunders, Harold H., "The Middle East 1978-79: Forces of Change," *Current Policy No. 77* (Washington, D.C.), 26 July 1979.

Seth, S.P., "Afghanistan in Global Politics," *IDSA Journal* (New Delhi), vol. 13, no. 2, October-December 1980, pp. 189-201.

Schlesinger, J.R., "Arabs Risking Use of Force," *International Herald Tribune* (Paris), 8 January 1974.

Shamarov, V., "Iran-Iraq: Constructive Dialogue," *New Times* (Moscow), no. 13, March 1975, p. 10.

Shwadran, Benjamin, "Middle East Oil," *Current History* (Philadelphia), vol. 66, no. 390, February 1974, p. 80.

Siddiqi, Abdul Rahman, "Western Oil-strategy, Soviet Geo-Politics and Gulf Security," *Defence Journal* (Karachi), vol. 7, no. 3, 1981, p. 5.

Singh, K.R., "Conflict and Co-operation in the Gulf," *International Studies* (New Delhi), vol. 15, no. 4, October-December 1976, pp. 487-508.

Skagestad, Gunnar, "Small States in International Politics: A

Polar-Political Perspective," *Nordic Journal of International Politics* (Oslo), vol. 1, 1974, p. 187.

Smith, Teresa Clair, "Arms Race Instability and War," *The Journal of Conflict Resolution* (Beverly Hill), vol. 24, no. 2, June 1980, pp. 253-284.

Smolanksy, O.M., "Moscow and the Persian Gulf: An Analysis of Soviet Ambitions and Potential," *Orbis* (Philadelphia), vol. 14, no. 1, Spring 1970, p. 82.

Speed, F.W., "Indian Ocean Rivalry," *The Army Quarterly and Defence Journal* (London), vol. 104, no. 4, October 1975, p. 459.

Stepanov, A., "New Fit of Pactomania," *New Times* (Moscow), no. 42, October 1979, p. 12.

Subrahmanyam, K., "Military Aid and Foreign Policy," *Foreign Affairs Report* (New Delhi), vol. 17, no. 11, November 1968, p. 109.

Subrata, Banerjee, "Indian Ocean: Massive US Military Presence Threat to India," *Peace and Solidarity* (New Delhi), vol. 2, no. 11, November 1980, p. 6.

Sullivan, Robert R., "The Architecture of Western Security in the Persian Gulf," *Orbis* (Philadelphia), vol. 14, no. 1, Spring 1970, p. 71.

Tahir-Kheli, Shirin, "Proxies and Allies: The Case of Iran and Pakistan," *Orbis* (Philadelphia), vol. 24, no. 2, Summer 1980, p. 352.

Tarabrin, E., "The Developing Countries and Disarmament," *International Affairs* (Moscow), no. 6, June 1977, p. 38.

Taylor, Maxwell D., "The Legitimate Claims of National Security," *Foreign Affairs* (New York), vol. 52, no. 3, April 1974, pp. 592-93.

Thabet, S.K., "Can Science Flourish in the Arab Middle East," *Scientific World* (London), vol. 14, no. 1, 1970, p. 16.

Thoman, Roy E., "The Persian Gulf Region," *Current History* (Philadelphia), January 1971, p. 38.

Turner, Louis and Bedore, James, "Saudi Arabia: The Power of the Purse-Strings," *International Affairs* (London), vol. 54, no. 1, July 1978, p. 408.

Ulansky, A., "The Iran-Iraq Conflict," *New Times* (Moscow), no. 39, September 1980, p. 11.

Vasin, N., "Iran and US Imperialism," *International Affairs* (Moscow), no. 5, May 1980, p. 72.

Von Imhoff, Christoph, "From the Persian Gulf to the Indian Ocean," *Aussen Politik* (Bremen-Nord), vol. 26, no. 1, 1st Quarter 1975, p. 47.

Watt, D.C., "The Persian Gulf—Cradle of Conflict," *Problems of Communism* (Washington, D.C.), May-June 1972, p. 33.

Weyand, Ired C., and Summers, Harry, "The Need for Military Power." *Military Review* (Leavenworth, K.S.), vol. 56, no. 12, December 1976, pp. 8-18.

Wheeler, Geoffrey, "Russia and the Arab World," *World Today* (London) July 1961, pp. 308-18.

Whitley, Andrew, "The Kurds: Pressures and Prospects," *The Round Table* (London), no. 279, July 1980, p. 247.

Wohlstetter, Albert, "Is there a Strategic Arms Race," *Foreign Policy* (New York, no. 15, Summer, 1974, p. 3.

Wright, Claudia, "Iraq—New Power in the Middle East," *Foreign Affairs* (New York) Winter 1979/80, p. 264.

Yorke, Valerie, "Security in the Gulf: A Strategy of Pre-emption," *World Today* (London), vol. 36, no. 7, July 1980 p. 242.

Yost, Charles, "Israel and the Arabs," *The Atlantic* (Boston), January 1969. Reprinted in *Survival* (London), vol. 4, no. 6, June 1969, pp. 180-81.

Zabih, Sepehr, "Iraq Today," *Current History* (Philadelphia), vol. 66, no. 390, February 1974, p. 66.

NEWSPAPERS

Baghdad Observer (Baghdad)
Keyhan International (Tehran).
Tehran Journal (Tehran).
Hindustan Times (New Delhi).
Indian Express (Cochin)
National Herald (Lucknow).
Patriot (New Delhi).
Statesman (New Delhi).
The Hindu (Madras).
The Times of India (New Delhi).

The Christian Science Monitor (Washington).
The New York Times (New York).
Washington Post (Washington).
Daily Telegraph (London).
The Guardian (Manchester).
The Times (London).
Observer (London).
Strait Times (Singapore).
The International Herald Tribune (Paris).

Index